The Cyclist's Companion

The Stephen Greene Press

Brattleboro, Vermont
Lexington, Massachusetts

Courtesy Schwinn Bicycle Company

The Cyclist's
Companion
by John Howard

First Edition

Text copyright © 1984 by The Stephen Greene Press

All rights reserved. No part of this book may be reproduced without written permission from the publisher, except by a reviewer who may quote brief passages or reproduce illustrations in a review; nor may any part of this book be reproduced, stored in a retrieval system, or transmitted in any form or by any means electronic, mechanical, photocopying, recording, or other, without written permission from the publisher.

This book is manufactured in the United States of America. It is designed by Irving Perkins Associates and published by The Stephen Greene Press, Fessenden Road, Brattleboro, Vermont 05301.

Distributed in the United States by E.P. Dutton, Inc., New York.

Library of Congress Cataloging in Publication Data

Howard, John.
  The cyclist's companion.

  Bibliography: p.
  Includes index.
  1. Cycling. 2. Cycling—United States. 3. Bicycles—Equipment and supplies. I. Title.
GV1041.H68   1984   796.6'0973   84–1648
ISBN 0–8289–0529–0 (pbk.)

TO THE MEMORY OF

Vicki Johnston

Contents

Acknowledgments ix

Preface xi

1 Cycling is for Everyone 1

2 Equipment 23

3 How to Bicycle 59

4 Clothing and Accessories 96

5 Bicycle Maintenance Made Easy 119

6 Recreational Cycling 140

7 Commuting By Bicycle 150

8 Touring 167

9 Competitive Cycling 191

10 A Brief Maintenance Manual for the Bicycle Engine 214

11 A Thumbnail History of the Bicycle 244

Recommended Reading 275

Appendix: Bicycle Contacts 279

Index 285

Acknowledgments

I'm happy to thank Christian Paul and Albert Gross, who provided invaluable assistance with the structure of this book as well as editing the entire manuscript in all its versions. I also want to thank Sally Rice, who read and commented on the manuscript. Her helpful suggestions improved every chapter. Kathy Shulga at The Stephen Greene Press was an extremely skillful and competent editor. Lynne Merrill and Elsa Sandberg were careful and diligent typists. And of course I thank Sandy Daggett, who was always there.

Thanks also to all the people and organizations who so kindly provided photographs and materials for inclusion in this book. And to all my sponsors and supporters, past and present, thank you for helping me pass the last 20 years doing what I most love to do—ride my bike.

Preface

When I first considered writing this book, two good friends tried to cajole me into representing their viewpoints on cycling. Peter is a racer, not just a weekend warrior but a 400-mile-a-week, hard-core, eat-sleep-and-breathe racing bum. He has no regular job. He works at menial labor during the winter so he can train and race full time during the summer months. He travels the racing circuit. Peter was excited about the possibility of a new book giving sophisticated training and racing information, but he was a bit chagrined when I answered that I didn't want to write an elitist book; instead, I wanted a book that would show the usefulness of cycling to all people, a book that would make them better cyclists.

Alex, on the other hand, is a lawyer. He has never attended a race, although he was impressed by the track racing on television during the last Olympic Games. His pride and joy is his shiny custom-frame touring bicycle with panniers (saddlebags), light clincher tires, and all the most expensive equipment. Alex wanted a comprehensive discussion of non-racing cycling—a kind of book that apparently doesn't exist.

At first I was loath to take either of their opinions to heart. There are already too many narrowly focused books on the shelves. Then I realized that Peter and Alex represent two points in a continuum of cycling perspectives. I had to find some way to express not just one end of that continuum, but whatever it was that was common to *all* cyclists, including Peter and Alex.

Peter had been highly competitive since he was a small child. He had run track, swum competitively in high school, and of course had played any number of high school team sports. He knew, however, he wouldn't make it to the top in any of these, and as the popularity of cycling grew in his hometown, he decided to take up the sport. His first bike was a $900 racing machine, and from his first race at the age of sixteen until the present, he had done nothing on the bike but train and race.

I wished to point out to him that his obsession with racing could burn him out if he didn't temper it with some enjoyable, noncompetitive bicycling. I maintained that riding a bike is intrinsically fun, and in his frenzy to be the fastest rider and to sprint for the line, he may have missed the sheer pleasure of the sport itself. Alex already shared my enthusiasm for the sport, but I felt he could become a safer and better cyclist simply by learning the skills and tricks normally used only by competitive cyclists. It was Alex who pointed out the common denominators between his cycling goals and Peter's; they both ride bikes to improve the quality of their lives with a planned program of fitness, and both base their programs on realistic expectations and physical discipline. The only differences between them were the nature of their expectations and the degree of physical discipline to which they adhere. Both expectation and discipline are intensely personal and individual.

So with completely different motivations, Peter and Alex are pursuing the same goals and engaging in many of the same activities. That's why I have tried to make this book useful and informative to all types of cyclists—racers, tourists, commuters, and others. It is also my goal to help the neophyte get started and the veteran bikie enjoy the sport even more.

1

Cycling is for Everyone

It is estimated that over 20 million Americans now jog or run. Bicycle purchases have surged during the last decade so that there are many more bicycles in America than automobiles. Our leaders and politicians make sure that we know about their own robust, vigorous physical activities. Of the past seven U.S. Presidents, one played golf to recuperate from a heart attack; one played touch football and swam; one hunted on his Texas ranch; another played golf; one collapsed at a 10-kilometer foot race; one rides horseback and chops wood; and one didn't regularly pursue any discernable physical activity and had to resign from office to avoid impeachment. (He did go for a walk once in an attempt to reconstruct his image, but looked ridiculous on the San Clemente beach in his wing-tip shoes.)

Politicians sometimes set the trends and sometimes they try to appear as though they had set them. We can only speculate about what caused the change, but in the past quarter century America's prevalent lifestyle has changed from sedentary to active. If participation and purchases of athletic equipment (including bicycles) are any indication, then many Americans seem to be adopting a fitness lifestyle. I'm an advocate of that change, and I feel that my sport, cycling, provides one of the most enjoyable ways to pursue a fitness lifestyle.

A change in one's self-concept seems to be central to adoption of the fitness lifestyle. Before reading any further, take a piece of scratch paper and make a list of the "things" you are. That list can provide some very good clues to your self-concept. Very likely your list includes such roles as family member or wage earner. If your list also includes such things as bicyclist, racquetball player, jogger, swimmer, or aerobic dancer, then your self-concept suggests you practice the fitness lifestyle. Even if your list does not include any athletic titles, the fact that you are reading this book suggests an interest in bicycling and fitness.

I am actively seeking new recruits for the fitness lifestyle. My hope is that after reading this book your new self-concept list will include the title "bicyclist." And my reason for writing this book is to teach you what you need to know in order to call yourself a true cyclist.

The benefits of the fitness lifestyle are easy to identify. Those who practice it seem healthier, more alert, and less vulnerable to disabling, debilitating disease than others. I find that those who engage in fitness activities lead a varied, interesting social life as they join others who follow their sport. Play is as natural and necessary for us as work, and fitness activities are fun as well as healthful. Moreover, I feel that those who pursue a fitness program are more energetic and effective in their work, and more likable in their social interactions.

Of course, I can't prove what my intuition tells me about the true health benefits of exercise. The physician and author Dr. Kenneth Cooper is one researcher who is conducting large-scale tests to discover the verifiable benefits of regular exercise. Perhaps before very long we will have evidence to back up my common-sense conclusions.

FITTING CYCLING INTO YOUR LIFESTYLE

April mornings are usually cool and gray in Buda, Texas. The sun rises at about 6:30 and the only activity you'll see then is an occasional train passing through. However, if it's Saturday morning, you can spot three cyclists just leaving town on Manchaca Road into the hill country. The leader of the three is 60-year-old Charles Pantaze. Charles is a successful publisher in nearby Austin. Every afternoon at 4:30 he sheds his business suit and dons his cycling costume like Superman in a phone booth. Then he heads for the hills, returning only as the sun is setting.

Charles started riding nearly 20 years ago when the pressures of a volatile business life pushed his weight up to 230 pounds and his doctors wrote him off as dead. Although he candidly admits his business would benefit from more attention, he recognizes that bicycling has saved his sanity and probably his life. Through regular cycling and a conscientious diet, Charles has lost 80 pounds and reversed 20 years of premature aging.

Riding with Charles are Ralph Halave, Assistant Attorney General for the State of Texas, and Paul Russel, employed at the Air Quality Control Board of Texas. On spring weekends, the three usually meet in Buda and spend the hours touring some of the most beautiful bicycling roads in the country. All three share a common appreciation of nature and a realization that a

All kinds of people ride all kinds of bicycles. Here's a gentleman who has customized his touring bicycle with a cushion seat, chest and chin rests, and a sporty automobile rearview mirror. (Courtesy Greg Siple, TOSRVPHOTO)

great deal of introspection, creative conversation, and decision making takes place on their rides. Charles spends about 20 hours—up to 300 miles—a week on his bike, and cannot imagine life (or sanity) without it.

Meanwhile, Houstonians Joe and Sissy Bentley and their daughter Hallie exemplify the family that has worked cycling intimately into its daily life. They commute individually by bike or, when they need to travel and arrive somewhere together, they ride a custom triplet (one step up from a tandem). The biking Bentleys have found what cycling commuters have discovered in towns all around the country: beneath those sprawling freeway ramps and limited-access highways lie quiet and untraveled back roads that, for the most part, predate the monster freeways but still get you from here to there. Every exit from a downtown turnpike is the beginning of a maze of roads that common motorists, intent only on making their way from the freeway to their destinations, never see. And these back roads aren't necessarily slower; many bicycle commuters in Houston can make an 8-to-12-mile trip in less time than a car can get through the clogged freeway system to the same place.

Commuting by bicycle offers hope of salvation from the looming contemporary nightmare urban planners have dubbed "gridlock," a theoretical automotive Armageddon. When a city's traffic jam becomes so bad that no vehicle can move to extricate itself, and traffic is permanently tangled, that city will be gridlocked. How remote the gridlock scenario would seem if more people followed the example of my friend Martina, who regularly rides the 11 miles from her house to her business by bike. With the money saved on gas, parking, car repairs, and insurance, she has put down a payment on a new townhouse in the inner city, where her bike has an even greater advantage over a car. She will probably never own a car again.

Fitting cycling into *your* lifestyle begins with realizing that it is not exclusively recreation but a viable means of transportation. Since the needs for recreation and mobility are so much a part of everyday life, the only prerequisite is a readjustment of priorities—away from the car and toward the bike. This may mean some inconveniences, such as allowing a few extra minutes in transit, keeping a spare set of clothes at work in case of rain, and justifying not being able to drive your kids and office mates to school or lunch. But when you remember that you are forsaking skyrocketing gas prices, automobile breakdowns, expensive repairs, insurance payments, and costly parking (if you can find parking at all), coupled with the fact that you are helping to reduce automotive pollution and economic instability, you are coming out ahead in the long run. For longer travel, you can take bikes on almost all trains, airlines, and buses. And you never have to worry about how to park or repair your auto in a strange city or on the empty highway.

Perhaps the most strident complaint against bicycle commuting comes from those who deplore arriving at work with perspiration on the brow and hair blown about by the wind. But the value structure of American society seems to be shifting from the opulent to the practical, a movement necessitated by increased energy costs and inflation. People are becoming more rational in their approach to economical modes of transportation.

The best way to accommodate cycling to your schedule is to look for every opportunity to ride. You might begin by using the bike for short errands, such as picking up small items at the grocery store or shopping mall. For most loads, a light nylon knapsack works perfectly well. If you have to bring a child along (one that is too young to ride his or her own bike), bike child carriers and trailers are now available that are sturdy, light, and safe.

Vacations are a great time to rediscover the bicycle. If you are traveling long distances by car, a bike ride over new rural roads near a roadside inn or motel can be a refreshing end to the day. If you are on a hectic business trip and cannot bring your bike, you may be able to rent one.

THE FAMILY

Perhaps no other sport can offer more possibilities for family activities than cycling. In the competitive end of the sport, I have seen families with members ranging from 8 years to veterans, all competing in their respective categories. Racing families such as the Bradleys and Stetinas have dominated much of American racing. Other families such as the Youngs, the Barczenskis, and the Doerings have contributed several strong racers from the same family.

Cycling with your child is a perfect way to instill an appreciation for the beauty of nature. Bike trips can provide regular opportunities to bring your children into a rural setting. From their parents' example, children learn safe cycling, personal attention to physical fitness, and responsibility for others.

Too Small to Ride?

Children can ride a bike as soon as they have the sense of balance to stay upright. Before that point, a child can enjoy cycling trips in a special seat mounted on a bicycle or in child trailers. Choice of bicycle seats for children is difficult; none of the seats available have all the features one desires. Frame-mounted child seats should be located behind the handlebars or behind the saddle, both for greater protection and for more equal weight distribution. The best seats are mounted behind the saddle and are made of molded plastic, with strong and secure straps for holding the child in and broad protective guards to keep the child's feet out of the rear wheel. The use of papoose sacks or knapsack-type child carriers is risky on a bike, since in a fall the child has no protection, and your center of gravity is elevated so that a fall is much more likely.

Never carry a child if you don't feel secure on your bike; you should be quite sure of yourself before you add the weight and the responsibility of a child to your ride. Riding in wet weather or at night with a child on your bike is just foolish. Commuting with a child is a proposition you must consider with great discretion; it calls for a lot of experience and presence of mind.

I recommend child carriers only for short-distance travel in good weather—for example, to a day school, to a nearby store, or for weekend family trips through parks or on quiet streets. I was quite intrigued, however, by a roadside encounter with a vacationing family of four on a triplet: the parents and the eldest child were pedaling in the three seats, with the infant doing the tour in a baby seat.

Child Safety

Young children on their first bikes do not belong on public streets, with or without their parents. The small bikes on which children first learn are only safe on sidewalks or on bike paths where motor traffic is forbidden. A responsible parent allows a child on the open road only if he or she is equipped to take the responsibility for self, other cyclists, and motorists traveling nearby. Riding skills must be sufficient to meet all needs on the road. The youngster must be able to ride a straight line at both slow and fast speeds, signal and make safe turns, start and stop in a straight line, and shift gears safely. A child also should have the endurance to make the ride in question without undue fatigue. An exhausted rider will not respond quickly to problems and will not be able to steer a straight and safe course.

Bicycles provide their riders less protection than any other vehicle on the road, so defensive bicycling is essential. Your child should know how to behave responsibly on a bike, and he or she should learn local cycling regulations well. Both adults and children should obey all traffic signs and ride in the same direction as traffic. Young cyclists must have a sense of where automobile interference may occur, understand when it's best to get off and walk a bike, and know when a road is too busy to ride safely. Much of this kind of responsibility is learned only by imitation of the cycling habits of adults, so parents wishing to inculcate safe cycling habits should spend sufficient time riding with their children.

I strongly encourage parents to support local school bicycle safety programs for their children. If you cannot spend sufficient time modeling safe riding to your children, at least you should encourage the schools to have such a program. Travelers Insurance Company has produced a film entitled "It's Your Move," which deals with bike safety for youngsters. Like a driver-education film, the movie confronts the child with a series of dangerous situations.

The Young Cyclist's Training

When a young cyclist decides to become serious about bicycling and wants to train in some organized fashion, much of the information elsewhere in this book will be applicable. Young bodies adapt quickly to training and progress comes very rapidly. A young rider may be tempted, however, to press on and overstress the body. I have known countless young riders who could have been great competitors but who followed overly vigorous training schedules, fell into chronic fatigue, and lost strength and energy with each successive ride.

Overtraining is not just a matter of lowered sugar levels in the blood; it is reflected—particularly in young riders—in muscle and ligament damage and in severe psychological trauma. The physical or mental damage may not be immediately obvious, but it can be very debilitating later on. A foundation of slow riding at moderate distances is essential before a youth can begin serious speed work or long-distance riding.

When your child is training hard, his or her diet will be altered drastically. If family schedules often conflict with riding schedules and meals are easily missed, the results will be disastrous. A child may satisfy the increased caloric requirements of hard training with junk foods, carbonated drinks, and candy, foods which supply the raw "energy" calories needed to continue riding, but which do not fulfill the body's elevated requirements for vitamins and other nutrients. The result is malnutrition.

No one can estimate accurately how much heredity predetermines peak performance levels, just as no one can accurately predict the effects of training programs. Many sports physiologists would agree, however, that 40 to 70 percent of final potential is determined by physical training and 30 to 60 percent by heredity. In the very early years (say, before 15 years of age), lung capacity and the ability to absorb oxygen from your lungs can be increased. After that point, very little improvement can occur, although other facets of cycling can be improved to circumvent this problem. Young lung capacity will have to be extraordinarily low for an active touring or commuting life to be denied you, so don't forsake all cycling if you don't have a racer's lungs.

Regardless of age, the youngster's legs and body are more important than the bike. Only when competing at the top of the sport do small changes in equipment make a winning difference. Remember instead that money will be needed for food, travel to tours or races, and perhaps for medical checkups. Because your child can outgrow an expensive frame, keep his or her equipment investments at a minimum until the young cyclist has reached the late teens.

AGE EXTREMES

Start Young!

Most of us are aware that older people are more likely than the rest of the population to suffer arteriosclerosis and high blood pressure. According to Professor Thomas Gilliam of the University of Michigan, however, high cholesterol, high blood pressure, obesity, and other factors associated with heart ailments in adults are becoming more common among children. Close to 50 percent of the elementary school children Gilliam has tested since 1975 have evidenced at least one such risk factor. To say the least, these are alarming statistics.

Gilliam asserts that these juvenile health problems can be corrected with a regular program of physical activity. He tested third- and fourth-grade boys and girls over a 12-week period of vigorous activity, with 25 minutes of exercise four days per week. A control group was given typical, less vigorous physical education classes twice per week. Students with high blood-lipid levels acquired normal lipid values within the 12-week period. Gilliam asserts that vigorous sports programs such as this should begin at preschool ages. He urges us to encourage youngsters to get an early start on a lifetime of strenuous activity which will benefit their health.

It's reasonable to assume that an exercise program begun early will enhance a child's chances of living a long and healthy

My brother Harry (on trike) and me on my fourth birthday. We spent a lot of time pedaling together as children. (Courtesy Harry Howard, Sr.)

life, but at what age and what level is a youngster best prepared to participate in physical exercise of this kind?

A few years ago I was attending a League of American Wheelmen convention in Denver. There I met an 8-year-old girl who had just completed a double century, a 200-mile non-stop ride. Although I once had cautioned young riders against riding too many miles either in one event or over a longer period, that girl provided good evidence that physical development and capacity in children can vary dramatically. Careful, progressive development in a sport can lead different children to drastically different levels of accomplishment.

The key to any manner of progressive involvement in physical activity is moderation. A child chronically worn out by hard riding can be susceptible to frequent illness, school absenteeism, psychological problems, and other complications. The pride and the willingness of young riders to push beyond normal pain thresholds often cause them to ride harder than adults. While riding in the 1979 National Cyclocross Championships, I watched Myron Lind, a 17-year-old West Coast competitor, put forth tremendous energy and tolerance for suffering—far more than I could ever hope to produce. He didn't finish as well as I did, but if he had fortified his motivation and endurance with the physical development I had acquired over the years, he could have been invincible. Among the midget (young) and intermediate age groups at national championships, one seldom sees

10

half-hearted efforts; they ride full-out and often more competitively and with more spirit than older participants. Regularly one sees parents quit tours while their children—though often exhausted—are still ready to persevere until the end of the tour.

The Over-the-Hill Bike Club:
Are You Ever Too Old?

In traffic, Charlie Morton rides with the style and grace of a man who has spent 50 years on a bike. He should; he *has* been riding that long. He is 69 years old, and he raced against the best European cyclists in the 1930's. According to those who remember Charlie's competitive career, he was the only American of his era who could match the Europeans stroke for stroke.

Charlie grew up in the racing era when derailleur changing mechanisms had not yet been perfected and riders competed in one gear, regardless of terrain. In 1936 Charlie made the Olympic Games in Berlin, and placed 19th after a crash (until very recently, the best-ever performance by an American). After the Games he turned professional, but with the advent of the second World War, American racing fell into total obscurity. Racing still existed in the United States, but it was practiced by a tiny handful of individuals like Charlie Morton.

There have been many serious riders who never entered a race. Harry Gallagher, 81, often rides 40 to 50 miles a day. Since his retirement he now has the time to ride the 118-mile round trip from his New Jersey home to Atlantic City and back. All through the years of the auto boom, Harry never owned a car; he has relied on a bike his whole life. "I got a strong heart and I got strong lungs, good breathing," he says. "You got to start when you're young."

What's the fitness problem for older people? The problem is in American attitudes toward the elderly. We don't treat our aged with the respect they deserve—we pamper them, then dump them. Long before they might conceivably wear out, we lose interest in them and they lose interest in themselves. Their mental and physical health begin to deteriorate.

What's to keep older people off a bike? NOTHING. Everywhere in cycling are allowances and special programs for older riders. The activities of the Over-the-Hill Bike Club in Los Angeles are an example. So if you are getting on in years you need not feel left out. If touring is your game, a number of organizations such as the International Bicycle Touring Society sponsor tours of all kinds designed specifically for the rider who is middle aged or older. These tours make concessions for weaker riders, busier work schedules, and preferences for finer dining and living accommodations.

A few years ago one such tour included a three-week ride through southeast France, touring castles and fortified towns built during the Crusades. Another tour explored the majestic mountains of Banff National Park in Alberta, Canada. Still another led riders down the coast of Mexico through seaside resorts

I have competed as a cyclist for 20 years. (Courtesy Will Van Overbeek)

and the myriad secluded fishing villages. You can find a tour aimed specifically at your age group, going almost anywhere in the world or leaving almost from your front door. You can ride tours that never travel more than 20 or 30 miles a day (and all of that mileage flat, as in recent tours of the Dutch dikes and of the Chesapeake Bay). You can stay in hostels or in the most elegant hotels if you like, and you can travel with just your cycling clothes or with a tux and patents to wear to the opera. About 10 years ago Keith Kingbay of the Schwinn Bicycle Company led a small band of cyclists across the country. A motorhome followed with all the amenities, leaving the bicycles unencumbered. How you tour is strictly up to you.

If you want to race, the United States Cycling Federation (USCF) has created age categories that allow you to compete against racers only of your own age range. This gives many racers now well into their 70's and 80's a chance to compete effectively again. Several studies have shown that riders' capabilities to cover a given distance don't decrease; only the speed at which they can finish the distance declines. With this in mind, the USCF encourages racing for competitors who are into their 70's and beyond. I myself have entered the veteran's division of the USCF, having now passed 35. I had already won six national championships in younger divisions, and in 1983, at the age of 35, I added my seventh. I intend to keep competing until I have bicycled in all the age divisions.

In Davis, California, there lives a man who started cycling at 58 and has been at it for nearly 20 years. He won his first race at 60, toured 2,100 miles in 23 days at 64, and toured 3,150 miles in 36 days in the following year. Ed Delano (Foxy Grandpa to his friends) raced in the veterans' world championships and in other veterans' races in his early 70's. For at least five years, he competed in the Senior Olympics in San Diego. He has won in his age category every year. Foxy Grandpa has twice competed in the national championships, winning gold medals in his category both times. Delano is only one of several "over the hill" pedal pushers who have proven that they can outride most cyclists a quarter their age. His recuperative powers, his ability to recover from injuries (he once broke his leg when hit by a truck), and his excellent physical condition are extraordinary examples of what cycling can do for an older citizen.

HOW TO REGAIN FITNESS

Most of us were more fit when we were youngsters than we are now. The key to regaining fitness is to reintroduce childhood physical activities into your life and to rekindle an interest in exercise or play. Most fitness experts now recommend a minimum of 20 minutes of aerobic exercises four to five times a week. For many fitness-minded adults the solution is to engage regularly in a solitary sport such as swimming, running, or bicycling. Then, when circumstances permit, regular workouts can be supplemented by a team sport or other competitive activity. Swimming, running, and biking are sports that the adult athlete can practice either at his or her own convenience or in a social environment.

Using your bicycle combines exercise with a practical means of transportation. Walking or jogging are too time consuming to be effective for daily commuting over anything but very short distances, and bicycle commuting may become more a financial necessity than a health one, as energy resources dwindle.

For many people, physical exercise is an interruption, incongruent with the rest of their lives. For instance, some people drive their cars half a mile to a running trail, park, run their regulation three miles, then return to their cars and drive home again. Bicycling is easier to integrate into your life because it gives you an easy command over distance, an inexpensive and potentially very enjoyable way to move about town, and a rewarding recreational activity. You can begin your bicycle exercise program at any level of exertion—coasting, if you wish—so very few people are excluded from cycling. A beginning rider can equip his or her bike with gears low enough to make most hills a breeze.

Today, running is by far America's most popular solitary sport. As a life-long bicyclist who has adopted the sport of triathlon, I am a runner too. Running is a very efficient way for an adult to get a fitness workout and promote fat loss in a short period of time. Advocates of running say that it is superior to bicycling as a fitness exercise, because runners almost always elevate their heart rate to aerobic levels, while cyclists sometimes don't. Something about running as an exercise makes you go faster and continue to get aerobic workouts as you get more experienced. Bicyclists don't necessarily do that; the machine is too efficient, and cruising on a bicycle is too tempting.

What some running advocates ignore is that, unfortunately, running is far more hazardous to joints, tendons, and muscles than bicycling. Therefore, I recommend *aerobic* bicycling as a gentler form of fitness exercise than running. I'm not recommending that you bicycle full speed as a beginner; merely that you learn how to get a fitness workout on your bike so you can avoid the injuries to which runners are prone. For fitness riding I recommend the following 40-minute workout four or more days a week: warm up by cruising slowly for 10 minutes (on level ground if possible), exert yourself by cycling briskly for the next 20 minutes (on level or moderate to difficult uphills), and then cool down by cruising slowly for the last 10 minutes (on level and downhill terrain).

This regimen is a minimum for fat loss and cardiovascular fitness. You *can* cycle longer and more frequently; as long as you avoid the four B's—psychological Burnout, Broken bones, Bruises, and the Bonk—bicycle aerobics is one area of life where more is better. (The first three B's are obvious; bonking is running out of fuel before you are done, or depleting all your glycogen supplies, the bicyclist's equivalent of when the runner hits the wall.)

Fitness as Preventive Medicine

Widely publicized research recently has linked heart disease to fatty, high-cholesterol diets and poor fitness, and this has motivated a lot of exercise. Preventive medicine for cardiovascular disease and therapy for recovering heart-surgery patients now usually includes dieting and exercise. This therapy was most persuasively advocated by Dr. Kenneth Cooper, who suggests that "aerobic" exercise and a low-cholesterol diet may prevent heart disease. (Aerobic exercise is an activity, such as walking, running, swimming, or bicycling, done vigorously enough to elevate the heart rate, but not so briskly that you are unable to replenish your oxygen. When you are in oxygen debt you are exercising *an*aerobically, or without air.)

There is an exclusive bicycling club in Los Angeles whose only membership requirement is that you be a heart-surgery survivor. At least one member of this club is reputed to have celebrated his long rehabilitation from a double-bypass operation by successfully completing a double-century ride. Chris, another heart-surgery veteran of my acquaintance, started running on his doctor's advice and now regularly trains for and runs full (26.2-mile) marathons. Doctors disagree among themselves about the wisdom of such endurance tests for recuperating cardiac patients. Most doctors agree, however, that a program of progressively more strenuous aerobic exercise will help prevent recurrence if the patient does not overexert by becoming too competitive.

A Few Tips for the Adult Cyclist

If you are over 35 or very much out of shape, consult a physician before starting an exercise program. The doctor may administer a cardiac stress test, among others. If your physician is generally negative on the subject of exercise, here are two suggestions: (1) Take a look at the doctor. Is this person a poor model of health, a fat slob who smokes like a chimney? Well then, physician, heal thyself! (2) Get a second opinion.

Most doctors will be very supportive of your athletic ambitions, unless you have some condition that makes the exercise an immediate threat to your life. Starting a bicycle fitness program is ideal for the person who has neglected physical activity because it is an aerobic activity you can start at any level of exertion. Most enlightened doctors would prescribe (or at least approve of) cycling as a way to avoid potential heart and circulatory problems.

Don't wait until you finish reading this book before you begin bicycling. Use the information elsewhere in this book to guide you on equipment purchases, cycling technique, bicycle maintenance, etc., but start your cycling program soon. Continue your research, turning to the information about commuting, touring, racing, and recreational cycling as you gain experience in the saddle.

As you work into a bicycle fitness program, don't overdo it. If your derriere and your leg muscles are sore from too long a ride too early in your cycling career, you'll be set back. It is much better to cycle short distances regularly—or better still, daily—than to try to prove how macho you are on one long ride. If you don't take it easy, you'll burn out long before you can improve.

The key to making your cycling interesting and challenging is to set ambitious—but *achievable*—goals for your cycling performance. Work toward something and you can improve, but don't let your goals become obsessive and take the fun out of bicycling.

Even during the winter months you can maintain your bicycle fitness program. You may be surprised how much fun a bike ride can be on a cold winter day, when you might otherwise be cooped up indoors. Ride at the warmest part of the day, if possible, and bundle up, remembering that on the bicycle you will be moving rapidly enough for wind chill to be an important factor. Take special care that your knees are warm by wearing cycling tights and/or leg warmers. (See the chapter on clothing and accessories.) You can even ride with snow on the ground, though it's difficult going. Rain clothes made from breathable fabrics are available for wet-weather cycling, but do keep in mind that wet pavement makes you vulnerable to falls and encounters with out-of-control automobiles.

The dedicated cyclist does need to have some other athletic interests to tide him or her over the winter. Cross-country skiing is excellent because it uses many of the same muscles as cycling and offers many of the same aerobic benefits. The cyclist can also pursue sports such as racquetball and indoor swimming to maintain aerobic fitness over the winter months. Competitive cyclists often practice weight training and ride on rollers or a stationary bike when the snow keeps them off the streets.

Fitness cyclists can do that too. Nothing stops the snowbound cyclist from doing yoga, stretching exercises, or aerobic dance either.

All of my advice on how to cycle works better when you are part of a group that supports your activity socially and otherwise. One of the earliest studies ever done in the field of social psychology showed that individuals are more productive when they work in groups. Triplett, who did the study in 1897, noticed from records supplied him by the League of American Wheelmen that cyclists ride faster in competition than they do in individual time trials. By cycling with others you will learn more about technique and equipment, and you will bicycle more frequently, faster, and over longer distances.

PARTICIPATION IN BICYCLING

Every year American racers and tourists have more and more events to enter. For racers, each year's total number of stage races has risen, from less than a dozen in the early 1970's to over fifty currently. Every day when I train on California's Pacific Coast Highway, I see individual bicyclists and small informal groups of cyclists loaded down with panniers and sleeping bags. These rugged individualists are on tours ranging from a few miles on a weekend to thousands of miles in several months. For tourists who want to enjoy their sport in the company of many other cyclists, the Tecate-Ensenada Bike Ride in Baja California, Mexico is a good model of what can be organized for any region. Each year as many as 10,000 riders, mostly from southern California, participate in that 72-mile adventure. Tours of new areas are regularly appearing.

In Colorado, bicycling event organizers have begun to recognize that there are problems in staging tours and races separately and have either run them concurrently or have made a tour and a race one and the same thing. The Super Tour of Colorado, for example, makes a figure-8 across the entire state, covering 2,000 km in eleven days. Racers form a fast group at the front, while more convivial groups adopt a leisurely pace

On rolling terrain, these riders are part of the huge annual Tour of the Sciota River Valley. Notice that most of these cyclists are wearing helmets and rain gear for their safety and comfort. (Courtesy Greg Siple, TOSRVPHOTO)

A food stop on a large organized ride. These preplanned stops give everyone a chance to rest or catch up to the group. (Courtesy Greg Siple, TOSRVPHOTO)

behind. In Iowa, the state-wide GABRAI* race attracts racers and tourists who wish to explore the beautiful countryside. As in long-distance running events, everyone can pick his or her own pace, and similar tour/races are popping up all over the country.

The world of cycling, however, includes more than just races and tours. According to the Department of Transportation, more new bicycles (103 million) were sold in the United States in the 1970's than automobiles (102 million). It has been conservatively estimated that 50 million Americans ride a bike, at least occasionally. Most of those millions of bicycle owners never enter a race or go on a tour. However, many of them do commute daily to work or school, and there is no way to count the millions of miles covered by weekend cyclists off on a recreational jaunt.

Keeping the Bicycle in Its Place

After competing in the Coors International bicycle race in Colorado in 1979, I was a spectator the following year and rode the Super Tour of Colorado. Cranking up steep climbs and peering between brake cables on sharp descents in the mountains gave me a desire to *see* this scenic grandeur rather than just race through it. After nearly two decades of addiction both to racing and to murderous training schedules, I now find I can enjoy racing and touring equally. I was lucky enough to find the aesthetic appeal of cycling before racing had completely burned me out.

Who Cycles?—Women as Well as Men

In such male-dominated sports as auto racing, horse racing, and distance swimming, women have regularly equalled men's performance records. In so-called power and endurance sports such as cycling and running, women have also steadily narrowed the gender gap.

The Ironman Triathlon, which I won in 1981, provides an example of the steadily improving performance of female endur-

*Des Moines Register's Great Annual Bike Ride Across Iowa.

ance athletes. Held each year on the Big Island of Hawaii, the Ironman consists of 2.4 miles of swimming in open ocean, followed immediately by a 112-mile bike race, and finally a marathon foot race (26.2 miles). In 1979, the only woman in the event—Lyn Lemaire—placed fifth of 15 competitors. In 1980, Robin Beck placed twelfth in a field of 111 in a time that would have taken second place overall in 1979. In the February 1981 race, Kathleen McCartney scored a heartbreak victory of 11 hours, 9 minutes over an exhausted Julie Moss, who crawled to the finish line. Julie Leach won the women's Ironman title in 1982 with a time of 10 hours and 54 minutes. In 1983 not only did Sylviane Puntous lower the previous record to 10 hours 43 minutes, but her twin sister, Patricia, who finished second despite a flat, also came in six minutes under the old record. In *The Aerobics Way,* Dr. Kenneth Cooper explains that the female

> disadvantage of less muscle (for speed) is compensated for. Women well trained have five to ten percent more body fat than trained men, and there are theories that they are able to burn this fat during a distance run. This theory, if proven, would mean that a woman would be carrying more "fuel" than a man and would have an advantage for long endurance events.

Cooper points out that in the marathon and longer running events women are rapidly approaching men's times; the improvement is attributed to finally adopting the same training techniques that men have used for decades. Women such as Diana Nyad are setting swimming records over long distances that men have yet to beat, and many of the best long-distance cyclists are now women.

In later chapters, which discuss equipment, human physiology, and protecting yourself from attack while cycling, I discuss the specific needs of the female cyclist. For now, though, I would like to point out that American women do much better in international cycling competition than their male counterparts. American men are still struggling for international prominence in cycling, while American women regularly return home with world-championship medals. I predict that American women will soon dominate international cycling competition. Perhaps by the time you read this book my prophecy will have been supported by the performance of women cyclists in the 1984 Los Angeles Summer Olympics.

2

Equipment

Today we have more types of bikes, more models of each type, and more manufacturers to choose from than ever before. With all the diversity and choice, there is a bicycle for every need and pocketbook, but it can be confusing for the uninformed shopper. Knowledge of bikes and components will help you get the most out of cycling. And although I can't make all the choices for you, I can at least try to steer you toward the right places to shop and the right kinds of equipment to look for.

TERMINOLOGY

Your bicycle is basically a frame with parts attached. The frame is made up of metal tubes of various sizes joined together either with or without lugs—sleeves that hold the tubes together. The horizontal bar between the saddle and the handlebars is called the top tube. It joins the seat tube and head tube; respectively, these are located under the seat and at the head of the bike. The remaining long tube of the frame is the down tube, running from the head tube down to the bottom bracket. As you can see, the head tube and bottom bracket are similar in that they both hold movable, rotating assemblies for steering or pedaling.

The rest of the frame holds the rear wheel. Two seat stays run down from the top of the seat tube to the rear dropouts, and two chain stays run from the bottom bracket to the dropouts. If you

23

This exploded bicycle shows all the 1200 or so parts that go into a single modern 10-speed bike. (Courtesy Cycles Peugeot)

trace the pattern made by the seat stays, chain stays, down tube, and top tube, you'll see they make a rough diamond shape, which accounts for the name "diamond frame."

Into the head tube goes the fork, which holds the front wheel and allows it to turn left and right. The ends of the fork blades are dropouts, while the tops are joined by the crown. The steering tube fits inside the head tube, secured by the headset, an assembly of ball bearings, races, and so on.

Fitting inside the top of the headset is the stem, which holds the handlebars. Handlebars may have tape, foam, or leather covering them so as to be comfortable and easy to grasp, or they may have rubber or plastic grips on the ends. When taped, the ends of the bars are plugged with plastic or metal plugs.

The saddle or seat attaches to the saddle post, which fits inside the seat tube.

Inside the bottom bracket is an assembly of bearings and a spindle that rotates. Attached on either end of the spindle are the crank arms, and at the end of each crank arm is a pedal. (Some less expensive cranks are made with spindle and crank arms all of a piece.) On the right-side crank are one or more chain rings, whose teeth or sprockets grip the chain and pull it around, thus moving the rear wheel.

24

The wheels are made of metal rims that support the tires, spokes, and the hub. The tires may have separate tubes, in which case they are called clinchers, or they may have the tube already inside, in which case they are called tubulars. The spokes connect the rim to the hub, which contains an axle and more bearings. It is the axle that fits inside the dropouts and keeps the wheels attached to the bike with either nuts or quick-release skewers. The rear wheel has one or more cogs for the chain to pull, thus forcing the wheel to turn when the crank arms are turned. The cog may be fixed, meaning it is impossible to coast, or free.

Most bikes have brake levers attached to the handlebars; pulling on a brake lever draws the cable and makes the brake pad close against the rim. The brake itself may be side-pull, center-pull, or cantilevered center-pull, depending upon how the cable and action are devised. The cables, like all bike cables, may run inside a housing or be bare, generally running between two fixed points of hardware that are part of or attached to the frame.

Bikes with multiple gears will have one or two levers with cables running to the gearing mechanisms. For a three-speed hub, a single cable connects a shift lever to a small chain that enters the hub itself. Front and rear derailleurs guide the chain to rest on one chain ring and one rear cog, respectively. Typically, these each have a shift lever mounted on the down tube, the stem, or somewhere on the handlebars, with the front shifter on the left-hand side.

Frames may have any number of different brazed-on attachments. Braze-ons reduce the mounting hardware necessary for parts, and so help to keep weight down. But just as important, they add to the beauty, efficiency, reliability, and usefulness of the bicycle. Cable guides, shift-lever studs, and water-bottle bosses are appearing more and more often as standard braze-ons even on relatively inexpensive frames. Brazed-on eyelets for front and rear racks are commonly found next to the dropouts of sport and touring bikes, but not on track or road-racing machines. Rear—and recently front—derailleur mountings are found on good frames, and often a small, mushroom-shaped stud will be brazed onto the inside of the right seat stay to hold the chain when the rear wheel is off for repair or transportation. This is called a chain hangar.

Any good shop can guide you to a competent person to add braze-ons to your bike. Some people with special needs have found it worth their while to get pump mounts, rack fixtures, extra water-bottle bosses, and such brazed on by an expert. The best time to do this is when having the frame painted.

Except for a little detail about cones, cups, and races—all of which are found in rotating parts of a bike and which are discussed under maintenance—these are the terms for various components of a bicycle with which you should be familiar.

TYPES OF BICYCLES

Since the bicycle has assumed so many different shapes and sizes in the last hundred years, a discussion of bicycle equipment could fill volumes. In the final chapter I give a history of the bicycle, tracing its development from the wooden hobby horse through today's amazing human-powered vehicles. That chapter will give you an idea of the diversity of bike styles conceived. In this section I will touch only on the nine most common bicycles found today.

The 10-Speed Bike

The most widely used and most popular bicycle in the United States is what many still call the 10-speed, others the sport bike, and still others the modern racing bike. The name 10-speed was first used to distinguish it from the 3-speed; it derives from the two chain rings and the five-cog freewheel used for the gearing system. As mentioned in Chapter 3 under gearing, 10-speed is a misnomer both because there are only eight usable gears on a 10-speed bike, and because many "10-speeds" have more chain rings and/or more cogs, and therefore more "speeds."

Unless otherwise stated, it is this type of bike that I refer to (and assume you ride). The 10-speed features the two-derailleur gearing set-up, dropped handlebars, straight frame tubing, nar-

Bikes were big business in 1900, just as they are today. This interior shot of the Peugeot factory at the turn of the century shows just how popular the mustache was then. (Courtesy Cycles Peugeot)

This racing bike sports full braze-ons, 12 speeds, classic lines, and top-of-the-line alloy parts. With good tubular tires and a racing saddle, as shown, this bike weighs about 21 pounds and goes like hell. (Courtesy Specialized Bicycle Components)

row rims and tires, and a racing-style saddle. The bike commonly has toe clips and straps to secure the shoes to the pedals, a cage for a water bottle mounted on the frame, a pump, and a bag under the saddle with enough goods and tools to repair the bike after a blowout or some minor mechanical problem.

On one end of the spectrum is the ultra-light road racer, with every superfluous ounce shaved off, a bike with price no object. On the other end is the touring bike, with racks and bags and a second water bottle, perhaps sporting mirrors, lights, safety flags, and geared low enough to climb the living-room wall. In between are the lightly loaded commuter bikes, the stripped-down sport bikes, the upgraded touring bikes, and the over-worked knockarounds that are filling up the bikeways and streets more and more.

The 10-speed has earned widespread appeal with its remarkable versatility. The range of available gears is so wide that every sort of terrain is manageable, given a decent road surface to ride on. And the same bicycle can reasonably be expected to carry its rider in a local race on Sunday, to work and back through the following week, and afterwards on an extended touring vacation. From a leisurely ride to a high-speed workout, over mountains or on the flattest plains, the 10-speed can transport the cyclist more efficiently and more thrillingly than any other vehicle on earth.

The Mountain Bike

A recent entry in the bicycle market, the mountain bike retains all the positive features of a good, lightweight 10-speed, but with added strength and reduced maintenance. The mountain bike, or all-terrain bike, usually has a strong touring-bike frame decked out with all the necessary braze-ons. The differences are found on virtually all other parts. The wheels are of alloy but are wide, with knobby tires that resist puncture and grip muddy, pebbly, and grassy surfaces. Usually they have cantilevered brakes and straight, reinforced handlebars. The saddles typically are wider than those found on 10-speeds, and most often they come with quick-release saddle posts for rapid adjustment. Many mountain bikes feature sealed hubs and bottom

This mountain bike has many of the features mentioned in the text. Notice the cantilevered brakes, triple chain ring, quick-release saddle and post, upright bars, balloon tires, and bare pedals. The frame has full braze-ons, incuding water-bottle bosses, just visible on the down tube. This bike weighs 28 pounds. (Courtesy Cycles Peugeot)

brackets, which relieve the owner of the burden of frequent overhauls.

Pedals on mountain bikes usually have no toe clips, since, in
theory, the cyclist will need to dismount frequently and/or may
take spills more often while on rugged terrain. The bikes usually come with 15- or 18-speed gearing, and at only about 28
pounds they really do approach the optimum in a strong but
light all-terrain bicycle.

Technological wonders that they are, mountain bikes are also
being sold as commuter and touring vehicles—to people who
may never attempt to test them in mountainous, off-road terrain—and I think this is a good idea. To many people, the all-
terrain bicycle looks more like the conventional balloon-tire
bike and is therefore less exotic and intimidating. And certainly
the well-built mountain bike is less troublesome to care for than
the typical 10-speed racer, if only from the standpoint of number
of flat tires per year. For the commuter or tourist who wants a
sturdy, dependable, light vehicle capable of carrying substantial
loads just about anywhere, nothing will beat a mountain bike.

An interesting phenomenon about the all-terrain bike is that
its arrival almost immediately spawned mountain-bike races.
These are conducted on cross-country courses that can be tra-
versed by bike, but only if the rider is willing to dismount and
push or carry the bike over obstacles and inhospitable surfaces.
Thus, a racer might have to ford a stream, climb a gravelly hill,
hop over a felled tree, or scramble through a thicket in addition
to riding over more road-like trails. Crashes and spills are more
common than in straight road races, thus the injuries are more
varied and interesting as well.

The BMX

Conceptually similar to the mountain bike, the BMX bike is
nevertheless radically different from it and all other types of
bicycles. The name, which derives from motorcycle racing, actually describes the bike: cross-country races on motorcycles are
called moto-cross races, or MX for short, and bicycles constructed to imitate MX motorcycles, and the bike races them-

Pioneering the blue tire and the heavy-duty fork blade, the BMX bike is one of the most popular models among children. This one features heavy-duty spoked wheels, reinforced handlebars, and side-pull brakes. (Courtesy B.M.X. Products, Inc.)

selves, have come to be known as bicycle moto-cross, or BMX. It makes no sense logically to keep the "moto" in the name, but a language's evolution seldom follows logic, so I suppose we'll have the redundant and inaccurate term "BMX bicycle" for some time to come. (The USCF recognizes cyclo-cross races rather than BMX races, but the participants may ride any sort of bike they wish.)

The BMX has enjoyed great popularity with the younger riders over the last several years, as anyone who has children will know. The bike is usually quite small of frame, with a high saddle post, high-rise handlebars, knobby tires, and, more recently, stronger 5-arm (not spoked), motorcycle-style wheels. Most have a single speed and coaster brake, and generally are rather heavy despite their small size.

BMX races are usually different from mountain-bike races in that the courses are less rugged and the obstacles more contrived. Jumps and banked turns are *built* into BMX courses, and usually they are designed as much for the spectator as for the racers. The BMX competitor must wear more protective garb and gear than the road racer, which I particularly favor since most BMX'ers are quite young.

The 1-Speed

When I was a kid in Springfield, Missouri, I used to earn money delivering papers from my red Schwinn Newsboy Special. It had wide balloon tires and upright handlebars, and its frame sported a curved down tube and *two* curved top tubes. It had a heavy, black iron rack on the back to hold my canvas saddlebags, and if that wasn't a sturdy, functional bike, then one has never been made. I jumped curbs without a second thought, and often I would ride it down porch steps rather than walk it.

The classic 1-speed bomber, complete with coaster brake, kick stand, balloon tires, and sprung saddle, is still a big seller, even with all the competition. (Courtesy Schwinn Bicycle Company)

(God knows it was safer to ride that bike than try to lift it; I wouldn't try it now without an assistant.)

Until the late 1950's, when the 10-speed first began to take a noticeable share of the American bicycle market, the 1-speed, coaster-brake, balloon-tire bomber was the consumer's favorite. Men and boys rode the standard model; women and girls had their own, with no top tube but a double down tube, supposedly to accommodate skirts. Most people where I came from knew of no other kind of bicycle, although a few had seen or at least heard of the 3-speed by the time I was 9 or 10 years old. (They seemed to think it was cheating to use multiple gears, though, so until I ordered my first 10-speed, at the age of 12, nobody else had anything but a 1-speed bike in my town, Springfield, Missouri.)

The single-speed has lost its grip on the market, but it is still sold in substantial numbers every year. Given all the lighter, stronger, more efficient machines available today, I suspect the days of the bomber are numbered. The last Newsboy Special rolled off the line years ago.

The Beach Cruiser

The modern beach cruiser is the more highly evolved descendant of the 1-speed bomber. The cruiser has the same curvy style to the frame, but the tubing is much lighter, and the paint job may be superior. There are foam grips all the way down to the stem on some brands, and the coaster brake has been replaced by hand brakes.

Although the beach cruiser has the same sort of balloon tires as its single-speed ancestor, they are now sporty whitewalls (and pinkwalls and yellowwalls) mounted on alloy rims. And the rims may be golden, pink, blue—anything but steel gray.

A few of these cruisers are actually 1-speed bikes, but most have a 5-sprocket freewheel and derailleur. About the only vestiges of its ancestor are the hard-rubber pedals and the chain guard, both essential to the casual cyclist. No special apparel or qualifications needed; you can ride one of these with bare feet while carrying a surf board, and many people do.

I could be getting a distorted picture of the popularity of the beach cruiser, living as I now do so close to a southern California beach, but it seems to me the cruiser is here in a big way. Maybe you are considering getting a beach cruiser. If so, let me just clue you in on the basics of cruiser etiquette. First, never rush anywhere on a cruiser. It is extremely bad form to ride one at anything faster than a brisk walking pace. Second, when you ride one, take every opportunity to stop and chat with acquaintances—and when you do, never dismount. Rather, sit on the saddle with one foot on the ground. Also, whenever possible ride with your arms in the official cruiser position, that is, each hand tucked under the opposite arm, and chin down. It is advisable to wear sunglasses and chew gum.

The 3-Speed

One of the most ingenious and enduring inventions for the bicycle was the Sturmey-Archer 3-speed hub. The arrival of this little mechanism permitted the cyclist to choose a low, medium, or high gear rather than settling for the lone gear then available. Suddenly the cyclist could climb hills and speed down descents much more easily and quickly than ever before, but with no real added cost in weight or maintenance. Unlike the external gear-changing mechanisms found on today's 10-speed, the Sturmey-Archer contains all its parts within the hub, protected from dirt, water, and objects that might break the mechanism. As a result, 3-speeds require almost no maintenance outside a little lubrication and minor cable adjustments from time to time.

The "English racer," as the early 3-speed was called, was quite different in appearance from the contemporary 1-speed, as it featured straight tubing, narrower wheels, hand brakes mounted on straighter, lower handlebars, and trimmer fenders. But at a hefty 35 pounds or so, those bikes were almost as heavy as a bomber, and when the marginally lighter, more versatile 10-speeds became available, the 3-speed lost its chance to dominate the American bicycle market.

Three-speeds are steady, low-volume sellers in spite of all the competition they have always had. They provide good, dependable transportation, especially in places where the terrain imposes little demand or when the weather is bad. I have a friend, Jean, who is a college student and an excellent cyclist. She usually rides an $1800 Masi, but it's her black Raleigh 3-speed, which she got as a girl, that she rides to class and back.

The Tandem

The man in the song who tried to woo Daisy admitted that he couldn't afford a carriage, and then he tried to appeal to her vanity by promising she'd look sweet upon the seat of a bicycle built for two. How times have changed in only 80 years. Nowadays the poor suitor would probably find himself hard pressed to pay off the bike, and he'd no doubt have to assure Daisy she'd get

These two on a tandem know how to get their exercise together. The "windshield" is a fairing, which makes the bike more streamlined and hence more efficient. Notice the racks, fenders, headlamp, and bags; this bike is set up for touring. Cantilevered brakes and two water bottles, seen here, are quite common on tandems. (Courtesy Greg Siple, TOSRVPHOTO)

a good workout riding with him, else she might just go looking for a stronger cycling partner.

A good tandem is an expensive bike, but one that may reward the cycling couple with health and relationship benefits as few other things can. Now that I no longer ride the race circuit, I spend a good deal of my cycling time on my tandem, riding with a friend or with my sweetheart. It's much different from riding with the same people on singles, since it requires close co-ordination of effort and goals.

Most people think "tandem" is Latin for "double" or "together" or something like that. It *is* from the Latin, but it's actually sort of a play on words. Its literal meaning is "exactly then," or "at length." If you take "at length" to mean "lengthwise," and "lengthwise" to mean "one in front of the other," then you have completely distorted a perfectly good Latin word to make a joke that nobody understands. You would think some other Latin word would have done better, but "duet" had already been taken.

Today's tandems are made of high-quality materials and built to last. They come with all the appurtenances of the best road racers, though they usually are geared more like a touring bike, and the wheels are typically spoked like touring wheels. Santana and Schwinn make most of the tandems, although they have some competition. When purchasing a tandem, be aware that no *one* bike can accommodate partners who are radically mismatched for height. If you are much taller or shorter than your companion, you may not find a machine to fit. And be prepared to spend $2500 to get a good bicycle.

Recumbents

The recumbent bike differs from all the other types in very many ways. You ride most bicycles by straddling them like a horse, but with a recumbent, you sit on it like a go-kart—or, more aptly, like a kiddie car, since there are pedals out in front. Therefore, you sit in a chair-like seat rather than on a saddle. The steering mechanism is usually quite different, too, with

cables running to the front wheel rather than the typical han-
dlebar-and-stem setup. They are much lower and longer than
upright bikes, and very often the wheels are of two different
sizes. Needless to say, the frame construction is nothing like the
standard diamond shape.

Many recumbents are homemade by amateurs who either reconstruct an old bike in a new way or purchase a recumbent kit.
There are also a couple of recumbent manufacturers who sell
various models at prices competitive with more ordinary looking
machines. My hunch is that the homemade bike will tend to be
much heavier and weaker than the factory model, unless the
amateur is already a knowledgeable frame builder. The non-
professional is likely to weld together heavy, straight-gauge
steel tubing, while the pro can solder lighter and stronger double-butted tubes specifically designed for the recumbent frame.
(See below for a word about frames and frame construction.)

*Here it's easy to see the differences between a good recumbent (the Ava-
tar 2000) and conventional bicycles. This rider has taken the manufacturer's suggestion to carry a flag for visibility. (Courtesy Greg Siple,
TOSRVPHOTO)*

Recumbent bicycles have some advantages over upright bikes, but there are drawbacks to them as well. Although the recumbent riding position looks peculiar, even inefficient to the cyclist's eye, it is very comfortable to some. It may even be more efficient than the standard seated position because the rider's lower back muscles can participate more fully in the stroke. The low profile of the recumbent bike is an indisputable advantage in terms of air resistance, since the rider's frontal area is reduced. But at the same time a cyclist who is that low to the ground is hard to see and so may be more likely to get in an auto accident. Recumbent riders are quick to point out, however, that if they fall, at least they'll land on their feet rather than nose first. With a lower center of gravity they are more stable and have less distance to fall if they do take a spill. Still, if you get rolled over by a semi, it's not much consolation to be squashed flat from 2 feet up rather than 5 feet.

Recumbents have their enthusiasts, but I don't see a great surge in recumbent popularity in the near future unless some things change to make the design more attractive to the everyday cyclist. Two major problems are lack of versatility and their peculiar status in races.

While a cyclist on a recumbent can go from place to place more efficiently than he might on an upright bike, he's limited in what he can carry with him. If you ride a recumbent purely for the exercise or transportation, you will be fine. But if you want to carry your lunch or clothes or camping gear or groceries, you'll have a hard time doing it, because your bike just isn't set up for the task. I've seen racks on recumbents, but a backpack is ruled out because of the seat and its proximity to the rear wheel. In short, the recumbent seems to be somewhat limited in its usefulness as anything other than pure transportation.

One further problem for the popularity of the recumbent is that it is the *machina non grata* of the racing world. The USCF allows racers to ride standard road-racing and track bikes in its sanctioned events, and that's it. A racer who showed up at a USCF race on his recumbent would be welcome only as a spectator—though I imagine he'd get so much kidding that he wouldn't stick around long enough even to see the start. Racers never ride recumbents because they can't race them, and they aren't going to train on a bike they can't race.

If recumbents were admitted in road races, however, they would have a double advantage over the upright racing bike. Because they are so low to the ground, recumbents are no good to pace from—that is, a rider on a standard bike cannot follow a recumbent and get any real wind block—so the recumbent racers would not help any other riders, although they could get help by riding behind standard bikes. Since a recumbent already takes less energy to ride, the recumbent racer could take it easy for most of a race and then sprint ahead of the competition at the end.

At present such a scenario is merely speculation, because the USCF* and the UCI* have banned recumbents from their sanctioned races. The IHPVA* sanctions open races, which recumbent riders could enter, but typically these events draw the most highly refined human-powered vehicles, against which an ordinary recumbent has no more chance than a child's tricycle. So don't look for the roads to fill up with recumbent bicycles in the next few months. However, recumbents could (and should) be more popular if the public were better informed about them *and* if they were made more practical. If I built or sold recumbent bikes, I'd be sure to have models fitted with racks so they could be used as commuting and touring vehicles. And I'd promote all-comer races with prizes for recumbent cyclists as well as upright riders. Recumbent enthusiasts might lobby the USCF for recognition, with perhaps a recumbent race or two in the regional and national championships. More to the point, they might lobby Congress for safe bikeways for their vehicles, as the open roads will not do. The recumbent is a good idea, but its time has yet to come.

The Track Bike

At first glance, the track bike looks like a 10-speed: dropped bars, narrow tires, diamond frame. But after a moment you see

*USCF: The United States Cycling Federation. UCI: Union Cycliste Internationale. IHPVA: International Human Powered Vehicle Association.

how sleek it looks: very bare, trim, and stark. The frame has nothing extra brazed on. There are no brakes, derailleurs, or cables or any sort. The saddle is very high, the bars quite low, with just enough tape to cover the last few inches of the handlebars. The track bike is the cheetah of the bicycle world.

Track bikes have a single fixed gear, and they are built for nothing but a track. I have ridden track bikes (equipped with a single brake) on the roads for training purposes, and now and then I'll see someone else do that, but in ordinary circumstances you won't see one outside a velodrome or a bike shop.

Since nobody but a trackie would buy a track bike, there's no point in making cheap ones. Like cellos, there is no such thing as a lousy track bike, though some are better than others.

Absence of all non-essentials helps keep the weight down on track bikes. Most are under 20 pounds, and some are down around 17. The fixed gear forces the rider's feet to move even when not actively pedaling, and it's a bit of a trick to ride one properly. You can actually ride backwards on a track bike, although USCF rules forbid it in competition. (Why even have such a rule? Well, in some races trackies try to force their opponents into the lead by stopping their forward motion in what is called a track stand. The rule is designed to prevent ludicrous and potentially dangerous situations in an already hazardous sport. Can't you just imagine two great cyclists both racing *backward* in an attempt to get behind their opponent?)

If you are already a trackie, chances are you know where to find the bikes, parts, and mechanics who cater to your sport. If you aren't yet, but would like to become involved in track riding, you should contact your nearest velodrome for information. Scout around for the bike shops that carry track bikes, and get to know other trackies. Not all cyclists are cut out for track bikes, but maybe *you* are.

COMPONENTS

No matter what type of bike you ride, the more miles you put on it, the faster you will wear out components. I hope by the time you have finished this book you will know enough about riding and maintaining your bicycle that you won't be put off when you wear parts out. Rather, you'll take it as a good sign: you've been riding your bike a lot!

Luckily, bicycle parts are relatively cheap. Although the most exotic, top-of-the-line components from the most exclusive, trendy manufacturers are expensive, it doesn't really cost that much to keep your bike in top condition if you shop carefully and wisely. I don't hold with those who say everyone should ride on the most fashionable parts all the time, because not everyone can afford to do that, and often there are quite adequate, less expensive, second-line or imitation products to be found. At the same time, you should use the best parts you can afford.

Ride the finest bicycle you can afford to ride—not necessarily the most expensive, but the best you can find. Buy the frame that fits you and meets your needs as closely as possible. Get the braze-ons you want, and mount the brakes, derailleurs, saddle, and handlebars that you like the most. I am convinced that you will ride more and enjoy your cycling to the fullest if you have absolutely the best machine for you. Ask any serious cyclist— once you've ridden on a good bike, you'll never be happy with an inferior one.

Here I want to mention a little about components to help you select parts, either as replacements on your present bike or as components for your next bicycle. I will talk a little about manufacturing processes where appropriate, and I'll recommend some brand names that have proven themselves. I won't mention model names or numbers, though, because these can change so rapidly, even within a season, that such information would be outdated by the time these words got to the typesetter. But I can give you a general rule to follow when looking for components: buy the pretty parts, not the ugly ones. Look at components carefully, feel them, before buying. Good parts look good; they feel nice and smooth. Quality components are beautiful, and lowlier parts are not so pleasing to look at. This holds true for everything on a bike, from pedal to saddle, fork to spoke; everything about the frame and everything attached to it. High-quality bike parts have been carefully made out of good materials; they are nicely finished; they work without sticking or whining; and they are obviously well designed.

Bike Framesets

There are several ways to tell good framesets from inferior ones. The best frames are built of the highest quality tubing—tubes made by Reynolds, Columbus, Tange, Ishiwata, and Super Vitus. Most frame builders use steel tubing, often chromium-molybdenum alloy, although other materials (graphite, aluminum, boron, titanium) are sometimes used.

Cheap, heavy frames are made of comparatively low-grade steel rolled into tubes, whereas better frames are made of steel drawn into tubes that are thinner, lighter, and yet stronger than rolled tubing. The better type of tubing comes in two styles. Straight-gauge tubes have walls of constant thickness throughout. These are mitered and butted together inside lugs to make up what is known as a butted (or single-butted) frame. The other, more expensive kind of tubing is not of constant gauge, but has walls that are thinner in the middle with thicker-walled ends, although the outer diameter of the tube remains constant. This is the kind that is used to make double-butted frames, which are lighter *and* stronger than the single-butted variety.

The more expensive frames are constructed of the costlier double-gauge tubing, but that isn't the only reason they are high-priced. Good frames must be carefully mitered and fitted together, then brazed at just the right temperature to ensure strongly bonded joints. Unlike cheap, mass-produced frames made of heavy steel, a high-quality frame cannot be welded together at high temperatures, and it doesn't rely on a heavy gauge of steel for its strength. Rather, the best frames are constructed individually by master frame builders who take the time necessary to make each one as nearly perfect as it can be. A joint heated just a little too much will weaken; one under-heated will not braze sufficiently. Improperly butted frames will never solder correctly and therefore will give way under stress. A correctly built bicycle frame is stronger, pound for pound, than any bridge or airplane ever built.

A frame jig such as this helps the builder fit the tubes together with precision. Still, no machine can save incorrectly mitered tubing. (Courtesy Cinelli)

When you shop for a good frame, look for a sticker that advertises the tubing used in its construction. Inspect all the joints to be certain there are no gaps where the tubes meet the lugs. If any joint is imperfect, forget buying that frame. Blisters around joints may mean the frame wasn't properly cleaned of brazing flux before painting, and such carelessness will mean a prematurely rusty frame at the least. Worse, it may well mean there are other, more serious structural problems with the frame as well.

Some framesets come with fork and headset installed; others may include the bottom bracket; and some bikes come complete from the dealer with all components. Forks, chain stays, and seat stays may be of better or worse quality than the tubing on a

Properly brazing a joint requires a high level of skill and a good deal of patience. After brazing, the frame must be acid-bathed to remove scale and flux, easily seen in this photo. (Courtesy Cycles Peugeot)

given frameset, so it is always a good idea to check with the dealer or builder about these parts. You should not pay as much for inferior fork and stay materials as for the better quality items. The dropouts on the best forks and chain stays are drop-forged separately and welded on, and often they are chromed rather than painted, as skewers invariably grind paint off dropouts. Cheaper dropouts are merely stamped and cut from steel plates. Campagnolo, Shimano, and Sugino make good forged dropouts and, if you have a choice, you should ask for them.

The bottom brackets made by Campagnolo, Shimano, Avocet, and Phil Wood are all excellent, reliable products. If you want to ride your bike for, say, five years without having to overhaul the bottom bracket, think about getting an Avocet or Phil Wood sealed-bearing bottom bracket. They're guaranteed, and the extra cost is often well worth it, although you should be aware that

A sealed bottom bracket like this one may take five years of hard riding without ever requiring maintenance. (Courtesy Champions Import-Export Company)

a sealed bottom bracket may not be as smooth as a standard one.

Modolo and Campagnolo headsets are also worth their higher prices, as there is nothing like the feeling of a perfectly smooth-steering bicycle. You may want to look into getting little rubber boots to cover the bottom of the headset. These are installed to protect the more vulnerable bottom race from water and grit, and they work.

The paint job on a new frame should be flawless. Check the lugs carefully as well as all braze-ons to be sure there is no blistering or chipping. Turn the frame over and run your fingertips along all the tubes; they should feel smooth, perfect. Many good frames come with an Imron paint job and several coats of clear coat over the paint. These coatings will withstand more miles of riding and more hours of nasty weather than ordinary paint alone, and you may wish to invest in this kind of extra protection. Remember, though, that paint has no effect whatsoever on the ride of a bicycle, and if a nice paint job hides an inferior machine, then it's doing more harm than good.

The frame is the single most important and expensive part of a bicycle, so it pays to be selective. Don't settle for less than the best frame for yourself if you can possibly find and afford it. To many people, the frame *is* the bike, since other components wear out so much faster. So if you want the bike that is best for you, get the perfect frame, even if it means postponing getting other components that you really want. You can always upgrade other parts as they wear out or as your finances permit.

There are those who believe that getting a good bike means buying a custom-made frameset, but I disagree. Granted, people with special requirements usually get their bikes made to order, but the majority of the biking public—even those at the top of their sport—will do just as well on a high-quality frame built on time-tested designs. The advantages of a custom-made bike are that you can be certain of getting exactly what you want, from angles to tube lengths to bottom-bracket height, and you can return the frame to the builder for repairs or complaints. The disadvantages are that you may pay more, you may still get a poorly made frame, and you may have to wait many moons for your bike.

Putting the finishing touches on a frame: the last paint details before assembling the bicycle. (Courtesy Cycles Peugeot)

I say *may* pay more because many American builders charge no more for a custom frame than the retail price of an imported factory frame. And yet the frame may be no better—could be a lot worse—than a factory frame. This is why finding the right builder is so important. A rookie could build you a pretty piece of junk, and then again he might be the next Michelangelo of bicycles. An experienced frame builder with a good reputation might be tired of his trade, more interested in your money than your bike, or he could still be at the top of his craft. Generally, though, experience helps. As Dave Moulton put it, "To be a good frame builder, one has to build a lot of frames." The best way to discover who is doing the best work in your area is to talk to racers and people in good bike shops.

The Drive Train

I've already mentioned one part of the drive train, the bottom bracket. What's left are cranks, pedals, chain rings, freewheels, and chains.

As with bottom-bracket sets, Campagnolo makes the best cranksets. Most people ride 170-mm cranks, but longer and shorter ones are available for tall and short riders. Criterium racers often choose shorter cranks for better clearance around sharp turns, and mountainous terrain usually calls for longer cranks for better leverage. Campy cranksets range from 160 to 180 mm, and they are quite good.

The lightest racing pedals are made by Campagnolo. If you are not racing, though, you'll probably want something a little heftier than these ultra-lights. Pedals by Shimano, Sun-Tour, and Campagnolo may fill the bill; they are light, strong, and reliable. I would avoid buying any pedal that cannot be overhauled, though. If you are in doubt, ask the salesperson before buying.

Alloy chain rings in a variety of sizes (number of teeth) are made by Campagnolo, Shimano, and SunTour. All of these com-

Light, stiff cranksets are a boon to all types of cyclists. These cranks are designed to take special light pedals that have no spindle. (Courtesy Shimano Sales Corporation)

A six-cog freewheel with a 13-21 range. This is commonly found on racing bikes, but the range of gearing is too narrow for most touring purposes. Individual cogs may be replaced when they wear out. (Courtesy Campagnolo USA)

panies make light, durable chain rings. As for freewheels, Mallard, Regina, SunTour, and Campagnolo are the brands I like best, with the most variety in 5-, 6-, and 7-cog combinations. Shimano makes a cassette freewheel that fits its own brand of hub, but no other, so be sure to check your present equipment before replacing your freewheel.

Light, strong chains are made by Sedisport. You will see chains in various colors—silver or gold—but that is just cosmetics. Your chain will be black soon enough, as it should be, so look for strength, not dazzle, in a chain. The Sedisport chain is smooth turning, light, inexpensive, and works on just about any bike.

The Wheels

Wheels are built of rims, spokes, and hubs. Anyone can build a wheel, but not just anyone can build a good one. Unless you are already an expert at wheels, leave it to an accomplished builder to make yours. You should get the wheels you want, of course, and your wheel builder should be able to help you decide exactly what you should have. Here are some decisions you can make before visiting your wheel builder.

Clinchers or tubulars? That is the question. Do you have the money to spend on sew-up tubular tires—and the patience to repair them when they puncture? Do you *need* sew-ups? Racers cannot do without high-quality, lightweight tubulars mounted on 700C tubular-tire rims. Even though they are expensive, sew-ups are much more responsive and reliable than clinchers, giving a superior ride in foul weather and fair. They are lighter (although some very light clincher tires are now available) and easier to change when they do go flat. You'll get nearly as many miles out of good sew-ups as comparable-quality clinchers if you repair them. It takes so much more time, skill, and patience to fix a flatted tubular than an ordinary tube, though, that they often are discarded sooner. If you are primarily a bike commuter or tourist, you will undoubtedly be better off with clincher tires designed for long miles and heavier loads. And many racers own

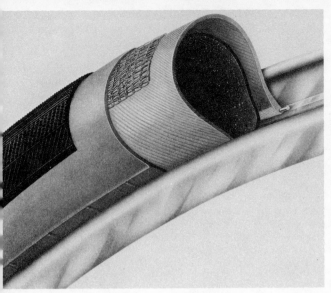

This cutaway shot reveals the construction of a clincher tire, with tube in place, mounted on a rim. This tire is different from most because it has some steel webbing for extra protection against flats.
(Courtesy Pneumatiques Wolber)

two sets of wheels, one of each type. They use clinchers most of the time and save their tubular tires for races.

Good tubulars are made by Continental, Pneudan, D'Allesandra, and Clemente. Specialized, Wolber, and Trim-Line make high-pressure clinchers that are lightweight and long lasting.

Rims for most bicycles (other than BMX and some 1-speeds) come in either 27″ or 700C diameter, the latter being just a bit smaller than the former. A 27″ wheel measures approximately 27″ in diameter from one edge of the inflated tire to the other, while a 700C wheel comes closer to 26½″ measured the same way. (This works out to about 67 cm. I believe 700C originally meant "not to exceed 700 mm," or 70.0 cm. The industry is in the process of changing to metric measurements for all wheels; when that happens, the diameters of wheels will be measured in either millimeters or centimeters, and from the inside edges of the rim rather than the outside of the inflated tire.) 700C rims are 25C wide—a little under 1″, or 25.4 mm—while 27″ rims are 1″, 1⅛″, or 1¼″ in width for 10-speeds. Wider wheels for mountain bikes and 1-speeds are also available. Rims usually are designed to accept either clincher or tubular tires, although a rim that can accommodate both types has recently been invented.

You can find rims in steel, aluminum, and alloys, and they may be bare, anodized or otherwise colored, or heat-treated for

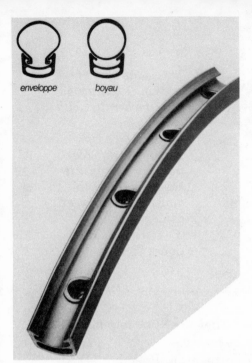

enveloppe boyau

A recent innovation in rims, this one will take either a clincher (enveloppe) or tubular (boyau) tire. (Courtesy Pneumatiques Wolber)

strength. I recommend alloy or treated alloy rims, as they are stronger and lighter than steel wheels, as well as more resilient. Alloy wheels even work better in rain. Whereas steel might dent, alloys are more likely to bounce back. Brands to look for are Araya, Assos, Mavic, and Super Champion.

Hubs, like bottom brackets, may be sealed or standard, and again it is Phil Wood and Avocet that make the sealed variety. Campagnolo and Sun-Tour hubs are good standard products. One choice to make is between low- and high-flange hubs. The flange is the plate around the end of the hub that carries the spokes. Higher flanges make for stronger, stiffer wheels, with consequent longer life span but a slightly more jarring ride. Another choice has to do with the number of spoke holes in the hubs—and therefore the number of spokes to the wheel. A light racing wheel may have as few as 24 spokes; standard wheels have 36; and some touring wheels have as many as 42 spokes. The spoke pattern may also vary between cross-2 (each spoke crosses only two others between the hub and the rim), cross-3, or cross-4. Usually cross-2 is used only for racing wheels.

I recommend that you use stainless-steel spokes, which resist corrosion, and discuss your riding needs and goals with your wheel builder before deciding on spoke gauge. The number and gauge of spokes used will help to determine strength and weight of the finished wheel, and in general you want to find the lightest yet strongest wheel that will work for you.

Derailleurs

The choice derailleurs are made by Campagnolo, Huret, and Sun-Tour. When shopping for derailleurs, you have to look for the sizes that will accommodate the number and sizes of chain rings and cogs on your bike. Touring bikes have a wider range of gears, and so they require rear derailleurs with longer arms and front derailleurs with longer cages than those for racing bikes. Top-quality derailleurs designed for racing bikes usually will work properly only if used with a fairly restricted range of tooth

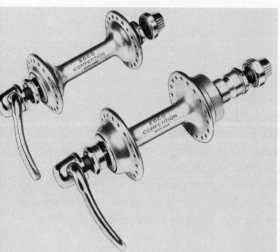

Front and rear hubs shown with skewers in place. Note threads on the right side of the rear hub to accommodate the freewheel. (Courtesy Champions Import-Export Company)

This front derailleur requires only minimal mounting hardware. The dark fitting shown here is brazed to the seat tube. More commonly, there is a circular clamp that embraces the seat tube to hold the front derailleur. (Courtesy Campagnolo USA)

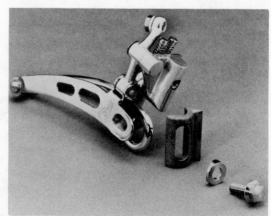

combinations, which are normally listed on the package. Be sure to use only the right size derailleurs.

The shift levers and necessary mounting hardware are sold with the front and rear derailleurs. If you do not already have brazed-on shift bosses, I recommend that you mount your shift levers on the down tube rather than the stem or handlebars. Mountain bikes usually have the levers on the bars near the grips, but 10-speeds will take them in several places. Some people find fingertip shifters (found at the ends of the handlebars) to be more convenient, but they are less responsive because of the very long cables needed to attach them. The same goes for shifters mounted on the stem, with the added fault that they are not at all convenient. It is easier to reach down to the down tube to shift than up to the stem, and derailleur cables are relatively short with down-tube mounting. Most good 10-speeds have the shift levers on the down tube.

Brakes

Everyone needs good brakes. The racer must be able to control his speed very precisely, else he endangers himself and his fellow racers. The tourist must also have sure stopping power, since he or she will ordinarily have greater mass and momentum. Campagnolo, Shimano, Weinmann, and Phil Wood all make fine brakesets. The Campy and Shimano brakes are side-pulls; Weinmann makes the best center-pulls; and Phil Wood manufactures disc brakes, which are found on some tandems.

I also would advise you not to buy brakes with so-called safety

This cantilevered brake is designed for touring, when extra weight makes slowing and stopping more difficult. The levers shown are the conventional alloy caliper (right) and anodized, cold-forged calipers for off-road use, to be used on straight bars (top) or dropped bars (center). (Courtesy Shimano Sales Corporation)

Stems come in all sizes to allow a precise fit. This photo shows both metallic and anodized finishes in alloy stems. (Courtesy Specialized Bicycle Components)

levers. These are extra levers attached to the calipers that allow the brakes to be applied with the hands on the tops of the bars. They originally were introduced to allow the rider access to the brakes from more positions. This flexibility supposedly increased the safety of riding. But the idea and the reality somehow never merged. Safety levers may give you a sense of security, but it is a false one because you cannot stop as surely with them as with the caliper. If your bike has safety levers on the brakes, I recommend you remove them.

Handlebars and Stems

Alloy handlebars and stems are preferable to steel, if only because of their lightness. Cinelli and Shimano make high-quality bars and stems in a wide variety of sizes and shapes. Men, especially if they are tall, usually prefer deeper drops and bigger hooks than women.

Saddles

Good saddles are manufactured by Brooks, Avocet, Cinelli, Concor, and Ideale. The so-called anatomical saddles made by Avocet and Selle Royal are much more comfortable for women than are the narrow racing saddles used by men. Women's saddles have raised ischial supports and a concave central ridge to better fit a woman's anatomy, but they couldn't be shaped any worse for a man. If you are a male, take heed: resist the temptation to try riding on a woman's saddle. You'll only get hurt.

PURCHASING A BIKE

Well, up to this point you have read all about the bikes that are available, and I've mentioned some of the choices you have in components. So by now you should know enough about bicycles to make it almost impossible to buy one. There are more choices than an ice-cream store, and right now you probably know only one thing for sure: you don't want vanilla. Maybe I can help you focus your search to a manageable number of flavors, and from there it's up to you to get a free taste if you can before purchasing.

The first step is to assess your needs. Do you already have a bike? What sort of riding do you do now? What kind of cycling do you intend to do over the next year, two years, five years? How much can you afford to spend?

If you already own a bike, you have a machine with which to compare your next bicycle. Maybe your present bicycle is just what you're looking for and you don't really need a new one. On the other hand, maybe anything looks good next to your Incredible Rusting Hulk. If you're already riding a fairly good bicycle, one that suits your current needs and those of the near future, consider keeping what you have and perhaps upgrading some of the components. If you wait to purchase your new bike this will afford you plenty of time to shop around, check parts and prices, and put aside the money for any tools or accessories you'll need. You won't regret any purchase that is carefully considered.

One variation on the wait-and-see approach is to buy new components for your present bike one by one until you have all the parts you want, but affixed to your old frame. Then buy a new frameset. This method is good if you can't find your preferred components on any single bike, or if money burns a hole in your pocket. You may pay more for the finished product, especially if you don't diligently hunt for bargains, but you'll have exactly what you want in the end. Why settle for less? If you are planning on getting a custom frame, very likely you'll have to wait some weeks or months for it anyway, and you'll probably have to buy the components separately in any event. Picking up parts individually, especially if you can shop around, makes good sense.

If you don't own a bike yet, or if your bicycle is completely unsuitable for your needs, then before looking you need to decide what kind of bike you should get. This means you have to think about—and explicitly state—what your cycling goals and needs are, which will help guide your choice of bikes. It might be a good idea right now to ask yourself what kind of riding you do or plan to do; what features you need in a bike; and how much you are prepared to invest in a new machine. Over the next few days, ask your present or potential cycling partners their opinions and discuss it with family members with whom you will (hopefully) be doing some cycling. Ask yourself what you would change about your present bike (if you have one), and what features you would keep. It might help to write some of these things down so that you can keep the high points in mind as you shop.

Before I get into the specifics of shopping for a bicycle, I'd like to state my own biases about bikes. I think the two most versatile, functional types of bicycle are the 10-speed and the mountain bike, in that order. You can find a fully equipped, rideable 10-speed for about $150, and it will take you up and down hills, with or without luggage, with efficiency and (at least a little) style. You can spend 10 or 12 times that amount on a custom-built racing machine with all the best components, and there is just about every imaginable gradation in between. What this means is that you can find a 10-speed to fit your budget and needs no matter what kind of riding you do—unless you are a track cyclist or the world's most dedicated beach bum. Mountain bikes are a bit narrower in price range, but they are otherwise comparable to 10-speeds for commuting and touring purposes, with the added benefit of off-road capabilities.

For most cyclists, then, some kind of 10-speed will be the bike of choice. Not that I have anything against other kinds of bicycles; they simply do not have the same functional flexibility found in the 10-speed. Single-speed bikes, for instance, are invariably heavier and less responsive than 10-speeds, and unless you live in a flood plain, that lone gear may not be enough; 3-speeds are also relatively heavy and have limited gear options.

Today's 15- or 18-speed touring bikes weigh about 23-25 pounds and can carry enough baggage for touring in any season. They have such a wide range of gears that virtually no climb is too steep to assault even when fully loaded down. And they can be put to use as recreational and commuting vehicles without making a single change in the bike. Against such versatility, most other types of bicycle look pretty limited.

In the upcoming chapters I hope you are inspired to use your bicycle in ways you may not have considered already, thus extending your list of cycling goals. Imagine yourself doing your shopping, visiting friends, commuting to work, taking vacations, and even racing on your bicycle. When you read about touring, actually envision yourself riding your bicycle on tour; when I talk about commuting, picture yourself riding to work on a bicycle, and think about such details as bathing facilities and routes to use. If you dismiss the idea of riding a bicycle where now you drive a car or take public transportation, you may never realize your own potential as a cyclist, and further limit yourself by the wrong choice of bicycle.

Familiarize yourself with the bike shops in your area. Find out what kinds of bikes each shop carries, whether or not they cater to a restricted clientele, and whether they carry a large variety of high-quality merchandise. Price and compare bicycles, clothing, and accessories. There is a shop near me that sells bikes and components for top dollar, but their clothing prices are very low. Guess what I buy in that shop. Just as important as price is the helpfulness and friendliness of the shop owner and employees. I don't mind spending a little more at a shop where I know the people treat me well. A good bike-shop salesperson won't try to sell you what you don't need, because he or she knows that you could easily take your business elsewhere.

Buy your bicycle from a reputable dealer, not from a mail-order house. First, a dealer will have a greater selection of bikes, and you can be sure the equipment has been correctly stored, assembled, and handled. You have no such assurances when you shop by mail. Second, it is difficult to register complaints if you are dissatisfied with a bike purchased by mail, whereas any reputable shop owner will make good on promises and guarantees made at the time of sale. Third, only a shop owner can help you in selecting models to test ride, in fitting the bike to your body, and in deciding among components available. Fourth, sooner or later you will need to replace worn parts or have repairs done, and you will have a head start on friendly relations with your shop owner if you buy a bike from him or her.

After you have decided on the type of bike, the kind of components, and the price you want to pay, visit the various shops and test ride some bikes. You should inform the salesperson of your cycling goals and the general idea of what you want, then listen to what he or she says. Your objective is to test ride and price as many different bikes as you can before making a purchase, but limit your search to the models that fall within your range of specifications.

You might make up a list of qualities you want in a bike, and rate the bikes you test ride for those qualities. Put down whatever is important to you—comfort, a certain brand of parts, color, price, lightness, whatever—and actually rate each bike on each dimension. Use a scale of 1-10 if you like, or A-F as in a report card. It actually *is* a report card, and one that will help you to narrow down the field of contenders for your money. With our limited memory, it makes good sense to keep score when going shopping for a bike—or anything else, for that matter.

With each bike you consider, inspect it very carefully before actually taking off on a test ride. Look at the paint job; it should be beautiful. If you see peels, bubbles, or scratches on the paint, then either the paint job was inferior or the bike was ill-handled. Take a close look at the lugs and joints. Are there any blisters there? Do you see any gaps between the tubing and the lugs? That means the frame wasn't carefully and correctly mitered and fitted. You don't want that bicycle, or one with dents or other abnormalities in the tubing. Anything that's supposed to be straight should be perfectly straight; if it's not, leave the bike where you found it.

How about the parts? Are they nicely finished and properly

mounted? The wheels should be perfectly true and round, and they should spin smoothly and easily. Nothing should be loose, dirty, worn, or scratched. If the bike doesn't look perfect, ask the dealer why. He or she should not let you roll out the door with a bike that isn't in absolutely top condition when new.

Your inspection should include lifting the bike to check its weight. With one hand at the rear of the saddle and the other at the head of the stem, lift the bicycle straight up to assess it. Don't heft it with one hand, or with two hands in some other position, because it will only feel heavier. Lift several contenders one after the other to get a good idea of how they compare on this rather crucial dimension. Although the weight of the bike often is listed in a brochure, you should check it yourself—on a scale if possible—because errors have been known to creep into advertising.

As to your test rides, take the bike through its paces, trying out all the gears and riding both up and down hill, as well as on the level. Listen for sounds; anything that makes any noise on a new bike is something that needs attention. Test the brakes several times for sureness and responsiveness. Notice how the bicycle handles. Does it steer easily? Is there any shimmy or wobble when you let go of the handlebars? Does it veer off to one side? A good bike travels a straight line even when you let go; you don't want it if it isn't at least that good.

When you have reached the point where there are only two or three models left from which to choose, you are in an enviable yet vexing position. You're close to actually getting a new bike, but you can't make a decision without some help. That's where your report card comes in. Look at your ratings for these last two or three bikes and see how they compare on paper. You might even rank the different considerations (weight, price, comfort, etc.) with the most important one at the top and the least important at the bottom. Then check the scores. Most likely, one will come out as the best bike for you.

3

How to Bicycle

"It's just like riding a bicycle—you never forget how to do it."
How many times have you heard that? For all I know, it's true;
you probably never do forget how to ride a bike. But you may not
have learned *how* to ride one properly in the first place! Cycling
may be a simple, repetitive activity, but that doesn't mean
there's nothing to it. As any good competitive cyclist can tell
you, good riding technique and style take years to develop and
refine, and you never cease learning more about riding a bicycle
no matter how many miles you have logged.

SETTING UP A BIKE

No matter what kind of bicycle you ride, it should fit you. Just
as your shoes must be a certain length and width to be comfortable and functional, so should your bike be the right height and
length to work properly. In fact, a bicycle must be much more
carefully fitted than a pair of shoes, because it will never stretch
or wear in to fit you.

There are, however, numerous minor adjustments that you
can and should make until your bike fits you perfectly. Since
there are so many kinds of bicycles available—BMX, mountain
bikes, track bikes, road racers, tandems, recumbents—I'll concentrate on the 10-speed sport bike, the most popular model, and
indicate where general rules apply to other kinds of machines.

The Frame

The smaller the frame, the stiffer, stronger, and lighter it will be. It's easy to see why. The main tubes of the 10-speed bike form a more or less perfect triangle, depending on the length of the head tube. The top, seat, and down tubes make three sides of the triangle, and on very small frames the top tube actually meets the down tube at the head tube. This triangle is very strong. It resists flexion and compression. On taller frames, the three main tubes are generally longer, and the head tube is also taller since the top tube remains parallel to the ground. The triangular frame then becomes a quadrilateral, an inherently less stable configuration than a triangle. Further, the longer four tubes will weigh more and the bigger frame will also flex more. Since every added ounce has to be pulled up every hill, bigger frames are less desirable if a smaller frame will fit. And that extra flexion means more energy that could go into forward motion is spent bending the frame.

There are several tests for the fit of a frame. The first rule of thumb is that there be *at least* one inch between the top tube and your crotch when you straddle the bike. Stand flat-footed over the middle of the top tube and see what happens. Did you groan or squeal in pain? That bike is too big for you! Is the top tube at about mid-thigh level? That frame is much too short.

You should be able to stand flat-footed while straddling your bike and still have 1–3" clearance above the top tube. (Courtesy Dave Ball)

This test shows that my top tube and stem are probably about the right length. With elbow on the front of the saddle, my fingers reach to just about halfway across the stem. Note that my saddle is a bit higher than most people would like, but that's how I prefer it. (Courtesy Dave Ball)

Shorter riders should be able to lift the bike about 1 to 1½ inches, while taller riders should have even more clearance—maybe up to 3 inches. I ride on a 59-cm frame (23¼″) even though I am 6′1″ tall.

Another rule of thumb concerns checking the top-tube length. Put your elbow against the front of the saddle and extend your forearm parallel to the top tube. If your fingertips reach about halfway across the horizontal stem, your top tube is probably right.

It seems that BMX and mountain bikes generally are sold with very small frames and longer saddle posts. If you buy such a bike, you'll want to check the fit with the salesperson—as, indeed, you should for any bike. BMX bikes and some other types of frames have non-horizontal top tubes, so the rules about clearance do not apply to them.

The Saddle

The saddle should be parallel to the ground, although it may be tipped slightly forward or backward to accommodate your particular anatomical idiosyncrasies. I would caution you to make only very slight saddle adjustments, and then ride the bike at least 4 to 5 hours before making any further changes.

The saddle post should not be too high—most of them have marks that indicate maximum allowable exposure—but neither should there be no post showing. If your saddle is right against the seat tube, your frame is undoubtedly too big.

When seated on the bike, you should be able to rest your left heel on the left pedal when it is at about seven o'clock, without either stretching or bending your leg too much. While riding in the seated position your leg should never be fully extended. You should have a little bend in the knee even when the pedal is all the way down.

How much bend is a little? How much is too much? The best way to tell is to watch other (good) cyclists as they ride. They don't fully extend their legs on the down stroke, and neither should you. You can ask others to watch you ride and critique your form. Since others may spot your flaws more readily than you can, why not make the corrections sooner rather than later?

There are a couple of indications of improper saddle height. If the rider appears to bounce in the saddle with every stroke, chances are the saddle is too low. If the hips rock back and forth, very likely the saddle is too high. You can use these tests to help your fellow riders. This is not to say that you cannot watch yourself ride, though. You can check that knee bend—and many other points—by riding past large, plate-glass windows and watching your reflection. When I lived in Texas, I used to make a point of riding by a particular department store every month or so to check on my form. The store had reflective windows near the curb that allowed me to see myself from the side. It was

You should always have some bend in your knee when riding. Full extension would be over-extension. (Courtesy Christian Paul)

while riding past that store that I first discovered how straight my leg appeared on the down stroke. I lowered my saddle and corrected a problem of which I was not aware until then.

Handlebars and Stems

The choice in handlebars and stems can really help the cyclist whose frame is not quite perfect. Are you stuck with a bike whose top tube is too short? Until you can afford that next frame, maybe a longer stem and more generous bars will do the trick. Are your arms so long that you can't crouch low and still be comfortable? A deeper set of drops might prove the easiest cure. I know a man who had some lower-back surgery that left him unable to lean as far down as he was accustomed. An extra-long neck stem was all he needed until he fully recovered.

Except in unusual circumstances, such as with my friend with the bad back, the stem should not be higher than the saddle. Lay a yard stick between the saddle and the stem, and if it's parallel to the top tube, at least your stem is not too high. Many riders, including myself, prefer the stem several inches lower than the saddle, and perhaps such an arrangement will suit you, too. Because I am tall, if I don't lower my handlebars that much I lose a good aerodynamic posture, and that could spell trouble in a race.

The bars should be positioned so that the drops are parallel with the ground or tipped down somewhat. This, like so much else about a bike, is an individual choice. It's worth experimenting until you are happy with your handlebar placement.

Mountain bikes, 3-speeds, and 1-speeds generally have bars that are not dropped, but are gripped at the ends at about the same height as the top of the stem. For these bikes, again, the stem should be no higher than the saddle, and the height of the stem and the tilt of the bars should be varied until they are right for you.

The placement of the brake levers also is important. As a rule, racers place their brake hoods lower on the handlebar than do tourists; whether you like yours low or high, be sure to position them so they are parallel to the bar and within reach. Some people with small hands have to be careful to find calipers with shorter reach.

THE PHYSICS OF CYCLING

Isaac Newton's system of physics quite adequately describes what happens when a person cycles. Riding involves the expenditure of muscular energy to overcome various Newtonian forces in order to propel both rider and machine forward. The four forces that work against the cyclist are inertia, rolling resistance, drive-train losses, and air resistance.

Inertia

A body at rest will remain at rest until some force moves it, and that tendency to stay at rest is inertia. If you want to move your bike, you have to put some energy into it by pushing off or turning the cranks. Once in motion, according to Sir Isaac, your bike should keep going at the same pace forever unless some other forces act on it to either speed it up or slow it down. More muscle energy will speed it up, but the other three forces will tend to slow it down, through wasted energy or through opposition to forward motion of the machine and rider.

Drive-Train Losses

Once you are under way, some of the energy you put into your bike will be wasted in drive-train losses. There is resistance inherent in a less-than-perfect chain traveling over less-than-ideally matched chain rings and cogs. Energy also is lost in the bottom bracket, derailleur pulleys, and pedals. Any part that goes round and round will have a little friction no matter how smooth and well-lubricated it is. Drive-train losses account for the smallest fraction of the energy you put into cycling from one place to another—maybe 5 percent in an off-the-shelf bike. A well-maintained bicycle is energy efficient. A dry chain clogged with dirt, a loose, ill-adjusted bottom bracket, and similar drive-train deficiencies will cost you energy with every revolution of the cranks.

Rolling Resistance

A more substantial amount of energy is used up in rolling resistance. This is really a combination of forces all acting to slow down the moving bicycle. One is friction in the hubs: even in an otherwise perfect environment, your bike eventually would coast to a stop due to the slight but ever-present friction inside the hubs. Another force is road-surface friction. Fatter tires, flabbier (i.e., under-inflated) tires, rougher roads, and deviations in wheel roundness and trueness all will tend to slow down the bicycle. The third force is gravity, which works both for you and against you, depending upon whether you're ascending or descending.

Air Resistance

At slow speeds (under 8 mph), and with heavy loads to bear, rolling resistance is the greatest impediment for the cyclist to overcome. But for the single rider on a light machine traveling at, say, 15 mph or faster, it is air resistance that presents the biggest problem. At 18 mph with no head wind on smooth, level ground, a good cyclist is using about 80 percent of all his or her energy just to overcome air resistance. At higher speeds, and with head winds, the percentage climbs higher and higher. So you can see that minimizing air resistance can make a big difference to a cyclist.

As you ride your bicycle, you will always feel some breeze in your face except on those rare occasions when you are traveling no faster than any tail wind. (Now you know why you always seem to have head winds: you do.) That breeze is not trivial. The typical cyclist has to push 1,000 pounds of air aside for every mile of progress—and that's in still air.

Drilling through the air will be more or less easy depending on how great a frontal area you project and how streamlined your shape is. The lower you crouch on your bike, the less your projected frontal area, and the less air you have to push aside as you travel forward. This is why a recumbent bike is more efficient than an upright machine; the recumbent has a smaller projected frontal area.

There is also aerodynamics to consider. The more "slippery" you are and the more aerodynamic your shape, the faster you will go even in a head wind. By slippery I mean smooth in texture and rounded at the corners, like a shark. You can get slippery by wearing a skin suit and a smooth helmet, and by shaving your legs. Your bike can be made slippery, too, by running cables inside main tubes, rounding off or eliminating all protrusions, flattening tubes, and so on. But the most important difference is to assume an aerodynamic shape.

As research and development of human-powered vehicles have shown, the teardrop shape is good for lowering air resistance. Fully enclosed bicycles and tandems with low profiles, teardrop shapes, and smooth outer shells can travel much faster than conventional bicycles, despite their greater weight. And your shape, even given the same frontal area, will affect how easily you slip through the air. Try varying your crouch by rounding your back, hunching your shoulders, holding in your elbows, and so on. You should be able to detect how these variations help or hinder you as you ride. And take into account the cargo you may be carrying. Panniers in front may make your

This aerodynamic bike was designed to cut weight and air resistance. All cables are buried within tubes, which themselves are flattened and smoothed. The brakes are hidden behind the crown of the fork and the bottom bracket and the shift levers are tucked behind the head tube, so as to prevent any extra turbulence. Notice the ultra-light, radially spoked wheels with only 24 spokes, and the platform pedals. Now if we could only streamline me. . . .
(Courtesty Cinelli)

bike more aerodynamic than placing them in back. A pack on your back could speed you up by making you more egg-shaped.

When it comes to fast and efficient riding, air resistance is the name of the game. If you pay attention to aerodynamics, it can pay off for you.

BASIC CYCLING TECHNIQUES

Signals

Every cyclist should know and use a few important hand signals. If they are not already familiar to you, they are simple enough to memorize as you read.

The two most elementary things you want to convey to motorists are change in direction and change in speed. When you want to go left, point left with your left hand. When you want to go right, point right with your right hand. This system is so simple that you don't even have to know your left from your right; all you have to do is point the way you want to go. Whether you use an exaggerated or a casual gesture, be sure that you unmistakably indicate where you intend to go next. If you have visual contact with an oncoming motorist at an intersection, for example, a brief pointing gesture may be enough. If there is heavy traffic behind you, and you want to move from the far right of the road to the far left, you may have to sit up straight and extend your left arm as you move from lane to lane, glancing back at traffic as necessary.

The other way to signal right turns to trailing traffic is with the left elbow bent and the left hand pointing up. It is the better signal to use if there is any doubt that your right-handed signal might be missed by drivers.

As far as slowing or stopping is concerned, you can signal that by bending your left arm down with palm facing behind you. If you wig-wag your hand left to right two or three times, you will clearly indicate that you are slowing down. Be careful not to signal so long that you cannot use your left brake, though.

You should be sure to signal your intentions when on a bike just as when you are driving a car, and these simple hand signals will suffice most of the time. But there will also be times when sound as well as visual signals will come in handy. If you cannot already whistle loudly and sharply, I suggest you learn how, so you can signal to drivers when they aren't already looking your way. A shrill whistle performs the same function as a horn on a car: to attract eye contact of others. Some cyclists actually mount small, very loud horns on their bikes, although they may be illegal where you live. Another possibility is the vocal signal—anything from a friendly "Yoo-hoo!" to a blood-curdling scream. If a negligent motorist's driving threatens your life, you will scream out of reflex anyway. But keep in mind that you also can make yourself heard in less life-threatening situations.

These signals apply to other cyclists as well as to motorists. When you are riding in a group, you will want to use these same hand signals, but perhaps more subtly. You can use either the left or right hand to signal that you are about to slow down.

Usually hand signals to trailing cyclists are most efficiently given by dropping your hand to your side, around the knee area, then signaling. The person behind you will be able to see your signal without looking up.

One additional hand signal useful for other cyclists is the "road hazard" signal for glass, potholes, obstructions, or other problems in the road ahead. The hazard signal also implies that you will be steering around the obstruction, so in most cases it obviates the need for a second, directional signal. When you see a problem in the road ahead, decide whether you are going to pass it on your right or on your left. If, for example, there is some broken glass ahead that you want to avoid and you decide to veer to the left, signal the problem either by pointing straight down with your right hand, or by putting your right hand palm down, and moving it in a slight wiping or scrubbing motion. This tells the cyclists behind you there will be something troublesome on the right very soon, and that you will be veering around it. You can also say something as you give the hand signal, such as "Glass ahead."

The last kind of signaling involves letting people other than motorists and cycling companions know you are coming through. Usually this means pedestrians, skaters, and other cyclists who are ahead of you or who may cross your path if they don't know you are coming.

If you have a horn or bell on your bike, make sure you use it to signal your presence when needed. I have often seen Sunday cyclists on beach-side boardwalks effectively use these signals when passing skaters or runners. Even if you don't have a bell or horn, you can let others know you are passing them by clicking your brake levers—my favorite way of signaling runners and other cyclists. If there is to be any doubt on which side you are going to pass, say, "On your right" or "On your left" as you approach.

Positioning

It's not enough to have a custom frame, the right shoes and apparel, a strong heart, well-developed legs, and the determination of a demon to win a race, or even to cycle efficiently. All of these will help but you won't get anywhere without proper riding technique. The more correctly you position yourself, the better you will turn your muscles' energy into distance traveled, and the more aerodynamic your posture will be.

Saddle Position

A racing frame has tighter angles than a touring frame. This means the saddle is more nearly over the bottom bracket (and the stem is more nearly right above the front-wheel hub) in a racing frame. A more efficient—and less comfortable—angle on any frame can be achieved simply by sitting closer to the front of the saddle or by moving the saddle farther forward. A good way to tell if your saddle is in the right place is to sit on the bike with your feet on the pedals, cranks parallel to the ground. Drop a plumb line from the back of your forward kneecap and see where the string passes in relation to the spindle of the pedal. The plumb line should just cut through the center of the pedal.

Many racers actually reposition the saddle closer for racing than for training, and such a practice may help you. But don't overdo it. The most stable and efficient position for the saddle is centered over the post, but a little variation may help you increase the power you send to the pedal. As with so many vari-

Checking saddle position by the plumb method. (Courtesy Dave Ball)

ables in cycling, you should experiment with both the front-to-back position of your saddle as well as the front-to-back position of your seat on the saddle.

Hand and Arm Positions

Maes-style drop bars have been very popular because they offer the cyclist many possible hand positions. Unlike mountain-bike or cruiser bars, which have only a single place to grip on either end, drop bars can be gripped in at least five distinctly different ways. The various hand positions allow you to relieve pressure on your hands without losing control of the bike, as well as to respond to the terrain.

The first grip is with the hands on the straight run of the drops, thumbs inside. The elbows should be bent, whether slightly (more upright body position) or greatly (very low crouch). With your hands in this lowest position, you can dodge the wind, break away from the pack, or chase down another cyclist without sacrificing any upward pull needed to balance forceful down strokes. If you are not already riding in this first position, perhaps you should try it. Remember to keep your elbows close in, especially when greatly bent. I see many riders hunching down with their elbows out, which destroys the aerodynamic advantage gained by their low crouch.

Next position is with the hands on the curve of the drop (the hooks), perhaps with one or more fingers resting on the brake calipers. This position has many features in common with the first, with the added advantage that you can apply the brakes without delay. I sometimes ride in this position when traveling fast in a group, as in a team time trial, because speed control is so critical then. (When your front wheel touches someone else's rear wheel, most likely *you* will go down without bothering that leading cyclist.)

Then there is my favorite hand position, the one with the hands resting on the brake hoods. Actually, there are two variations. The more common is with thumbs hooked over the hoods, fingers down or draped across the brake levers. This position offers quick access to the brakes and a slightly higher posture than either the first or the second position. But I prefer the second variation, with the palms more or less facing the ground and index fingers crooked over the hoods. With my very low handlebar position, I can crouch down as far as I need to with my arms closer in than if I used any of the other positions mentioned. I don't necessarily recommend this style to you; if it were comfortable for everyone, you would see more people using it. But it works for me, and you might try it and see whether it works for you.

The fourth position is palms down on the top curve of the bar. I usually use this when I am far from traffic and in need of a rest. You can sit up a bit, straighten your arms and back, and stretch your fingers, letting them recover from pressure. This position is not good for riding in heavy traffic.

In the fifth position, fingers are over the straight portion of the tops, with thumbs below. Often you will see riders using this position when they are not so interested in high speed, but that doesn't mean you can't go fast in this position. The only problem with the fifth position is that you might strike your elbows with your knees if you crouch too low. This hand position, and its variation, is also good for coasting down steep descents in what is called the tuck position described below.

Foot Positioning

Although some people teach that you should cycle pigeon-toed, I ascribe to the theory that you should ride using your natural foot plant. It is possible that pigeon-toed people are naturally better at cycling, as some have claimed, but I tend to doubt that. Your best bet is to use your natural foot plant on the pedals, with the ball of the foot over the axle of the pedal. This will allow you to transmit maximum force to the pedal with each down stroke. Toe clips and cleats should be exactly placed so as to ensure that you are pedaling with the proper foot plant.

Pedaling

There is a lot more to cranking than just stepping down on the pedals. Most cyclists do, in fact, spend most of their energy step-

This is how I most like to sit on level ground. I usually put my hands on the brake hoods, elbows well in, and forearms parallel to the ground. Also note that my knees are just even with the top tube when the cranks are parallel to the ground, as they should be. (Courtesy Dave Ball)

ping on their pedals, but they are not pedaling in good form. Even though one revolution of the cranks (one stroke) is perfectly circular, we can think of it as being composed of four different components: a down stroke, a back stroke, an up stroke, and a fore stroke. Most cyclists, even the best, concentrate only on the down stroke, but you can approach maximum efficiency by working on all four stroke components.

With toe clips and cleats, you can do more than just step on the pedals. As you ride, think about your strokes. Work on each stroke component in turn, concentrating on just the back stroke for a while, then just the up stroke, then the fore stroke. Feel how the hamstrings, the muscles in the back of the upper leg, are used to pull the pedal back and up; notice how the quadriceps, in the front of the thigh, work to push the pedals forward and then down. You will probably find that such practice tires you out, and your legs may be a bit sore at first. That's all right, because it proves you are using both your hams and your calf muscles to turn the cranks, rather than the quads alone. The soreness will last only a short while; bear with it. You are getting stronger and better at riding.

Although it's useful for training purposes to think of stroking in a square pattern, what you want is to pedal in a perfect circle, with constant pressure on the pedals and thus constant speed of the rotating cranks. You can approach a more circular cranking

Look closely at these chain rings—they aren't round. Since most riders put more into the down stroke than anywhere else in pedaling, bio-mechanical engineers have come up with various oval shapes to take advantage of the powerful quadriceps. I'm not so sure I buy that theory. Oval chain rings have been in and out of fashion since the 1890's, and they haven't proven themselves yet. (Courtesy Shimano Sales Corporation)

and involve your lower leg muscles, too, by adding ankling to your stroke. Ankling is the purposeful up-and-down motion of the foot at appropriate points in the stroke of the cranks. On the down stroke, keep your heel down; on the back stroke, point your toes down; on the up stroke and fore stroke, keep your foot level with the ground.

Ankling is probably the most important difference between the cranking styles of top riders and casual cyclists. It seems to be a trick of the trade the general public doesn't know about, but should. Not that all good cyclists ankle all the time—they don't. But if all riders would practice ankling more, they would be better cyclists. Again, since it will involve more extensive use of your lower leg muscles, ankling may tire you and make you sore. But soon all your leg muscles will be involved in turning the cranks, and your stroke will be more powerful and efficient than ever before.

When you ride your bicycle, think about your pedaling. Notice whether you are putting more force into the down stroke than the other three strokes. Feel whether your ankles are stiff or fluid, working for or against the perfect circular motion you want. I usually can feel which part of the circle is getting less attention if I think about it, and then I can work on that. With proper pedaling, your cycling will improve tremendously.

Gearing

The multiple-gear bicycle offers the cyclist the possibility of riding over varied terrain and in various wind conditions much more efficiently than with a single-gear machine. I say "possibility" because, unless they are used properly, multiple gears will do you no good at all.

The two basic ways to achieve multiple gearing are the Sturmey-Archer 3-speed hub and the derailleur system, as mentioned in Chapter 2. Both systems allow you to vary the number of wheel revolutions that result from each revolution of the cranks. Lower gears (or small gears) require less effort to push, but they take many strokes to travel a given distance.

Higher gears (or big gears) are harder to push, but they don't take as many strokes to travel that same distance.

Just as with a car, you start out in a low gear and gear up as you accelerate. You want to select the proper gear for the terrain and velocity, changing whenever necessary. You wouldn't drive on a highway in first gear or start out in fourth; in the same way, you want to ride your bike in a gear that allows you to pedal at the right speed, neither too fast nor too slow.

Pedaling speed is called cadence, measured in revolutions per minute. The most efficient cycling is done at cadences between 60 and 110 rpm, or one to two down strokes (counting one foot only) per second. Optimal cadence efficiency has been measured at 85–95 rpm.

Three-speed hubs have a single cog and an internal mechanisms that varies the stroke-to-wheel ratio. A single lever attached to the handle bar connects to the inside of the 3-speed hub via a cable. To shift gears, you momentarily quit pedaling while you move the lever to the desired gear—usually labeled Low, Medium, and High, or 1, 2, 3.

Derailleur systems have all the shifting components external to the hub. Typically there are two or three chain rings and a freewheel with five, six, or seven cogs, with both a front and a rear derailleur to guide the chain to the chain ring and cog. By multiplying the number of chain rings times the number of cogs, you arrive at the theoretical number of "speeds": thus, the 10-speed has two rings and five cogs; and a 15-speed touring bike has a third chain ring; and so on. There are 5-speed cruisers (a single chain ring with a 5-cog freewheel) as well, and most recently the 7-cog freewheel has been mated to a triple chain ring to arrive at the phenomenal 21-speed bike! (In fact, the actual number of available gears is always less than the theoretical number of "speeds" because of cross gears and gear overlap, as explained below.)

Shifting gears on a derailleur-type system is simple enough: there is one lever for the front derailleur and one for the rear, and you move the appropriate lever *while pedaling* until the chain is on the desired chain ring and cog.

The lowest gear is the one with the chain on the small chain ring and the largest cog—both of which are the closest to the frame of the bike, or far left from the rider's point of view. In the highest gear, the chain is on the largest chain ring and smallest cog. All other gears fall in between.

There are only a few rules to know about gearing. First, don't ride in a cross gear, that is, with the chain on the smallest chain ring and smallest cog, or largest chain ring and largest cog. You will see when looking down at your chain that a cross gear twists the chain a great deal, so it's not a good idea ever to ride that way.

The second rule to remember is that as you gear up, shift the chain onto smaller and smaller cogs, and from the smaller to the larger chain ring(s). Conversely, down shifting means shifting to larger cogs and/or onto the smaller chain ring(s).

Third, remember to maintain proper cadence, or pedaling rpm. To do this, you have to shift up when pedaling becomes too easy (too fast) and shift down when pedaling is too difficult (cadence too slow).

Finally, it's a good idea to shift to a low gear before coming to a complete stop. That way you can start up again in the proper gear. Note that you don't necessarily have to start out in your lowest gear, just in a relatively low gear.

If you follow these basic rules, there's no reason for you to worry too much about gearing, since you will always ride in a comfortable gear and you won't be doing your gearing apparatus any harm. If, however, you are serious about cycling, you'll probably want to know more detail about gearing.

First some terminology. The number of teeth on a chain ring or cog determines its size. Chain rings range in size from about 55 to 24 teeth, but most 10- and 12-speeds come with 52 and a 42, which is written 52-42 (say "fifty-two forty-two"). Freewheel cogs can go from 12 to 36, but except for true racing or Alpine touring bikes, usually you'll see them no smaller than 13 or larger than about 28. A common 6-cog freewheel is 13-15-17-20-22-24, but there are many other possible combinations.

A given gear is the combination of chain ring and freewheel cog. For example, 52 × 20 (say "fifty-two twenty") or 42 × 17. (These just mean a 52-tooth chain ring and 20-tooth cog; and a

42-tooth chain ring with a 17-tooth cog.) If you divide the chain-ring size by the cog size, you arrive at the gear ratio, or number of wheel revolutions produced by each stroke. Hence, in a 42 × 21 gear, you have (42 / 21) = 2 wheel revolutions per stroke, or 2:1. In a 52 × 13, it's (52 / 13) = 4, or 4:1. And halfway in between, at 3:1, would be 42 × 14, since (42 / 14) = 3.

These gear ratios are directly comparable. A 4:1 ratio will take you twice as far as a 2:1 ratio for the same number of pedal strokes. Most people in the United States calculate gear inches, though, figured by multiplying the ratio by the diameter of the wheel in inches. For a 27″ wheel, a 52 × 13 works out to (52 / 13) × 27 = 108 gear inches, while a 42 × 14 gear would yield (42 / 14) × 27 = 81 gear inches. If you know all of your gear inches, you can compare gears with other riders and figure the best shift pattern for your bike.

A slightly more complicated way to talk about gears is the English method. There they multiply the inch gear by π (3.14) to calculate the distance traveled for each revolution of the cranks, also known as the rollout. My preference is actually to measure the circumference of the rear wheel and multiply *that* by the gear ratio. That will give you the most accurate figure no matter what the exact diameter of your wheels. Let's suppose you have the 52-42 and 13-24 set-up mentioned above, and your wheel's circumference is exactly 84½ inches. Then your high-gear rollout is (52 / 13) × 84.50 = 348.0″; your low gear has a (42 / 24) × 84.50 = 147.875″ rollout. An easy way to measure wheel circumference is to lay down a small start line in talcum powder on a level surface (say, a sidewalk or a parking lot) and run your rear wheel straight over the line and beyond until it leaves a mark on the ground, then carefully measure that distance.

Steering

Smooth form in riding requires good steering. The rider who steers better rides more efficiently, comfortably, and safely.

Watch a child learning to ride a bike. He or she has to balance, pedal, and steer all at the same time, and these require lots of attention. Steering is erratic, the course jerky. In trying to steer a straight line, the child turns one way, then over-corrects, pushing the handlebars back and forth. As riding skill increases, the child's steering becomes straighter, but there are always traces of those first erratic miles. A *perfectly* straight course is impossible, but that should be your aim.

A truer course is safer because you aren't likely to strike a curb or be struck by a vehicle if you stay a constant distance from the edge of the road. And when riding in groups, keeping a straight and true course insures that you and your companions won't collide.

A straight line is most efficient as it is the shortest distance between two points. A wobbly approximation to the shortest distance from start to finish may not matter much on a trip to the grocery store, but in a race it can mean the difference between first place and out of the money. If you rode a perfect S-shaped line rather than a straight one, you would have to ride 1.57 miles for every mile of the trip. Let's use that as an extreme case of wobble. A very minor amount of wobble might add, say, a tenth of a percent to the distance—a negligible increase. But in a 100-km time trial, that's a tenth of a mile, or 52.8 feet! In a sport that often decides winners by hundredths of a second, 52 more feet is too much extra to go. Clearly, smooth steering is worth working on.

You can check how straight your steering is as you ride. Look down to where your front tire touches the ground and see what happens to the shadow. The more variation in the shadow, getting thicker then thinner, the more erratic your steering. You can get the same information by sighting down the top tube or watching the rear wheel's shadow. Or you can judge how much wobble you have by looking at your track after passing through water.

To improve your steering, follow painted lines or seams in the road at a two-inch distance for 20 or 30 strokes. Keeping your shoulders relaxed, watch your front wheel following that straight line. Another method is to fix your gaze on a distant object and concentrate on "pulling" that object straight toward you. This technique allows you to steer straight without thinking too hard about what your hands are doing.

Notice that wobble can be attributed to poor pedaling. Overreliance on the down stroke causes the bike to sway side to side. This sway very commonly causes side-to-side steering as well, as is easily seen in sloppy hill climbing.

As you ride your bike, strive for that perfectly straight line. Seek perfection, even if it can't ever be achieved.

Climbing Hills

Very few places are so flat that they can be said to have no hills at all. There are vast stretches of Florida and the Great Plains where the land is as flat as a table, but most of the country has more surface variation. Most bicycle jaunts, from a trip to the local grocery to a summer-long bike tour, will involve some climbs. Many people dread hills because they demand more work and more time than the flats. But you may as well look forward to them and get the most out of them, because they are always going to be there.

There are several benefits of climbing hills that may not be obvious to you. First, they give you a chance to change riding position. This alleviates pressure on the seat and hands, and gives the leg muscles a different set of demands, which acts to rest them. Hills also afford you a chance to increase your workout, since gravity increases your rolling resistance. Further, terrain variations force you to work on your techniques, both physical and mental, on overcoming challenges. Because hills slow you down, you have time to take in the view, smell the vegetation, and think about where you are going much more thoroughly than when riding on level ground.

There are conflicting theories about how to take hills in terms of riding position and technique. I'll give you all the facts and some opinions, and let you make up your own mind on the matter. There's no dispute about needing lower gears to climb hills. Any ascent worthy of the name will be too steep for higher gears because the pull of gravity is too great. As you begin a climb,

When the terrain demands it, don't be afraid to get up out of the saddle and crank it. (Courtesy Dave Ball)

you should gear down appropriately, maintaining cadence just as you would on level ground. As you approach the hill, it's much more efficient to go down one or two gears at a time, rather than to crank in high until you are forced to shift into low for the remainder of the ascent.

Some people advocate staying in the saddle for all but the very steepest hills, and others claim you should get out of the saddle for every ascent. The standing, or hill-climbing, position is less efficient than the seated position, because it relies on a very forceful down stroke and relatively little on the rest of the crank cycle. This makes for a rougher cadence, although typically the rider can take the hill in a higher gear. You will not necessarily ascend the hill faster; just in a higher gear. You can prove this to yourself by doing repeats up some nearby hill with a friend, alternating standing and sitting as you climb.

Climbing hills out of the saddle raises your center of gravity and makes you more unstable, especially if you are carrying any gear on your bicycle. Furthermore, if you are fighting a head wind, you will increase the wind resistance by standing up. So why do so many riders climb hills that way? First, especially on short ascents, it is possible to maintain a higher cadence without shifting down very many gears and, once at the top of the rise, the rider can return to the higher gears more quickly. The cyclist is propelled up the hill much faster than would be possible by staying in the saddle and shifting down further. Note, however, that this applies mostly to short climbs taken at high speeds. It's just not possible to power up long climbs the same way, since such slow cadences are very inefficient, and fatigue sets in very quickly.

Another advantage to standing on ascents is that you can relieve pressure on the seat, because pressure is increased on climbs when you stay seated. Long rides can cause decreased circulation and consequent pain and numbness in the seat. Slight shifts in saddle position while riding the flats will help to alleviate this pressure, but only for short periods. Nothing works so well as actually getting out of the saddle, and that is done most naturally when climbing a hill. Also, the leg muscles get a rest of sorts when you ride in hill-climbing position. Although you use the same muscles for climbing as for level terrain, you stress them differently on a climb. Each down stroke throws much of your body weight as well as some muscle action into pressing the pedal, which allows the opposite leg to rest much more than usual.

Some people take every hill standing because it looks professional or trendy, but that's not a very good reason to do anything. I recommend varying your hill-climbing style according to the specific conditions. If you have a stiff breeze right in your face, you will probably do better to stay on the drops and in the saddle, so as to cheat the wind as you ascend. And if you are on tour and carrying lots of gear, you should probably limit yourself to less frequent stands. But if you're feeling frisky or racing someone up a hill—and if you don't care about getting tired—then get up and crank it. It's best to practice climbing both ways, testing different grades in different gears, and seeing how head winds and tail winds affect you. Whether you are the most casual recreational rider or a world-class racer, you will face those hills wherever you go, and you should be aware of how to take them. This awareness comes only with practice.

When you climb a hill standing, you have various options as to positioning. Typically, cyclists grasp the brake hoods or top curves when in hill-climbing position, but you will also see riders holding the drops. You should try both. I have found that the drops are too low for me to climb efficiently, but I set my handlebars very low, so you may not have a problem. Generally speaking, the amount of forward lean will depend upon the steepness of the hill. You probably will find you can get a more forceful down stroke when you lean forward a bit, but if the hill is too steep, you already will be leaning forward a good deal.

Although the standing position emphasizes the down stroke at the expense of smooth turning, you should not neglect the rest of the crank cycle. When climbing hills, concentrate on pulling up with each stroke; you may be surprised how much faster you can crank simply by thinking about your calf and hamstring muscles. This holds true whether you stand or remain seated on an uphill. If anything, good form on the pedals is more crucial when ascending than on the flats. This kind of concentration need not prevent you from enjoying the climb; you can almost ignore the down stroke, if you pay a little attention to the up stroke.

I have already mentioned that good form in cycling means riding a true and straight course, taking smooth turns, and minimizing sway. These all hold true for the hill-climbing position, although it is more difficult to maintain form when you are off the saddle. Just as on the level, if you sway, you may wobble and so ride a longer distance, following an endlessly repeating "S" line. Although some people encourage drastic sway on hill climbing, others claim it should be eliminated altogether. Excess sway does waste energy, but the best hill climbers have practiced and mastered the art of climbing, and can dance their way up hills with some sway but no wobble. To imitate their style, deliberately pull up on the handlebars or brake hood with each down stroke. As your right foot presses down, pull up with your right hand—not so much as to pull your bike off-course, but just enough to keep yourself perpendicular to the ground. Then as your left foot begins the down stroke, pull up with your left hand. With practice, you will feel a constantly changing, smooth tradeoff between right and left hand. Even though the bike sways from side to side, you will remain upright. The precise hill climber can take a hill in just as straight a position as on the level. True, ascending without looking sloppy is more demanding and more difficult, but good form on the uphills returns even more benefit than it does in the flats.

Descents

All the extra work necessary to overcome gravity on the ascent is returned on the descent, when you can trade in those low gears for high, or just sit and coast, taking a well-earned rest.

Descents are pleasant, but they are also potentially dangerous, and they can be deceptive. Although they require less work than level terrain, descents demand no less skill and concentration and they certainly demand more care. Quite often steep downhills are accompanied by high winds, which can be hazardous in and of themselves. Add the increased speed so easily achieved on a descent and you can see how disastrous a carelessly ridden descent can become.

The first rule is never to take a steep descent with hands off the bars. I have seen several nasty crashes caused by wind and road roughness on steep downhills that could have been avoided if the cyclists had held on to the handlebars and maintained good position. You don't want to experience a high-speed downhill crash, believe me. The worst crash I ever had was just that: I was shooting down Feedlot Hill in Austin, a fairly steep half-mile grade, doing about 45 mph, and I sat up to adjust my sun glasses. The next thing I knew I was regaining consciousness on the side of the road. I had abrasions from head to foot, and my bike was no better off. How I escaped breaking bones, I don't know. I couldn't ride for at least two weeks, and I spent most of that time ruing my stupidity.

When you go speeding down a hill, ride the same as you would on the level with a head wind—on the drops. You will be able to ride in high gears, and your speed will create a head wind, so you should crouch as you descend. When your velocity is higher than you can match in your highest gear, or when you don't want to pedal, you can coast effectively by "tucking in." The tuck position involves streamlining the body: cranks parallel to the ground; knees together; hands close to the stem if not on the brakes; elbows close in to the body; head down next to the stem. Some riders lift off the saddle just a bit when they tuck, for a better aerodynamic shape or to relieve pressure on the seat. Often you will see the hands very close to the stem of the handlebars, palms down, but some people can get more compact still by gripping the tops of the bars palms *up* and using the elbows to fill in the space between the legs and the torso.

On descents, practice varying your own shape to find your best position. For many people, this means slightly rounding the back and keeping the nose down low to better assume a teardrop shape. You may be surprised what a difference little things like pulling the knees and elbows together will make.

Of course, on some descents you may want to slow down to take in the view, for safety reasons, or to wait for a companion. To do so, sit up and gently brake to control your speed. It is a good idea to turn the cranks from time to time even on long, coasting descents, to prevent chills or loss of circulation to the legs and feet.

Avoiding Obstacles

Fewer flats, fewer accidents, fewer bicycle repairs—wouldn't we all like that? The best way to achieve all these is to ride around obstacles, not over them.

As you ride, always look ahead for chuckholes, glass, branches, wet leaves, sand, debris—and steer around them! I don't know why it is, but it seems to me that many cyclists just trust to luck and roll right over anything in the way, with predictable results.

An obstacle that cannot be avoided because of traffic or because it was noticed too late must be jumped over. With a little practice, anyone can learn to take a little hop with a bike. All you do is raise off the saddle and lift the handlebars to get the front wheel over the obstacle. If it is small enough and/or you are traveling too fast to do anything more, a little hop will prevent damage to your front wheel at least, and might save you from a crash. If the obstacle is large and you are going slowly enough, you also can try to clear it with the rear wheel by pulling up with both feet as you lean forward onto the front wheel. You have to keep the cranks parallel to the ground as you pull up, and the forward lean at just the right second is crucial. Many good cyclists can hop up curbs this way with no danger to their wheels, but beware: if you haven't practiced this technique sufficiently and you try to take a curb on the fly, you may end up with a heart-shaped rear wheel. Don't say I didn't warn you.

Riding with Others

When riding in a group, the first rule is never to overlap wheels with a leading cyclist. If you are following someone and decide to pull up parallel or go ahead of him or her, that's one thing; but otherwise don't let your front wheel get ahead of someone else's rear tire. If you should collide with that cyclist, most likely you will take a spill, and you might take others down with you. Instead of overlapping, ride a few inches behind your leader, and make sure your follower is at least as far behind you.

In racing, training, or casual riding, it is common to ride single file, in what is called a pace line. The idea is to let one person at a time lead the line at a fast pace. When the leading cyclist has gone the prescribed number of seconds, feet, or crank rpm's, he or she pulls off to one side and rejoins the pace line at the end. The standard practice is to pull off into the wind, thus shielding all the other riders temporarily as they pass. If there is a distinct side wind, and the traffic conditions allow, the pace line often becomes an echelon, with each trailing cyclist behind and off to the side of his or her leader, on the protected (leeward) side. When riding in a pace line, it is up to you and every other cyclist to be constantly on guard not to run into another bike; it is so easy to take down an entire group with one momentary lapse of attention.

A group of riders not riding single file is usually called a pack. Riding in a pack often means taking up a whole lane of traffic, which should be done only if there is plenty of room for auto traffic in the remaining lanes. The signals given by leading riders should be passed back by successive riders so that nobody is left ignorant of hazards or turns coming up. Further, the hindmost riders in a pack are responsible for informing others about any dangers such as approaching trucks.

Dealing with Dogs

The bane of the avid cyclist is an overly excited dog. Especially in rural spots, such as where I was raised in Missouri, dogs are apt to chase cyclists, barking and snapping, and, like as not, biting the innocent pedaler. I love dogs, and I appreciate their loyalty and devotion, which is what prompts them to chase me away from their territory. But I don't especially like being bitten, so I usually try to out-sprint my barking adversary. Dogs won't chase you too far beyond their own territory, so if you can get past that imaginary line faster than they can, you'll probably be safe.

If you can't beat your tormentor to the next dog's property, you have several alternatives. One is the squirt-and-run trick, where you squirt the dog in the face with your water bottle and *then* sprint like mad. Plain water will do, but if you happen to have some juice or an electrolyte-replacement drink in your bottle, you're more likely to discourage the dog. Some cyclists carry the same sort of spray repellent as mail carriers, but I don't know of anyone who was able to retrieve, aim, and spray it fast enough to be of any help.

Some people advocate charging straight at an attacking dog

and yelling. Dogs are more likely to chase you than attack head-on, however, so it's not often practical to face them down. Other people claim that many dogs will halt if you raise your hand or jump as if to strike them, but I've never tried that.

The most unique and effective method I've heard of to ward off a canine was invented on the spur of the moment by a couple of friends of mine, Al and Cosette. They were on tour, and they stopped for some take-out beef ribs for lunch one day. Since they were only one day from home, they kept their leftover rib bones for their dogs—and were soon glad they did. After they had been back on the road an hour or so, a huge dog gave chase, intent, it seemed, on chomping off one of Cosette's legs. Almost reflexively, Al pulled the rib bones out of his handlebar bag and flung them at the dog, which accepted the trade without hesitation.

SAFETY IN TRAFFIC

There are very few cyclists who emerge from auto-and-bike collisions with fewer injuries than the motorist. If you want to spend more time in the saddle than in the emergency room, you will have to ride safely and defensively.

Many collisions between cyclists and motorists occur because the exhilarated cyclist forgets or ignores the very real danger of other vehicles. But many more accidents are due to drivers who fail to accord the cyclist the same road courtesies they give other motorists. They may not consider the bicycle a threat to their own safety, or may not realize how fast a bicycle can go and how much distance it requires to stop. We all have seen autos pull out in front of a fast moving bicycle, and we also have seen bicyclists running stop signs and traffic signals, heedlessly cutting across lanes of traffic.

I hope you will remember and practice the safety tips I have already given. But for riding safely in traffic, there are three general rules to follow and instill in your children: be visible, be predictable, and be careful.

Be Visible

It is obvious that a lone cyclist, or even a group of cyclists, will never be as easy to spot in traffic as an automobile. The beauty of a bicycle lies partly in its narrow form, which helps to minimize the projected frontal area of the rider-plus-machine and so increases its aerodynamic efficiency. When the cyclist is moving down the road in a low crouch, however, he or she presents only two or three square feet of visible area to the approaching motorist. This is not a very large target compared to automobiles, trucks, and buses. Compounding the problem of visibility is the fact that the cyclist usually rides at the edge of the roadway, where he or she blends into the landscape. The driver of a car or truck therefore may not see the bike as another vehicle to be reckoned with.

Visibility is a problem especially at night. Even with several reflectors and light-colored clothing, you may not be seen by a motorist until you are dangerously close to one another. Without lights and reflectors, the average cyclist is virtually invisible except on very brightly lit streets.

There are a few ways to increase your visibility as a cyclist and so improve your chances of making it through the year without any harrowing experiences. One way is to dress in brightly colored clothing so as to stand out from the background. There is a wide variety of multi-colored jerseys and non-black (even tiger-skin) cycling shorts to choose from. Consider wearing bright yellow socks and applying some reflective material to the back of your cycling shoes. The feet, which move faster than anything else on a cyclist, can act as attention-getting flags. When traveling through heavy traffic in town, you will probably hit a light or stop sign every couple of blocks anyway, so ride in a more upright position to give the motorists a greater visible area than your feet and back pocket.

You should also get into the habit of using your hands to attract attention. When you ride down a street and see a car coming out of a driveway, sit up tall and wave until you know the driver sees you! Sometimes I look at drivers who are about to turn in front of me and give them the traffic cop's sign, an open palm pushed decisively toward the vehicle. So far I have found drivers to be surprisingly obedient to my traffic directions; I hope motorists obey you, too.

Riding at night demands that you pay attention to how visible you might be to motorists. Besides reflective material on the back of your shoes, you should have at least one light to the rear and one to the front, reflectors, and reflective clothing. A small leg lamp strapped just below the knee is an excellent warning device that can be seen by motorists coming from ahead or behind, and the up-and-down motion instantly identifies it as belonging to a cyclist. Another good, attention-attracting light is the flashing white or amber lamp that attaches to the rear of the bicycle or shorts. Usually these lamps flash at one-second intervals, and they are bright enough to be seen from a great distance at night. You should also have some sort of white light for illumination on the front of your bike. It will identify your vehicle as a bicycle since it will appear to bounce and wobble from side to side as it approaches.

Reflectors are a must at night since they help the motorist to judge direction and rate of travel. If your bicycle does not already have front, rear, and side reflectors (many cyclists prefer not to carry the extra weight during daylight hours), you can wear some on your clothing or on any bags or racks on your bike. Since it is usually cooler after dark, you might consider sewing some small reflectors right onto the windbreaker or sweatshirt you usually wear riding at night. Reflectors are best used in combination with lamps; alone, they may not be readily seen, and they may be indistinguishable from reflectors on fences, shoulder markers, and mailboxes. You don't want some weary (or, heaven forbid, intoxicated) driver to mistake you for a stationary object.

White or yellow apparel can be spotted more easily at night than black or blue clothing. When you ride after dark, plan to wear light-colored shirts, jackets, shorts, or leggings. Even white stockings help here. You can increase your visibility even more by wearing clothing that is designed to be highly reflective, or by putting reflective tape on your attire. An isosceles triangle taped to your back in orange reflective tape will be of help. That, of course, is the symbol for the slow-moving vehicle.

Finally, your helmet should do more than just sit on your head in case you fall. If it is light in color and has some reflective material on it, your helmet will help make you more visible day or night.

Be Predictable

Besides being visible to motorists, you want to be predictable, too. Being easy to spot doesn't help if your riding is erratic. This is the main problem with many children's bicycle riding: the driver can't tell where they will go from one moment to the next. Motorists don't know whether to drive slower or faster, to veer or not, and so on. But many adult cyclists are guilty of this same unpredictability.

Riding predictably need not take any more concentration than riding correctly. In fact, that is what proper riding technique entails. The cyclist whose smooth form indicates expertise will be the one whose intentions can be "read" by motorists and other cyclists with a minimum of error. The basic idea is to ride smoothly, obey the laws and rules of the road, and give clear, definite signals to motorists and other cyclists.

The mark of a novice cyclist is the snaky, erratic trail he or she leaves when going at any speed. Before anyone becomes expert at steering a straight course, he or she weaves left and right, only approximating a direction. The experienced rider can follow a straight line at any speed, and turns in graceful, sweeping arcs, ceasing to pedal at just the right moment and recommencing as soon as possible. If you can ride a straight line and do so in traffic, you will show motorists that you have control of your bike, that you know where you are going, and that you will not dart out suddenly in front of them. As you encounter obstacles—potholes, parked autos, debris or glass in the road, vehicles nosing out into traffic—steer around them smoothly and gracefully, returning to your former location relative to traffic as soon as you have passed the obstruction. The motorist who sees you riding that way does not fear that you will do anything rash as he or she passes, because you are evidently following an efficient and predictable course. If you follow the suggestions I have made about riding form and technique, your steady improvement will pay off not only in cycling pleasure and efficiency, but in safety as well.

Your signals should be clear, definite, and accurate. Point the way you want to go, then go there. If you have to go around an obstruction in the street, and you must get in front of an auto to do so, give a hand signal, pass the obstacle, give another hand signal, and resume your previous lane. If you are a good cyclist, your signals and turns will be both crisp and unmistakable, and the motorists will have no problems understanding what you are doing.

Signals to other cyclists should be equally precise. Whether you are riding with a friend, are joined by a stranger, or are training in a group, you must ride predictably or risk hurting yourself and others in a pile-up. One difference between signaling to motor vehicles and signaling to other bicyclists is that you can speak to cyclists in addition to giving hand signals. Thus, you might say "Glass" as you signal "Hazard," accurately informing your fellow riders of the nature and location of the problem ahead. Another difference is that signals meant only for trailing cyclists can be more subtle. Whereas you may want a full-arm point to signal a turn to automobile drivers, you can clearly signal your turn to the cyclist behind you by dropping your hand to your knee and pointing briefly just prior to the turn.

Predictability also means obeying the rules of the road. Don't ride on the wrong side of the street unless you want to endanger yourself, other cyclists, pedestrians, and motorists all at once. Only where there are separate bikeways with clearly labeled directions is it permissible to ride counter to auto traffic. Don't run stop signs and stop signals, either. You can be ticketed, at the least, and you could be struck by some massive vehicle driven by a perfectly law-abiding citizen. In the Great American Bike Race I had to stop at hundreds of signs between Santa Monica and New York. I hated every one of them because all they did was slow me down in a *race*. But we racers couldn't be above the law any more than anyone else, nor would any of us have survived a crash better.

All the rules of the road should be observed by the cyclist. If you ride through a state where right turns are illegal on a red light, you should of course obey that law. Everywhere there is the rule that slower vehicles stay right, and the rule that the vehicle on the right proceeds first through an intersection. Get in the habit of riding your bicycle as if it were a car—but a very slow, very narrow, very quiet car. You must follow the rules so as not to surprise drivers of those other cars—those faster, wider, noisier, and more dangerous ones.

Be Careful

If you ride predictably and make yourself visible to motorists, you automatically will be riding more carefully. But there is still more you can do to prevent nasty encounters. If you ride defensively and intelligently, you will have many happy, safe miles, even if you ride in traffic daily.

First, be certain that you can see and hear motor vehicles as well and as clearly as possible. This means no headphones with music drowning out traffic noise: if you cannot hear autos or other bikes as you go your way, how on earth can you cycle defensively? With traffic noise muffled and drowned out by music, you are actually deaf to a great deal of important information. You have only sight and feel to guide you, and that's not enough. I don't mean to say that deaf persons cannot or should not ride bicycles, but the deaf have practice at getting around without their hearing, while hearing people do not. When I have tried wearing headphones, invariably I have found myself surprised by passing cars and trucks.

Just as your hearing should be unimpeded, so should your vision. Wear sunglasses or goggles when it is too bright out, but take them off when you don't need them. If your helmet has a visor, be sure that you can see under or through it. Otherwise, remove the visor.

Being careful also implies watching out for other vehicles and obstacles, and taking no undue chances with either. If you see a grate in the road ahead, ease around it smoothly and well ahead of time, rather than waiting to see whether you will have to jump it in order not to get stuck. If you see a car coming from an intersecting street or driveway, watch to see that the front end dips, indicating braking. Don't assume that the driver will stop or even slow down just because there is a stop sign or cross traffic. When crossing at an intersection with a four-way stop, be sure it is your turn before proceeding, then go. And if you have a bike lane or at least some shoulder to ride on out of traffic, stay far enough away from the auto lane to minimize close scrapes. Some drivers have difficulty judging how closely they hug the right side of their lane, and if your bicycle is at that edge, you could be in for an unexpected bump.

And watch for opening doors from parked cars. If you are riding between cars parallel parked and the rightmost lane of traffic, you have only a narrow path—one that is scarcely wider than a car door. When that door opens and you are not prepared for it, it matters very little that you technically were not at fault.

Sight down the windows of parked cars as you ride, continuously monitoring them, and always look for someone seated behind the wheel. When you spot that person, make sure you will have clearance in case that door opens, and be prepared to warn the driver if you suspect (or see) that the door is opening. I sometimes whistle as soon as I see the shoulder move—the tip-off that the driver is working the door handle. You should also refine your skills at looking in side-view mirrors and trying to glimpse inside driver-side windows on vehicles that don't afford you a clear view through a rear window. Don't be afraid to give a warning as you cycle by. I would rather sound a hundred false alarms than be stopped dead once by someone's ill-timed open door.

You should also be extra careful when your bike is loaded more heavily than usual—such as when going on tour—as you are then much more likely to be buffeted around by the wind. Practice with the bike encumbered to help you become more skilled and confident. Remember also that a heavily laden bicycle can be more dangerous than a stripped model because your vision can be somewhat obstructed. Front bags, for example, prevent you from seeing the road immediately in front of you. If you know these things, you can proceed with a little more caution than usual. Further, a bike loaded with panniers is substantially wider than a bare machine, and this can cause you difficulties in passing through straits, trying to avoid obstacles, or leaving room for passing motorists.

A final point about being careful. Consider restraining the impulse to make rude gestures to motorists whose driving causes you a problem. I know it's tempting to insult the intelligence of the careless driver, to suggest things about his or her mother's behavior, or to make an obscene gesture. But try to resist these temptations. I have heard many a horror story about the confrontations between the indignant cyclist and one or more motorists who took exception to the cyclist's words or gestures. It seems to me that in most cases the cyclist ended up getting the worst of it.

4

Clothing and Accessories

The clothes you wear when you ride will make all the difference in your comfort, safety, and enjoyment of cycling. We cyclists dress in somewhat unusual looking garb, not because we like to stand out in a crowd or shock the public, but because these clothes are made specifically for cycling. Although you can wear just about anything short of a suit of armor on a bike, you'll find that the "official" shorts and shoes really are superior to any substitutes.

Wool jersey, cycling shorts (inside out), shoes, cap, gloves, helmet, and leggings—most of these things will make bike riding safer, more comfortable, and more efficient.

CLOTHES FOR CYCLING

The well-dressed cycling fanatic in full-combat regalia sports Italian shoes, fingerless gloves, and a cap worn backwards with the bill turned up. If the weather is foul, he or she will have black wool tights and a long-sleeve wool jersey with a club name if not a sponsor's logo emblazoned across the front and back. In fair weather, our bike enthusiast may wear a multi-colored skin suit or a blinding cotton jersey and cycling shorts.

Two distinct sub-species of the well-turned-out cyclist are the clashers and the blenders. Blenders are color-coordinated with their bikes, their cycling partners, and their handlebar tape. They even match their sweethearts, right down to the shoelaces. Clashers, by contrast, resemble nothing so much as a bulletin board in a kindergarten, for every piece of clothing and equipment is a distinct color—a bold, bright, vibrant color not found in nature.

I admit to being something of a clasher myself, since I ride in clothing suited to the weather, without regard to color. I'm only a blender when I happen to wear something that by chance matches my bike. The most sensible approach, I think, is to buy and wear clothes of the proper fabric, weight, and cut for you and for the weather. If you can find the colors and designs you want, so much the better, but don't let fashion get in the way of practicality.

Shorts, Tights, and Leggings

The "official" pants for cycling are those close-fitting shorts made of wool, acrylic, spandex, or a blend. Black is the classic color for these, although turquoise, flamingo, crimson, and canary are now available. I may be old-fashioned, but I still think black is the best color for shorts, since it hides grease smudges and sweat stains.

Cycling shorts have a piece of chamois (or some imitation fabric) sewn into the crotch to prevent chafing from the seams. They are made to be worn without underwear. It's best to have

Cycling shorts come in several colors and fabrics, often with a pocket for keys or money.
(Courtesy Cool Gear)

at least two pair of shorts, so the chamois has a chance to dry between uses. You'll find that your own sweat will keep the chamois soft and comfortable while you ride, but dry chamois is stiff, so you might want to put a little petroleum jelly or skin cream on beforehand. Talcum powder also helps.

Cycling shorts are long enough to prevent the leg from chafing against the saddle, and they fit snugly but without restricting motion. The waistband, which will have either elastic or a drawstring, is high, to help keep the lower back covered. No other kind of shorts combines fit and comfort for cycling so well as real cycling shorts, which explains their popularity. Once you ride a bike any distance wearing them, you'll never revert to your former shorts or pants.

You have to hand-wash and line-dry cycling shorts, turning them inside out to dry. You should be a bit careful when you don or doff a pair, because the fabric of the shorts stretches more than the chamois, and it's easy to rip the chamois at the stitching. With a little care, however, cycling shorts will last many a mile.

Long-legged cycling pants, designed for cold-weather riding, are known as tights. These are not the same as dance tights; they are specifically designed for bicycle riding. Some tights have a chamois crotch, and some don't. The ones that don't are meant to be worn over a regular pair of shorts, and they can be pulled off in public without causing a stir. Tights are made out of the same fabrics as regular shorts.

Leggings are just wool tubes that go from thigh to ankle, and, like tights, are meant for cool weather. Leggings don't always stay up on the thigh, so many riders resort to safety pins when they wear them. Again, leggings are not the same as dance warm-ups, although they work similarly. And some cyclists do wear dance leg warmers when it's cold.

It's a good idea to wear some kind of protection on the legs, especially over the knees, whenever you ride in the cold. Because of wind-chill damage to knees, some people recommend tights or leggings whenever the thermometer drops below 70°F. A pair of tights or leggings can always be stashed under the saddle or in a jersey pocket, so it's wise to take them along in case you need them.

Shirts, Jerseys, and Jackets

The classic cycling jersey is made of wool and has short sleeves. It's cut long to prevent the back from being exposed to the elements, and there are two or three pockets in the back,

Leggings are good to have when the air temperature drops below 70°F. This cyclist is taking no chances—he has "armies" on as well. (Courtesy Cool Gear)

A well-outfitted cyclist will have a comfortable and safe ride—especially if he or she remembers to wear a helmet. (Courtesy Cool Gear)

often closed with buttons. There is only a crew collar, though it may have a zipper or buttons at the throat. Wool is a great fabric for a jersey because it wicks off moisture (read sweat and rain and anything that may splash you) while keeping the wearer warm. Even in relatively hot weather, a thin wool or wool-cotton blend jersey is the favorite of many cyclists. Jerseys also are made of synthetic materials such as nylon. These are easy to care for and can be very warm in cool weather, although they can't match wool for staying dry next to the skin.

It's not necessary to wear an "official" cycling jersey, though, especially in very warm weather. A plain cotton T-shirt or sleeveless shirt is often quite adequate. Long- or short-sleeved T-shirts are good to wear beneath a wool sweater or jersey in cold weather for an extra layer of protection, and they help reduce the itchiness of the wool. In particularly bitter cold, I wear a cotton shirt, a wool jersey or a sweater, and a nylon wind-

breaker as an outer shell. I also pin a piece of cardboard or
some newspaper to the outside of the T-shirt under my jersey to
protect my chest. Old manila file folders and large envelopes are
handy for this purpose, and I sometimes add a sheet of plastic for
good measure. If I get too warm wearing my paper chest protector, I just toss it in a trash can, where it was headed anyway.

Your wardrobe should include at least one nylon windbreaker
or light jacket. These are excellent both as the outermost layer
and as emergency rain or cold protection. They take up very
little room when folded, and they can save your skin when it
turns chilly or wet, or if you are forced to stop for a while. Your
body temperature can drop rapidly if you stop, say, to repair a
flat, so it's good to carry extra protection to help retain body
heat. Furthermore, if you are going to be doing any serious
riding in the rain, you should think about investing in rain
pants, jackets, or ponchos. I don't mind a little rain when the

Dress for the weather. This rider is able to keep going through the rain by wearing rain gear and a large plastic trash bag. It's low-rent protection, but it works. (Courtesy TOSRVPHOTO)

weather is fairly warm, but I don't think it's a good idea to go touring or commuting in the rain without some protection.

Skin Suits

A combination of shorts and shirt, the skin suit is basically a pair of cycling shorts that extends to the shoulders. Skin suits usually are made of spandex for quick drying, a snug fit, and wind protection. Spandex is particularly nice in hot weather, too, for it breathes better than most other fabrics.

The skin suit is popular among triathletes as well as cyclists. A smooth, tight-fitting skin suit is much more aerodynamic than any loose or flapping clothing, and racers are turning to them in greater numbers every year. Triathletes have found they can save precious minutes of transition time if they swim, bike, and run in a skin suit rather than change between events.

Because they lack pockets and are made of such light fabric, skin suits have more limited uses than some other items of apparel. But if you're looking for comfort and reduced air drag, a skin suit is worth the investment.

Gloves

The fingerless gloves of a fashionable bikie are not just for looks. A good pair of cycling gloves serves two functions: comfort and protection. Because they're padded in the palms, cycling gloves are much more comfortable than thinly taped handlebars, and they greatly reduce the chance of damage or pain due to pressure on the hands. Gloves also offer excellent protection in a fall, when the automatic reaction is to hit the ground hands first. I've been lucky enough to have gloves on during all my really bad spills, I'm happy to say.

In addition to reinforced, padded palms and no fingers, most cycling gloves have a loose-woven back with a Velcro closing at the wrist. For cold weather riding, you can wear another pair of gloves over them. It's important to protect the hands from the cold and damp, so whenever you expect inclement weather you should consider wearing some kind of glove. (Military surplus

The loose weave helps keep cycling gloves from getting too hot to wear, while the padded, reinforced leather palms ease the pressure on the hands and protect the hands in case of an accident. (Courtesy Cannondale Corporation)

stores carry inexpensive but quite adequate wool and leather gloves, by the way.) Probably the best thing about store-bought cycling gloves is that they already have padding on the palms, so it isn't necessary to reinforce them. They're also good for picking raspberries, I'm told. The fingers are free to pick the berries, while the rest of the hand is protected from the thorns.

Shoes

Much less versatile than gloves, cycling shoes are practically worthless for anything other than riding a bike. But they're great for that. With the cleated cycling shoe, coupled with a toe clip and strap, the rider's foot virtually becomes a part of the bicycle, the key to minimizing the amount of energy wasted in turning the cranks. It's just about impossible to walk comfortably or gracefully while wearing cycling shoes, and anyway

103

walking in them ruins the cleats and/or the soles of the shoes. They are fine when you are out strictly for exercise or transportation, but if you get on and off the bicycle a lot, you probably won't like having to change your shoes so frequently.

Most cycling shoes have leather uppers and either wooden, plastic, or stiff leather soles. (Lately I have noticed more variety in the materials used for the uppers: nylon, mesh, and suede are now often combined with leather.) The better leather-soled shoes feature a steel plate in the sole to guarantee stiffness, the idea being to prevent energy dissipation in flexing the foot or bending the shoe. Hard plastic and wood soles, of course, don't need any steel plates.

Cleats may be affixed by nails, screws, or bolts. I prefer the adjustable kind, because after breaking in the shoe, I sometimes like to move the cleat a little for a better fit. With nail-in cleats, this isn't so easily done. To properly locate the cleat, it's best to ride the bike with the cleats off until the pedal marks the sole of the shoe. First-time users of cleats are likely to fall over at least once when they forget (or fail) to pull their foot out of the pedal in time to stop. If you've never worn cleated shoes before, be extra cautious until you're used to riding in them.

Since cleats are so bothersome everywhere but on a bike, many riders wear touring shoes. These resemble running shoes, in that they usually have suede-and-mesh uppers, but the soles are made of relatively stiff rubber, and they have ridges rather than cleats to fit on the pedal. You can walk quite comfortably in touring shoes, but doing so weakens the soles. Touring shoes don't quite grab the pedal as well as cleated shoes, and the soles aren't nearly so stiff, making it a less efficient shoe. But if you aren't looking to become the fastest cyclist in the territory, and you don't want the little inconveniences that come with cleated shoes, then perhaps you should think about wearing touring shoes when you ride.

I don't recommend riding in other than touring or cleated cycling shoes. Running shoes, tennis shoes, and deck shoes are all right for a mile or two, but over a distance the shoes may cause injury to the foot due to lack of support. It takes stiff soles and properly reinforced uppers to keep both the shoe and the foot

Touring shoes are comfortable for walking and biking. They are as light as running shoes but stiffer in the sole and reinforced across the ball of the foot for long wear. (Courtesy Cannondale Corporation)

from being mistreated. Good brands to look for are Vittorio, Detto Pietro, Duegi, Sidi, and Bata.

For snowy, rainy, or cold weather, you can get overshoes and booties of various sorts, many of which are filled with down and made of rip-stop nylon, like sleeping bags. Overshoes may be attached to the pedal or just slipped over your regular shoes. Some people make their own overshoes out of wool stockings coated with snowseal. Cut a little hole in the bottom for the cleat and you're ready to go.

Helmets

I have a little collection of cycling caps that commemorate various races of the past, and I keep them hung up on a beam in my living room. They protect my head there as much as on the bike: a sporty cloth cap will not help at all if you go down. If you crash and strike your unprotected head against *anything,* you may never be the same again—assuming you live. In most United States Cycling Federation (USCF) sanctioned races, helmets are required, and any rider who removes his or her "brain bucket" before finishing the race is disqualified.

New cycling helmets come on the market practically every month. You should shop around, ask your friends, and look for the manufacturer's information on test crashes. Some helmets pass most of the tests, and some fail miserably. You should at least know how much protection to expect before you buy. Many racers effectively skirt the helmet rule by wearing little Naugahyde racing helmets patterned after the sort of helmet made of

105

leather tubes stuffed with lamb's wool. Although some leather ones are excellent, their flimsy Naugahyde imitations are strictly for show. This little subterfuge often is defeated by race rules that specifically disallow inferior helmets, and this has encouraged manufacturers to design race-worthy helmets that racers will wear.

The ideal helmet is sturdy, light, and comfortable. It protects the wearer from sun and precipitation as well as from injury in a collision or crash, so when shopping, keep comfort in mind. Ventilation makes a huge difference on a warm day. One brand of helmet might have only one or two holes in it, while another kind might have many flow-through slits in it. The more air that can pass through the helmet, the more comfortable it will be, and the more likely you are to wear it. Also consider how much protection from rain, snow, and sun your prospective helmet can provide. Some helmets have visors to cut glare and keep precipitation off the face; some are made so that your head will stay dry in a downpour even though there is good ventilation.

BIKE EQUIPMENT

Pumps

A light, reliable pump on your bicycle is indispensable. You never know when a tire will puncture or blow out, but when one does, there are only three ways to inflate the replaced or repaired tire and tube. One way is to use a CO_2 cartridge designed to be used once and then discarded. The first such device made was the Qwikfil and I have used them often since they were invented. If you rely exclusively on CO_2 cartridges you could run out and have to find another method of getting air, i.e., from a gas station. There is no guarantee, however, that a filling station will be nearby when you flat. Another consideration is that air hoses at gas stations work only on Schrader valves—the ones that look like automobile-tire valves—and not on the thinner Presta valves, which require an adapter. Still another problem with compressor pumps is that they are so variable. Some won't give you the 95 or 100 psi you need, and others are so powerful

Foam handlebar covers are popular items with many dedicated cyclists. They reduce pressure and pain in the hands, and can help prevent potential vascular or nerve damage on long tours. (Courtesy KBC Corporation)

they explode the tire before you know what's happening. This leaves us with the third way to inflate tires: using a pump you carry with you.

Generally, the longer the pump the better, since more air will be forced into the tire with each stroke. Pumps come in many different lengths to accommodate different sizes of bicycles. They may be mounted beneath the top tube or on the down tube, but the best place for them is on the seat tube. Frame-fit pumps are designed to sit between the top tube and the bottom-bracket shell, and I recommend this type for two reasons. A frame-fit pump will be relatively long and it won't require any mounting hardware. Whether or not you buy a frame-fit pump, though, be sure to look for one with a quick-release or pull-off head. Threaded, screw-on valve attachments allow too much air pressure to be lost in removing them. Zefal and Silca manufacture excellent ones.

An under-the-saddle pack like this one is perfect for a few tools, a spare, and some money—the minimum on a ride. (Courtesy Kirtland Tour Pak)

For at-home use, I recommend a stand-up floor pump with an easily read pressure gauge. It's hard to judge the amount of air in a tire by feel, and small pressure gauges may not be accurate. A good floor pump will give you an accurate reading even as you inflate the tire, and it will be easier to use than a hand pump. If you use tubular tires and deflate them somewhat between rides, you will almost certainly need a floor pump.

Bags and Racks

There are various kinds of bags that can be mounted on bicycles or on cyclists, any of which you might need to transport goods. You could wear a back pack to carry small, light items; I don't like to do it much, but I use back packs when I have to. Fanny packs, which are basically belts with a large zippered

A handlebar pack with a map window comes in handy for both the tourist and the recreational cyclist. (Courtesy Madden Touring Equipment)

Front panniers, used alone, can make a bicycle more aerodynamic than the same size panniers on the rear. Whenever very heavy loads are taken, it's advisable to put 40 percent of the weight over the front wheel. (Courtesy Kirtland Tour Pak)

pocket in the back, also come in handy for the cyclist who has just a few small things to carry. They don't cover much of the back and aren't as cumbersome to wear.

Most cyclists carry spare tubes, tires, patches, or tools in some sort of seat bag mounted beneath the saddle. There are bags made just for this purpose, but you could make your own or use a plastic bag and a leather strap. I often ride with two spare tubular tires folded up under my saddle and held there with a toe-clip strap.

These rear panniers have several nice features: cutaway design to keep them far from the cyclist's heel; internal structure to prevent the bags from touching the spokes; and multiple pockets. Note the brazed-on rack studs. (Courtesy Kirtland Tour Pak)

Handlebar bags, which ride between the hooks and in front of the stem, come in a variety of sizes. The larger ones have small mounting arms and stabilizers, and they carry a surprising amount of stuff. Tourists often use these kinds of bags, as they usually have a map window on the top and are easy to open even while riding. The advantages of using only a handlebar bag are that the bike is no wider, as it is with side-mounted bags, and the mounting hardware is likely to be lighter than a rack.

The bags that mount on racks over the front and back tires are called panniers, a word that means breadbasket in French. Panniers, like most other kinds of bags, come in many sizes, so it's a good idea to consider your exact needs if you are thinking about buying some. A month of camping/touring in the summer might call for larger bags than you need for your daily commute, for example. Good panniers carry cargo relatively low to the ground for a lower center of gravity and better stability. They are designed not to interfere with pedaling and to remain clear of the spokes of the wheels. Panniers protect cargo from the weather

Racks to support panniers and other bags may be made of aluminum, steel, or an alloy, and may be either plain or anodized. (Courtesy KBC Corporation [rear rack] and Cannondale Corporation [front racks])

and yet permit easy access to the contents. Current thinking about touring is that both front and rear panniers should be used, with 40 percent of the load inside the front bags. Some people advocate using only front panniers for light-duty touring or commuting, on the theory that improved aerodynamics and savings in weight over rear panniers more than make up for any handling problems caused by front bags.

Both front and rear panniers require racks, and it's important to make sure that the racks and bags are compatible. Some racks are designed to take only certain panniers, and vice versa. Blackburn and Eclipse products, for example, are incompatible without adapters. Your racks should be securely mounted to the bike before they are used. Brazed-on mountings are the best; some touring frames come so equipped and others are modified to take racks. If your bike doesn't have the braze-ons, be sure the mounting hardware works properly for your frame. Some racks are perfectly adequate in themselves, but are sold with poor-quality hardware.

Bags that ride atop the rear rack can be combined with panniers to increase the luggage capacity. When used alone, they provide the commuter with an easily removed carry-all that won't increase the width of the bicycle. (Courtesy Cannondale Corporation)

This handy sky bag allows the traveler to take his or her bike on any plane, bus, or train. The model shown is made to take a bicycle with front and back racks; other models are available for recumbents, racers, and tandems. (Courtesy Chamberlain Design Systems)

Bicycle Carriers

Bikes can be transported on top of or behind automobiles on bike carriers. Most people don't trust the rear carriers, because the bike is so vulnerable to damage. I have to agree that a bicycle is a poor substitute for a rear bumper. The one good thing about a rear carrier is that it doesn't cost much.

Your bike is less likely to be demolished if it rides atop the car. Roof carriers typically can accommodate two bikes, either upright or upside down. I use the latter kind. Those carriers that hold the bicycle upright usually have a quick-release device to hold the fork dropouts and some sort of cradle for the rear wheel.

113

One important thing to look for is the security of the quick-release device. Make sure that the fork will be firmly held to the carrier, or your bicycle may end up on the road. Also consider whether and how your bike may be locked when on the carrier. Models with built-in locks might be worth the extra money.

Trailers and Child Seats

There are several brands of bike trailers on the market, some of which are designed for passengers, some for goods. On a long tour, you might find it more convenient to tow your belongings rather than (or in addition to) carrying them. And children too young to ride along also can be safely transported in a trailer.

I have seldom ridden a bike with a trailer, but I've talked with people who use them regularly. It seems luggage trailers are not worth the extra weight unless you are carrying substantially more baggage than you can safely manage in panniers. In that case, a trailer offers at least three advantages: the tires on the bike last longer due to less weight; handling is much easier,

Trailers that carry goods or passengers (or both) are useful to the recreational cyclist and the tourist with extraordinary loads to tote. (Courtesy Cannondale Corporation)

Be sure to buckle Junior into his child seat and put his helmet on him before going riding. A leg shield prevents the child's feet from touching the rear wheel. (Courtesy Bell Helmets)

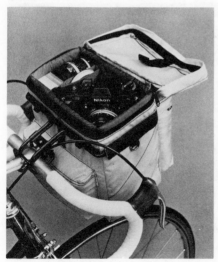

It's easy to combine other interests with cycling, especially if you're willing to put a little thought and imagination into it. And you may find accessories, like this camera bag, perfectly suited to your needs. (Courtesy Kirtland Tour Pak)

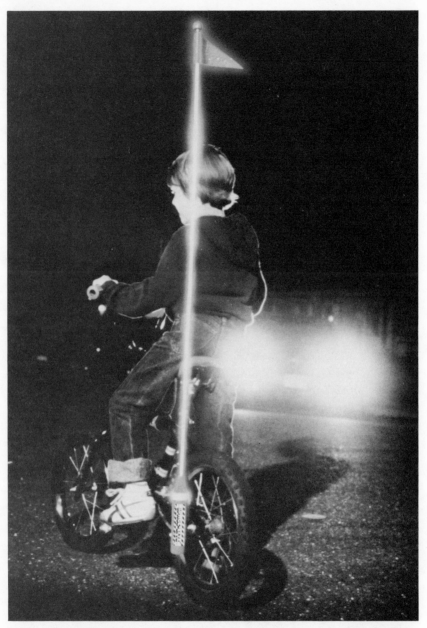

Flags and lights are great ways to increase visibility in traffic and after dark. This flag, a flexible pole that can be illuminated, helps to identify a cyclist day or night. (Courtesy Space Lyte International)

since there need be no bags on the bike itself at all; and the load doesn't seem as great, even though you may be carrying much more than in panniers.

Child trailers offer the tourist or recreational cyclist a safe, convenient way to take a youngster along for the ride. The best ones are stable and well padded, and they have a safety belt to keep precious cargo from spilling out.

Besides lightness, strength, and safety features, a good trailer should have high-quality wheels and hubs, and narrow, high-pressure tires. The last thing you want in a trailer is a lot of rolling resistance, so be sure to look for good parts.

When the weather is too harsh to ride outdoors, I still get a workout on my ergometer. This Criterion trainer is made by Hooker Industries. (Courtesy Ken Hougen)

Children can also ride on seats mounted behind the saddle over the rear wheel. Child seats should be equipped with seat belts, which should be used at all times. Before buying a child seat, check whether its design prevents the child's feet from getting near the rear tire or spokes, and be sure that it can be mounted on your bike securely. If you use a child seat, make it a habit to check it regularly to be certain it is firmly attached to your bike, set at the right angle, and still big enough for your passenger. When transporting a child this way, remember that your center of gravity is very high, so cornering is potentially more hazardous than usual. Needless to say, whenever you ride with a child as a passenger, either in a seat or inside a trailer, you should proceed slowly and cautiously.

5

Bicycle Maintenance
Made Easy

One nice thing about the bicycle is that it is relatively easy to maintain in good repair. Everything—well, almost everything—on a bike is right out in the open, all ready to check and fix, if need be. The bicycle is such a simple machine that even the most non-mechanically inclined rider can master its maintenance challenges with a minimum of effort. If you don't already know how something on a bike works, you can see it and study it for a while without having to take anything apart; and most likely you'll figure it out all by yourself. Anything beyond your mechanical reasoning power can be learned from a friend or a book. In fact, I recommend that you get a good general bike-repair manual and read it once you've finished this book. Whenever you need to do any maintenance, you can re-read this chapter and/or look it up in your repair manual, and eventually you'll know all about keeping your bike in top condition. See the Recommended Reading section for repair manuals.

No single chapter can turn you into an expert bike mechanic, but I think you can learn a lot about caring for your bicycle by reading about it first, then working on any problems that come up. If you follow my suggestions about keeping your bike in good shape, you should be able to keep it rolling for quite some time at minimal cost.

A few spare parts and tools are shown here. Spare wheels and tubular tires are often owned by racers who don't want to wear out expensive parts on training rides. Also seen are extra cables, derailleurs, and freewheels; a floor pump with a dial gauge; oil and grease; and various tools.

FLATS

Flat tires are the curse of the cyclist. Everyone who rides a bike will eventually get a flat, but some people get them only once or twice a year, despite big miles, while others seem to spend more time seated on the curb than on the saddle.

Every cyclist should be able to get his or her bike back into operation after a flat tire. Those flats will happen to you sooner or later, and, unlike the motorist, you will have no tow truck to call. Whether you're halfway across the country or just rolling down your own driveway, when your tire won't hold air anymore, you either have to fix it or walk.

Chances are your next flat tire will be on the rear wheel. Even though the odds *should* dictate a 50-50 chance for either wheel, you'll hardly ever flat the front tire, the easy one to change. This is because your rear wheel carries more than 50 percent of the weight and so is more likely to press a sharp object into its worn surface. Further, you are more apt to steer the front wheel around obvious hazards, but the rear may roll over glass or metal despite your best efforts. If I were to look for the good in having more rear-wheel flats, I guess I'd have to say at least your steering is not so negatively affected when the rear tire goes flat. A high-speed blowout on the front wheel could test your cycling skills at the most unexpected time.

If you ride on tubular tires, always carry one or two with you. I never go anywhere without two spares because I have had two flats in a day, and I've sometimes had a new sew-up fail to hold air. Just think how upset you would be with a flat tire and a flat spare, too. If you use clinchers, you can carry one or two spare tubes, or a patch kit, or both. It's much nicer to put in a new tube and get underway, perhaps patching the flatted tube after your ride if it's worth saving. When on tour, you might even carry a spare tire, since they wear out rather fast under heavy loads.

When a tire blows, pull over and remove the wheel, taking care to set your bicycle down so as not to damage the derailleur, saddle, or the paint. Don't turn it upside down to work on it; rather, shift into your highest gear, loosen the brake with its quick release, then pull the skewer lever to free the axle from the dropouts, holding the bike with one hand and the wheel with the other. If you have a riding companion, he or she can give you a hand with this part. Usually you can lay the bicycle down on its left side without harming any parts. When the flat is on the front, you can stand the bike up on the fork dropouts, but if it's a rear flat, standing it up could harm the rear derailleur.

If you have sew-ups, you have to roll the tire off the rim and install the spare. Stand with the wheel between your feet, valve near the ground, grasping the top of the tire as if it were a steering wheel, that is, with thumbs across top of the tire and pointed toward each other. Pinch the tire between your thumbs and forefingers, then roll it off the rim away from you. If you have trouble getting it off right away, that's probably because you haven't had a flat in a long time. Isn't that nice?

On large group rides, when one person has a flat or mechanical problem, the usual procedure is for the group to continue. The lone rider, perhaps helped by a friend, will fix the problem and catch up to the group later rather than hold everyone up. Self-sufficiency not only pays off; it's a must. (Courtesy Greg Siple, TOSRVPHOTO)

Next step is to clean off the rim, with solvent or at least a rag. Stretch the new tire by making it a figure-8 and looping it over your shoulder and knee, just until you hear the stitches cracking a little. All you want to do is make sure it will fit the rim properly. Spread a thin coat of cement on the rim and another one on the inner side of the tire and wait for them to get tacky before attempting to mount the tire. If you're in a big hurry, as in a race, or if you don't have any cement with you, you can skip the gluing stage, but you should be extraordinarily careful until you can remove the tire and cement it back on the correct way.

When the glue is tacky, stand with the rim resting on your feet (off the ground, at least) and the valve hole at 12 o'clock. Put the valve in first, and pull the tire equally on either side of the valve to position it against the rim. Work carefully and slowly so as to get the tire on as symmetrically as possible. When you have got it a bit more than half on, turn the wheel over and work your way up. After the tire is on, inspect it all the way around to be sure it is centered on the rim. You'll be able to position it properly before the cement dries, but the job won't be so easy if you wait too long. When you're satisfied the tire is properly seated, inflate it halfway and check it again for evenness and roundness before filling it all the way. Then be sure to wipe off any excess cement prior to reinstalling the wheel.

As to repairing the punctured or blown-out tubular, you should first decide whether it's worth the trouble it will take. If there are only a few miles left in the tire, you probably will want to throw it away. But if it's a relatively new tire, you can repair it by undoing some of the stitches, patching it from the inside, and re-sewing the tire. To do so, you should consult the tire manufacturer's recommendations before trying to repair a sew-up tire.

If you have clinchers, you must remove both tire and tube, check for foreign objects, repair or replace the tube, and re-mount both tube and tire on the rim. Some peoply try to get away with pulling out just enough tube to patch, perhaps not even removing the wheel, but they often end up with another puncture because there is something inside the tire putting a hole in the tube. As my grandmother used to say, "Lazy man works twice."

To remove the tire, you can use essentially the same technique as for a sew-up, trying to lift and push the tire over the edge of the rim. But not everyone is strong enough to do this, and you may have to use tire irons. These are little metal spoons used to pry one edge of the tire over the rim; once the entire side of the tire is off the rim, it's easy to remove the tube and pull the tire completely off. If you use tire irons, resist the temptation to use them to install the tire also. Most likely you will puncture the tube before you're done, and that's no fun.

Once the tire and tube are off, look and feel for the nail, glass, staple, or whatever it was that caused the flat. If you can find the offender beforehand, you will save yourself some time. If you can't find what caused the puncture, pull the tube out of the tire and look inside the tire. You may find something that shouldn't be there, in which case, pluck it out. Or you might find something still stuck in the tube. Before you do anything else, take a cloth and run it all along the inside of the tire and the edge of the rim once or twice to be sure you have dislodged any other objects.

If you have a spare tube with you, all you have to do is put that and your tire back on. Otherwise, you have to repair the tube first; but I'll postpone talking about patching a moment here and assume you have a spare. Put one edge of the tire around the rim first, then put the valve stem into its proper hole. Imbed the tube in the tire, perhaps letting a little air in the tube first by depressing the core of the valve. Next, using your thumbs, press the remaining edge of the tire little by little inside the rim until you have it all. This is easier to explain than to do, but with a little patience and the appropriate facial expressions you'll get the job done sooner or later. If you really have trouble with the last two inches or so, and you promise yourself to be extremely careful, you may use a tire iron to pop the last bit into place. But you could very easily either puncture or pinch the tube, and that means another flat to fix, so try to do it with your hands alone.

After you have the tire on, check it all around for proper seating, then fill it halfway up. You might find it helpful to press the valve stem part way back *into* the tire before filling it; otherwise, you might get a bulge and even a blowout near the valve. With the tire half-filled, check it all around again for proper seating and deflate it if necessary before pumping it to full pressure.

Repairing a punctured tube is a simple matter. Buy a patch kit from your bike shop and follow the instructions. Rema makes good kits; the patches are especially good because they are thinner toward the edges than in the middle, so they don't make too bad a bump on the tube. Generally, to get a good patch job, you have to have a little patience and wait for the cement to get tacky before placing the patch over the hole. If you put it on too soon, it may not bond properly, and when you fill it up with air you get a surprise.

TRUING A WHEEL

I have cautioned against building a wheel unless you already know what you are doing, so let me say here that I don't suggest you try to straighten a wheel that is radically out of true or out of round. Take it to a good wheel mechanic and get it done right. However, from time to time a little adjustment in trueness of a wheel will be in order, and you should know how to do it if you have to.

Take a look at a wheel, at the spoke pattern, and you will see that alternate spokes attach to the rim from alternating sides of the wheel. A spoke from the right side pulls the rim toward the right, and one from the left pulls it to the left. If all the spokes pull with about equal force, the rim should be true, since left and right side will balance each other out. But imagine what would happen if one spoke, say on the left, "let go." Then there would be two spokes from the right side pulling without the (left-side) spoke between them pulling against them. The wheel would be out of balance, and this would show up in a small section pulling to the right as the wheel spins past a fixed point. The wheel would be out of true.

How would you fix such a problem? Obviously, you would have to tighten up that one spoke that "let go" until it was pulling about as much as all the other spokes. When you have a wheel that is a little out of true, then, what you have to do is decide which spokes are pulling too much and which too little, then correct the imbalances until your wheel is true again. Part of the correction process is simply checking the tension on the spokes to find which ones are looser or tighter than its fellows. You can squeeze them in pairs all around the wheel, comparing them as you go, and you can pluck them like strings and listen to the "ping." A new, true wheel will have a fairly uniform ping to all the spokes, and they'll feel equally tight.

To tighten or loosen a spoke, you have to turn the nipple at the rim end of the spoke with a spoke wrench. Spoke wrenches come in various sizes and styles; all I can say is that you should buy one that fits your nipples, and use it sparingly. Turn the nipple clockwise (from the point of view of the rim) to tighten up the spoke, and counterclockwise to loosen it. Never tighten a spoke too much at a time, as you could over-stress it or pull your rim out of round. Go easy on it, checking the results in small steps.

DERAILLEUR ADJUSTMENTS

Both front and rear derailleurs will require adjustment now and then, especially if the cables are relatively new, as cables tend to stretch with use until they reach their maximum length. The symptoms of improper derailleur adjustment are (1) throwing the chain off the chain rings or cogs and (2) the inability to shift to all the gears. It is best to make the adjustment as soon as you have any problem in shifting, because you can seriously damage spokes, cogs, and the chain by throwing the chain.

Since all a derailleur does is move the chain left and right, adjustment involves fixing the mechanism so that it will take the chain only as far left and right as necessary, and no farther. This means pulling the cable taut with the shift lever in its most. forward position, then setting the high and low limit screws to their proper places.

For the front derailleur, shift into low gear, that is, left shift lever full forward, right lever full back. (On some bikes, this configuration won't be low gear. In any case, what you want to do is take the tension off the front derailleur cable.) Check the cable. Is it relatively taut, or is there a lot of slack in it? If there is slack, you'll have to pull the cable a little tighter. Look where the cable enters the front derailleur. It will be held there by some sort of nut, usually either an acorn or an Allen nut. Loosen that nut enough to pull the cable taut with a pair of pliers, then tighten the nut up again. Now look at the derailleur closely and find the two limit screws on it. One of them (probably labeled "L") stops the cage from moving any farther left than it is now; the other (either "R" or "H" for right or high) limits the rightward movement of the cage. If your front derailleur is throwing the chain too far left, the left limit screw is too far out. Screw it in a little bit and test it by shifting up a couple of gears and then shifting the chain back and forth between the small and large chain rings several times. Naturally, if your problem has been failure to get the chain onto the small chain ring, you should back that left limit screw out a little bit. The same procedure holds for the right limit screw: tighten it down a little if you have been throwing the chain off the large chain ring, and back it off a little if you've had trouble getting the chain onto the large chain ring. Test the adjustments several times with your bike on a stand or with a friend holding the bike off the ground, and then again on the road. Take a screwdriver with you and fine-tune the derailleur until it works perfectly.

The rear derailleur should be adjusted in a similar way. First shift into your highest gear so as to take all the tension off the cable, and then tighten the cable just as you did with the front derailleur. Now locate the two adjustment screws. The one labeled "H" should be right up against some part of your derailleur, and you should be able to press the arm toward the wheel a little and so put some distance between the limit screw and the derailleur's interior. If your problem is that the chain wants to jump off the freewheel when you shift into high gear, then you'll have to turn the high limit screw down a little bit; if you can't quite get into that smallest cog, then back that limit screw off a little. Test it by shifting down a couple of cogs and then back into high. By now you should be able to tell me how to do the adjustment for your largest freewheel cog, even if you've never had a screwdriver in your hand before.

When a cable needs to be replaced, be sure you have the right replacement before doing anything rash with the old one—like cutting it or tying it into a bo'sun's knot. Put your bike into low gear for replacing a front cable; high gear for the rear. Then loosen the bolt that holds it in place and draw it out through its various guides and cable housings until you can pull it off the shift lever. Match the head of the cable against the new one, and if they are identical, then cut the new cable a little longer than the old. Before threading the new cable through its intended path, coat it with bearing grease to protect it, but stop short of the spot where it will attach to the derailleur itself. After you have the new cable in place, pull it taut and tighten up the nut that holds it in place. Test it, and when it works properly, cut it so that only about 2″ are left over. Then crimp a spoke nipple or one of those specially made aluminum caps over the end of the cable to keep it from fraying and/or stabbing you.

HANDLEBARS AND STEM

The handlebars will need only the most occasional adjustment, since they don't loosen or move much, but the stem should be attended to a little more often. The bars are held onto the stem by a bolt through the stem. Yours may require only an Allen wrench, or it may take two spanners (or else two adjustable wrenches) to do the trick. Loosen the bolt by turning counterclockwise, and tighten by turning clockwise. It's a good idea to set your bars at the desired angle and then tighten them down well, because you don't want them moving around while you ride.

The stem, on the other hand, shouldn't be all that tight. You will see a bolt, either Allen or hex, at the top of the stem. This bolt reaches the length of the stem and into a wedge-shaped nut (binder bolt) which mates to the bottom of the stem. When you tighten the bolt, you draw the binder bolt up toward the top of the stem, which in effect jams the stem inside the head tube. If you tighten the stem down too much and then spill the bike, you risk bending your handlebars up; but if you leave the stem a little loose, the handlebars will more likely turn in a crash, thus sparing them at least a little. Every six months or so, take your stem out and coat the wedge-shaped nut with bearing grease to keep it safe from corrosion.

BRAKES

Since brakes are used so often and are so important to your survival, you should pay particular attention to them. Check them every time you ride, and take notice if they act up. You always have enough time to repair your brakes.

The most common problem with brakes is that the shoes wear down just enough to make braking "soft." When you have to squeeze the brake lever a little too much to slow or stop, it's time to make a simple brake adjustment. Most side-pull brakes have an adjustment wheel of some sort on the upper arm. This wheel will, in effect, make the cable slightly shorter or longer and so move the shoes closer to or farther from the rim. All you have to do is press the shoes closed with one hand and spin the adjusting wheel with the other until you have the desired effect. Some brakes have a set nut as well as the wheel, so you may need to use a small wrench to loosen the nut first, then twirl the wheel and reset the nut.

If the adjustment wheel won't help, most likely your brake cable is stretched and needs to be tightened. Here is where a friend or a third hand comes in handy. If you don't have a friend conveniently nearby, then you can use a tool called a third hand. A third hand may not be as good company as a real friend, but then it won't drink your last beer either. This tool grips the brake shoes and clamps them closed, freeing you to loosen the nut that holds the cable, pull the cable taut with a pair of pliers, and tighten the nut again. Experiment with the adjustment wheel a bit to see whether you should twirl it one way or the other before applying the third hand (or your friend's hand) to the brake shoes. And, as with derailleur cables, coat them with grease to protect them, cut them about 2 inches beyond the holding nut, and crimp a spoke nipple or aluminum cap onto the ends so they won't puncture your skin.

If your brakes are off center, but your wheel is on center, then you have to center the brakes. Center-pull brakes can easily be centered by squeezing the shoes and centering the brake cable where it meets the short center cable. Side-pulls are a little trickier, but basically you will need to turn either the front or the rear nut to center the brake; the remaining nut is for tightening the brake onto the fork or frame. If you have trouble with this, take your bike to a good shop and let them fix it for you and explain how your brakes work. There are many design variations for side-pull brakes.

AXLES, SPINDLES, AND BEARINGS

Nearly all the parts of a bike that spin around and around rely on the spindle-and-bearing assembly to allow low-friction, smooth turning. There are plenty of people who find the concept of spindle and bearing beyond their powers of comprehension, but you don't have to count yourself in that number.

Pedals, wheel hubs, headsets, bottom brackets—all these have revolving parts that use ball bearings. (Other turning parts that don't use bearings are derailleur shift levers and jockey wheels, and brake levers.) The spindles for each of these four parts are known as spindles (pedals and bottom brackets) or axles (wheel hubs), though in the case of the headset it is the steering tube of the fork that acts as the spindle. In each case there are caged or free ball bearings that surround either end of the spindle. The ball bearings can revolve around the spindle because they are seated between a concave inner surface called either a race or a cup, and a concave outer surface called either a cone or a cup. Basically, you can think of a cone as being a movable cup, and in fact that's what the "cone" in a bottom bracket is called. A spindle set-up is properly adjusted when it rotates smoothly, with no binding, yet has no play. If you can move a wheel from left to right, when the axle is secure in the dropouts, then your hub needs adjustment. The same goes for your headset, bottom bracket, and pedals if there is any play when you jiggle the fork, cranks, and pedals.

When you overhaul any part that has a spindle and bearings, you need to take a few precautions. Put newspaper and/or cloths down before disassembling the parts, and keep a jar handy to hold them. Be sure you already have new bearings and some good bearing grease at hand before starting the overhaul, unless you plan to return the present bearings to the assembly. In either case, you'll need a good solvent, such as kerosene, and some rags to clean off all the parts. Also, be sure you have the right tools to do the job. All these parts require more or less specialized tools, which aren't usually found in a non-cyclist's tool box. If you want to overhaul your hubs, you'll most likely have to buy a freewheel remover and the right spanner for the cones. Your bottom bracket will need a special bottom-bracket wrench for the lock ring and the fixed cup, and another one for the adjustable cup. Your headset will require at least a large adjustable wrench. If you don't have the right tools, get them, or you risk ruining parts and putting yourself in a bad mood.

Hubs

To overhaul wheel hubs, remove the wheel from the bike and take the skewer out of the axle. If it is the rear wheel, remove the freewheel. Remaining in the hub, starting from the end of the axle, will be a thin nut, a washer, a cone, bearings, and a cup. Surrounding the bearings and cone will also be a dust cap, which is just a ring that fits onto the hub to protect the bearings from the elements and to prevent them from falling out. Begin by removing the nut, washer, and cone from one side only, using the proper size thin spanner to hold the cone still while removing the thin nut. You can then remove the washer and cone by hand. Once these parts are off one side, gently pry off the dust cap and remove the bearings. At this point, you should have all the parts off one side of the axle only, and it should be obvious that all you have to do to remove the parts from the other side is to turn the wheel over, pull the axle out (without removing anything from it beforehand), pry off the dust cap, and remove the bearings.

Thoroughly clean all the parts you have removed from the hub as well as the interior of the hub itself. You don't want any dirt inside your wheel. If you are replacing the bearings, you can just toss out the old ones, but be sure you have the right size and number of new bearings first. And if any of the other parts are worn out, they too should be replaced.

This exploded view of a Campagnolo hub and skewer shows how all the parts are arranged. (From *Glenn's Complete Bicycle Manual* by Clarence W. Cole and Harold T. Glenn. Copyright © 1973 by Harold T. Glenn. Used by permission of Crown Publishers, Inc.)

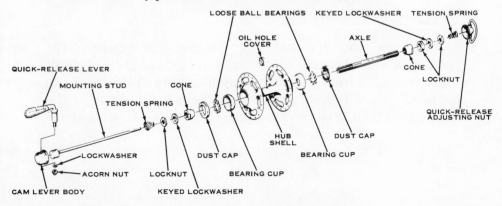

Before you put your hub back together again, take a good look at the axle and the parts that remain on it. Let's call the cone that you left on the axle the left cone. You can see that the left-side nut and cone are jammed together pretty tightly—or if they aren't, they should be, so get them that way before reassembling the hub. You also will want the cone and nut on the right side to be tightly backed against each other eventually. The thin nut and cone have to be able to stay together and in one place to keep the bearings in place. When you put the entire assembly together and adjust it so there is no play yet it spins freely, you will have to freeze the cone on the right side in place by tightening the thin nut against it, just as the left-side cone and nut are frozen in place now.

To reassemble the hub, first put a coating of bearing grease on the left cone, just on the concave bearing surface, as well as on the left race, inside the hub. Now carefully imbed the new or clean bearings inside the left race. Replace the dust cap, then put the axle through the hub until the left cone rests against its bearings. Turn the wheel over, so that the right-side race is up, and put some grease on that race and the right cone. Then imbed the bearings, replace the dust cap, and thread the right-side cone onto the axle.

Here is where the real adjustment comes in. You want to turn the right-side cone down just enough to eliminate all play in the axle but not so much as to restrict the motion of the bearings. You may have to experiment with it a little, but with some patience you will get the hang of it. After you have discovered just where the cone should rest so as to give you the perfect adjustment, you'll need to replace the washer and thin nut. And of course tighten the nut against the cone to freeze it in place.

Pedals

Pedals are much like hubs, but simpler. The spindle of the pedal is so shaped that it has no need of a cone on the end closer to the crank. There is a cone-and-nut assembly on the outer end of the spindle, however, and this can be seen by removing the cap that covers it. You can follow the instructions for wheel hubs to overhaul pedals by substituting the inner end of the shank for the left-side cone. Pedals don't require much attention, but they do sometimes loosen up or run dry of grease, so it is a good idea to check them every six months or so and overhaul them whenever they act up.

Headsets

The headset has an arrangement of cups and races at the bottom of the fork tube (that is, right at the crown of the fork) and another at the top of the fork tube. It is the lower cup and race that are fixed in a headset, while the uppermost cup is an adjustable race. Typically the upper, adjustable cup, which threads onto the top of the fork tube, has a washer above it and a

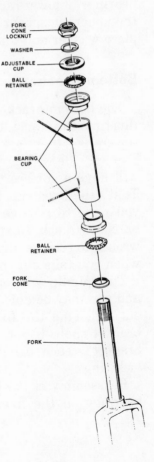

This shows how all the parts of a headset are arranged. (From Glenn's Complete Bicycle Manual *by Clarence W. Cole and Harold T. Glenn. Copyright © 1973 by Harold T. Glenn. Used by permission of Crown Publishers, Inc.)*

nut above that, and so is analogous to our right-side cone, washer, and nut on a wheel axle.

In order to overhaul a headset, you have to remove the handlebars and stem, and often the job is made easier still by taking off the front wheel as well. After spinning the top nut off and pulling off the washer, lay the bike down on a cloth or newspaper and grasp the fork and head tube with your left hand while you remove the adjustable cup. Free bearings that don't fall out should be removed from the top race and counted. Then pull the fork straight out of the head tube, taking care not to damage the threads. Bearings will spill all over the place once again, so be warned.

As with axles or pedals, clean everything up and put it back together again in reverse order: grease on lower race and cup; bearings in lower race; carefully put the fork in place; grease on the upper cups; bearings in place; thread adjustable cup on; replace washer and top nut. Gets easier every time, doesn't it?

Bottom Brackets

The bottom bracket also has a fixed and adjustable end, but this time the adjustable side is the left. You first have to remove the cranks, then look at either side of the bottom-bracket shell. The left side will have a notched lock ring, while the right side will have a surface that is more circular with two flat edges. That's the fixed cup. Before you can get to the adjustable cone, you have to remove the lock ring using the special bottom-bracket wrench. Next off is the left cone, which requires its own wrench to remove. Bearings, unless they are caged, will spill out when you take out the adjustable cup, so be prepared.

The spindle will come out when you pull it from the left side, and you may be able to clean and reassemble everything without removing the fixed cup on the right side of the bottom-bracket shell. If not, the fixed cup comes off with the bottom-bracket wrench, using the opposite end from the one used for the lock ring.

Reassembly of the bottom bracket proceeds with grease and bearings on the fixed cup; insertion of the greased spindle;

grease on the left-side race and adjustable cone; and replacement of the cone. Once the cone is in the proper place to hold the spindle just right, replace the lock ring. To keep the cone still while tightening down the lock ring, use the cone wrench and the lock-ring wrench at the same time.

TOOLS

Your tool kit should include at least a few basic tools, and it can be as elaborate as you wish. Every bike will require a slightly different tool kit because of its own peculiar components. A cyclist who owns a bike identical to yours may have a different kit because of the range of tasks he or she may feel competent to undertake. Your best bet is to buy high-quality tools as you need them, and stay away from pre-packaged tool kits unless they contain few tools you don't need.

You will need Allen keys to fit all the Allen bolts and nuts on your bike (and this could range from none to four or five), a 6″ adjustable wrench, a pair or two of pliers, both flat-blade and

Spare tubes and tires, patches, tire irons, Allen keys, air-pressure gauges, wrenches, screw drivers, and other necessities can be carried in a seat bag. Add a pump (seen here) and you will be prepared to keep your bike rolling even if you have a breakdown on the road. (Courtesy Cannondale Corporation)

Phillips screwdrivers, a good cable cutter, a third hand, and several open-end wrenches or spanners to fit various nuts and bolts. You should also have a chain tool, so that you can remove and replace your chain, and a spoke wrench, just in case. If you plan to do any adjustments of your headset or bottom bracket, you will need tools especially made for those areas specific to the brands on your bike, so shop carefully for those. If you want to overhaul your hubs, you'll need just the right spanners to fit the cones, so again, be selective. You may also want to invest in a stand to hold your bicycle while you work on it. You will need various rags and cloths, some good bearing grease, oil for lubricating, and kerosene for cleaning. Phil Wood, Campagnolo, and Bullshot make good grease, and Tri-Flow (or Tri-Flon) oil is just about unbeatable, but expensive.

ROUTINE MAINTENANCE

Mile for mile, the bicycle requires more maintenance than the automobile, because it is relatively fragile and much more exposed to the elements. The amount of time needed for daily

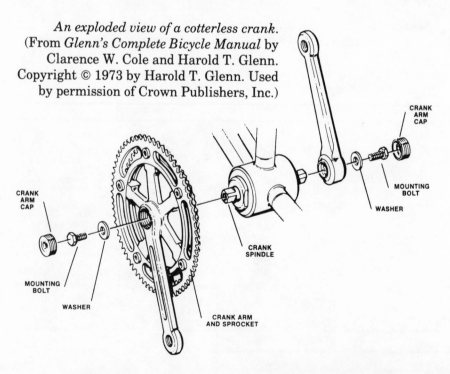

An exploded view of a cotterless crank.
(From *Glenn's Complete Bicycle Manual* by Clarence W. Cole and Harold T. Glenn. Copyright © 1973 by Harold T. Glenn. Used by permission of Crown Publishers, Inc.)

CRANK ARM CAP

CRANK ARM CAP

MOUNTING BOLT

WASHER

MOUNTING BOLT

CRANK SPINDLE

WASHER

CRANK ARM AND SPROCKET

routine maintenance is minimal but important nonetheless. At regular intervals, much more frequently than for a car, the bike will need close attention. Luckily, even major repairs or maintenance on a bicycle require very little time or money compared to motor vehicles, and they generally are more fun. Usually you can diagnose the problem correctly and figure out its solution immediately, and if you perform the work yourself you have a much higher chance of doing it right the first time. A bike may require a bit more tinkering than a car, but working on one is much more rewarding.

The cardinal rules to follow to keep your bicycle in good repair are to inspect it every time you ride it, be on the lookout for symptoms of wear or breakdown, attend to any problem as soon as you notice it, and follow a regular schedule of overhauls.

Whenever you roll your bike out for a spin, you should look it over to be sure nothing has changed since you last put it away. Is the air pressure right? Are the handlebars and saddle aligned? Are both wheels centered and secured to the dropouts? Do you have your pump, spare tubes or tires or patches, and a filled water bottle? This kind of inspection takes only a minute to complete, but it can make the difference between a pleasant ride and a miserable one.

When you return from a jaunt, you should clean your bike up before putting it away, and fix any problems you may have noticed while out on the road. Cleaning need not be too involved; a cursory wipe-down of all the tubes and parts will suffice most of the time, with perhaps a shot of oil where needed. If you wipe the bike off with a soft cloth every time, you will be sure of removing any harmful dust, water, or chemicals that may be on the frame, keeping the parts free of grit and sludge, which wear them down and reduce their efficiency. If the chain is dry, spray a little oil on it, checking for sticking links as you do so. Squirt a bit of oil onto the moving parts of both derailleurs and brakes, but wipe off any excess so as not to attract dirt. The chain should have a slight sheen of oil, but other parts should be basically free of oil. Spin the wheels, checking for wheel trueness, noise in the hubs, and wear on the tires. If you have tubular tires, you should let out some air, perhaps down to 50 pounds, to prolong their life.

If there is nothing wrong with your bike, you can put it away knowing your next ride will start out trouble-free. If you do spot a problem, then you should correct it before riding again.

Whenever you ride your bicycle, pay attention to any changes in its performance. If you hear a sound you never noticed before, or feel some bumping, or see something out of alignment, something is wrong, however minor the problem might be. Don't ignore that chain that occasionally skips on a cog; it's a symptom that your chain and/or freewheel are worn. Listen critically when that brake shoe starts rubbing; it's telling you that your wheel is misaligned or out of true, or your brake is off center. Is there a squeak developing somewhere whenever you stand on a hill? Maybe your brake levers or handlebars need to be tightened. Do you feel a little looseness in one crank arm when you pedal? Possibly your cranks need to be tightened or a pedal requires an overhaul. You should actively listen and look for such signs of problems when you ride your bike so that you will be able to fix them before they become overwhelming.

Every month or so, you should go over your bike part by part, tightening up nuts and bolts and checking spindles and spokes. Be sure the nuts and bolts that hold on water-bottle cages, racks, derailleurs, brakes, saddles, and handlebars are properly tightened. Check to see whether any cables are so stretched, frayed, or worn that they should be replaced. Check all the spokes for tautness; they tend to loosen as they age, and an old wheel may be true but have spokes that are too loose. Finally, check all the spindle and axle parts to be certain they are spinning freely but aren't too loose. If any of these things needs adjustment, don't put it off; do it right then.

Depending on your mileage and the quality of your equipment, you will need to perform more major overhauls every 4, 6, 9, or 12 months. These include all spindle parts, and freewheel and chain, which should always be changed together. I recommend that you keep a running list of such repairs, with the date and nature of the overhaul, so that you can schedule the various repairs more easily. One friend of mine writes down everything from major overhauls to flat tires on his repair calendar because he likes to know how many miles he gets on various brands of tires and how long it's been since he worked on his derailleurs. You may not be that compulsive, but I do recommend that you record the more important overhauls.

Any repair that you cannot do yourself can be done at a good shop for a price. If you want to pay someone else to do all your bike maintenance, that's possible too, and I won't say you shouldn't do it. But I hope you will do most of your own repairs and maintenance on your bike, because it's fun, and it only increases your self-reliance. Besides, when you are your own mechanic, you always know the exact condition of your bicycle.

6

Recreational Cycling

Although I have spent most of my youth and all my adult life as a bicycle racer, having competed in many different kinds of races all over the world, I don't expect all my readers to try (or even want) to be racers themselves. But I do expect you all to be recreational cyclists—it's almost impossible to ride a bike and not get recreation out of it.

I conceive of cycling in four different but overlapping categories: recreational cycling, commuting, touring, and racing. Although they share common features, each has specific ends and aims, and each is approached differently. The most general type is recreational cycling, which encompasses all facets of cycling and includes all cyclists. Most specialized is bike racing, to which few aspire and in which fewer still can hope to excel. I devote one chapter to each of these types of bicycling, and in that order.

The dictionary defines recreation as the diverting activities we do to have fun, to play. Mark Twain called it whatever we do that we don't *have* to do, which to my mind describes bicycling in a nutshell. It may be work at times, it may even be arduous or painful, but it is always play. Your bicycle, whether it's a brand-new Italian racer or a rusted cruiser, is so efficient and so liberating a machine that it can take you nearly anywhere at a much faster clip than walking and yet with far less energy. The thrill of zooming around town with a pal is just as real as the

Even in the heart of a big city, the recreational cyclist can enjoy the benefits and pleasures of riding with friends. (Courtesy Schwinn Bicycle Company)

kick of a head-to-head race, and it's there every time I put foot to pedal.

I have yet to meet a dedicated bike racer whose work and play were not completely merged in cycling. But even if you don't race, even if you hardly ever ride your bike, even if you don't *own* a bicycle (yet), I'm willing to bet you know in your heart what I mean. Bicycling is a simple skill you probably acquired before the age of reason, and even if you put your last bike away "for good" years ago, you remember the fun you had on it—the only vehicle you had control of and mastery over until you learned to drive. Perhaps it is this association of the bicycle with childhood play that has prevented most adults in the United States from cycling, and this is truly a shame. The type of play adults usually turn to tends to be more sedentary and competitive. Where is it written that we must abandon everything from childhood, particularly if it was fun? Why should it be better to have "fun" betting on horses (i.e., losing money) than to get out in the open air and spin the pedals?

Luckily, there is an unmistakable trend in this country toward fitness and health, and many more people than ever before are getting involved in such sports as cycling, running, swimming, racquet sports, and aerobics. I see more riders out on the road every day, and I think the upswing is going to continue for a long time. Cycling as a sport, once much more popular than baseball, is now enjoying a revival nationwide. Now that America can boast some of the world's best cyclists, it's likely we'll all see and hear more about cycling in the future. The move toward fitness has prompted many people to try biking vacations who otherwise might have traveled by car in the past. As touring cyclists become more commonplace sights, they can only encourage public acceptance of the bicycle as a legitimate means of transportation for adults.

The same can be said about the growing number of people who do their commuting by bicycle. More people will consider riding a bike to work as bicycle commuting becomes more common (and as fuel costs and traffic jams increase). Further, as people come to consider the bicycle as a useful, functional vehicle, they will tend more and more to think about cycling instead of driving when they shop, visit friends, go exploring, and run errands.

EXERCISE AND STRESS REDUCTION

Bicycling is one of the few truly pleasurable activities with no bad side effects. Nothing harmful comes from cycling—and yet there is much good in it for the cyclist. (I am assuming here that the cyclist stays on the bike. A nasty spill would be harmful, but that's true for every other activity too.) Riding is good exercise, even at a slow pace, giving the legs (at least) a good workout. The harder you ride, the better the exercise, since the heart gets stronger only if it beats for extended periods at moderately high levels. But the leg muscles benefit at any speed; and I believe it's better to begin riding at a slow pace and work up than to forego cycling at all. If you ride purely for the exercise, or if you are thinking about taking up cycling for that purpose, I applaud you for your choice. Nothing compares to cycling for the variety of speeds you can achieve, the diversity of places you can go, or the number of things you can accomplish as you get your workout. Only top-level distance runners at full effort can approach the speed and distance easily within reach of a moderately fit, middle-aged cyclist; and the runner has no breath to spare for conversation, no extra attention to give to the scenery as the cyclist has. Other forms of exercise, such as swimming or tennis, can burn a lot of calories, but they offer no changing scenery, no leisurely chats, no mobility. The bicyclist out to exercise is truly a participant-observer in the environment. When you ride you are going places, and you can explore the world with a great deal of freedom on every outing.

Exercising by bicycling is particularly easy because you can rest even as you roll. If you get tired, you can slow down your pedaling and coast on the down grades until you feel peppier. If you run out of steam you can stop and eat and stretch, and soon you'll be renewed and ready to set out again. Unlike many other aerobic activities, you can eat and drink before and during your workout—and you should. I regularly eat breakfast before my morning ride, and I almost never go on a long ride without taking some food with me. On a bike, food won't slow you down or give you a cramp; it will just give you fuel.

Riding is also a good way to release tension. I believe bicycle riding is a perfect exercise for reducing stress for two different reasons. Not only are the various non-cycling activities associated with a bike ride themselves inherently pleasant and relaxing, but this simple, repetitive exercise tends to soothe jangled nerves, as do many other aerobic activities. There is something about exercise that leaves the person refreshed and clear-headed, calm and relaxed. Even a very strenuous aerobic workout will reward you with that warm glow of peacefulness soon after you stop. People talk a lot about runner's high and positive addictions, but no one seems to know why getting a workout should make you feel so good. I never am so free of stress or so clear-headed as after a hard ride. This so-called positive addiction is all right with me; certainly that's better than the opposite.

To repeat, both exercise and stress reduction are automatic benefits of riding a bicycle, though either could also be your main reason to cycle. Any time you roll out Old Sturdy you can expect to get something good in return, and I think that's fine.

Even if your cycling objectives are solely to get exercise and peace of mind, you have many choices to make. Route, distance (or time), and number of companions are the main things you'll have to decide each time you set out. I recommend varying all these over the course of time. Some of my friends ride their bikes over only two or three known routes. They time themselves and record their progress on the different courses. Although I do time certain routes—such as a particular 10-mile section of roadway near my house—I don't limit my routes and rarely do I take exactly the same ride two days in a row. Some days I'll ride somewhere I've never been, either alone or with companions. The novelty of the route is always interesting, and sometimes unknown territory presents challenges or surprises I'm glad I didn't miss. I even purposely get lost sometimes, just for the fun of exploring.

So be on the lookout for new routes. Knowing a variety of routes comes in handy particularly when riding with others: there is always some indecision whenever two or more people plan to take a ride together. But as soon as someone says, "I know a really good ride," especially if it's a new route, the prob-

Bicyling with friends is a great way to get out and do some sightseeing.
(Courtesy Cannondale Corporation)

lem is solved, and most often the ride turns out to be a great success.

Also vary the number of people with whom you ride. Ride alone sometimes. It's good to face the wind and the road all by yourself, to concentrate on your riding without having to worry about a companion's pace. When you ride solo, it doesn't matter if you're sluggish or particularly energetic. You can set your own goals for the ride and never worry if they conflict with someone else's. And cycling alone reinforces one's self-sufficiency.

But ride with friends sometimes, too. With another companion, you can train hard together if you're of equal ability, or make your ride more social. If you set out on a ride with several people, you can socialize and still not hamper your training, for the others can help spot your strengths and weaknesses. You can share information on good places to buy tires or which brands of shorts are on sale. You can make new friends or maintain longstanding friendships. Like singing, riding a bike can be fun when done alone or with others. And it's most likely to stay fun when it's done both ways.

SHOPPING TRIPS AND ERRANDS

I'm willing to bet you can do a lot of your shopping by bike, if you stay alert to the opportunities to do so. How often do you zip over to the grocery for one or two small items for a recipe? Do you drive there, or do you pedal over and back? When you go get your hair cut next Saturday, don't you think you could get there just as easily on your bike? When you run out of stamps, can't you make the trip to the post office an adventure rather than a chore by rolling over there on your bicycle? And how about your next trip to the bank? Won't it be more fun if the pedals you step on are attached to your bike rather than your car?

Most shopping involves only short excursions from home with only a few small items to transport. Does it really make sense to take a 3000-pound automobile even a couple of miles just to carry one person and a few parcels? Certainly most of the people in the Third World would consider such use of a car as an unnecessary, extravagant waste, and they're right. In places where the bicycle commonly is used for transportation and for bearing much greater loads than milk and eggs, nobody would consider it odd to ride a bike to the grocery store.

For most such errands, nothing more is needed than a light backpack and perhaps a bike lock. Unless you are doing some serious shopping—although I do know people who do all their grocery shopping by bicycle—you won't need a full set of panniers or even so much as a rack. You probably will need a lock, however, if your bike is going to be out of your sight.

Begin thinking of your bicycle as a vehicle and you'll use it as such. Every mile you pedal doing errands is another mile of exercise. And every time you ride your bike to run an errand, it's like money in the bank.

Like this couple, you may find that cycling to and fro adds to your other recreational activities in a unique way. (Courtesy Schwinn Bicycle Company)

FAMILY EXCURSIONS

People talk about spending quality time with their children; but they seem to miss many opportunities for recreational excursions with their friends and family. I hope you will think about traveling by bicycle the next time you take your kids to the zoo or the museum, or take in an afternoon concert or movie with your spouse or sweetheart. Consider riding along with your daughter when she goes to soccer practice. Think about making your next family picnic a bicycling trip. Cycling to and from such outings makes the entire excursion fun, and it can do wonders for family relationships, for parents who ride with their children are giving them time of the highest quality.

Mary and Abby are a mother and daughter who live in a small California town. They are a familiar sight as they bicycle around, Mary in the saddle and Abby strapped in her child seat. They ride to the library to get a new storybook. They pedal over to the shoe store to get Abby some sandals. They ride to Abby's pre-school on days when Mary substitutes at the local junior high school. It's a pleasure to ride with them, listen to them chat and joke, and observe the interactions between a parent and child who so obviously love each other. Mary's bike is nothing special, but what happens when she rides with Abby is.

Many parents could have a closer, deeper, more entertaining relationship with their children if they would take them out on excursions through the week. Pre-schoolers whose days are spent largely in front of the television set and with neighbors' children could have a much more enriched upbringing if they went more places with Mom or Dad. These excursions can be absolutely free of charge and more fun if they are biking expeditions.

If you have children, maybe you can work some bike excursions with them into the next week or two. Consider missing the game on TV next Saturday in favor of a family outing to a park or the zoo. Take a little ride with your son tomorrow afternoon to play catch at his school or to listen to the marching band practice, or accompany your daughter to her scout meeting. You may not discuss anything of importance; you could end up wasting time going the long way around; but you might have a great time together.

These little excursions can do as much for sweethearts and spouses as the children. Don't you think you and your honey deserve a ride together next weekend? You could spin over to visit another couple across town. If you have a favorite restaurant for Sunday brunch, you can ride there together, have brunch, and have a leisurely ride back home. Who cares if you spend half the day?

TRAINING

Whether you ride purely for fitness, for commuting, to go on tour, or to race, you are always in training to reach, maintain, or exceed some level of performance. One good reason to ride every day is that you will *stay* in shape even if you don't race or ride to work or take a long tour.

Training for commuting and touring requires daily workouts that progress from quite easy to more taxing sessions, with never too great an increase from one ride to the next. If you are working up to a 10-mile ride to work, ride short distances every day until you can do, say, five miles at what feels like 80 percent effort. At that point you should have the stamina and confidence necessary to crank 10 miles to work—and back—without strain.

Training for tours demands long miles and simulated conditions to prepare you for the rigors of the road under what may be adverse conditions. Even if your projected vacation plan is to travel relatively few miles per day, you should have solid training behind you before departing. Now and again you should ride hilly terrain with your bike loaded as for your trip. You want to practice maneuvering, climbing, and descending while fully packed so that you will have no rude surprises during the trip itself.

No one could hope to finish in a respectable position, much less win any race, without adequate training. Training is recreational riding and should be just as fun, just as enjoyable as any other kind of cycling. Get out there and ride your bike!

7

Commuting By Bicycle

Unless you live in your office or are within walking distance of work, you do what most Americans do every working day: you take a car or a train or a bus to work and back. Commuting by bicycle, however, saves you time and money, and keeps you healthy and happy.

Bike commuters are a small but growing minority. The U.S. Department of Transportation predicts there will be 2½ million of us by 1985. One friend of mine took up cycling to work after suffering a mild heart attack. He makes his daily 11-mile commute by bicycle, and he rarely takes longer going his side-street route than the trip used to take him by car. Why? Because he avoids the daily freeway snarl. This friend has missed only six days of cycling to and from work in the past three years, and he is trimmer, fitter, and less harried now at age 38 than he's ever been in his life.

Another Houston friend, Joe Bentley, is also a bicycle commuter, as are his wife Sissy and daughter Hallie. Several years ago the Bentley family car suddenly died, as cars are wont to do, and Joe and Sissy naturally thought about how to replace it. The Bentleys own a Houston bike shop, so they had ready access to vehicles while they made up their minds on their next car. But it didn't take long before they both realized that they didn't *need* another car. They still haven't bought one, but they did invest in a custom triplet for the whole family, as well as one bike each for transportation. Even in Houston, a city that is above average in freeway jams, air pollution, and inadequate public transporta-

150

tion, it is possible for commuters to get to and fro by bicycle. It can hardly be worse where you live.

I can hear the protests even as I write: "I live too far from work!" "I'm no athlete!" "I need my car in the city!" "I have to work late too often!" "I'll smell like a goat all day!" "I can't work in my biking clothes!" "What will people think???" Phooey! I've heard those excuses and hundreds more, and I still say you can do at least some of your commuting by bicycle if you try. And you will reap many benefits if you do.

THE NUTS AND BOLTS OF COMMUTING BY BIKE

Bathing and Changing Clothes

It seems the biggest problem for some potential "bikies" is that of bathing once they get to work. How on earth can you cycle more than just a hop without working up a sweat? How can you work all day smelling like you want to be alone? And where do you change?

These questions aren't really as tough as they seem. There are very few occupations that will absolutely prevent you from cycling to work and getting dressed and groomed before beginning your work day. It just may take a little effort and imagination.

Some people are lucky enough to be employed by companies with an enlightened view toward physical fitness. These people will have no problem getting in a good workout before putting on the tie and vest, because their company has provided them with a gym and lockers, and maybe even a full-time fitness coordinator who will record blood pressure and mileage. If you are so fortunate, you have no reason not to ride your bike to work *tomorrow*.

More likely you will have to make do with something less than a fully equipped gymnasium, such as a nearby fitness club, your own office, or the company restroom. Do not despair: you have everything you require right there. You will *not* stink to high heaven if you shower before leaving home and take a "spit bath" after arriving at work. Some people keep nothing more elaborate than a sponge and a towel at work for a cursory ablution before putting on their work clothes. Any perspiration you have will be clean sweat borne of plain old exertion—nothing that won't come off with clear water. It is perspiration sweated during periods of anxiety that is particularly malodorous. So if it takes you more than 10 minutes to sponge and towel off and change clothes, you are probably dawdling or spending too long gazing into the mirror—unless, of course, some puddles got in your way.

Two minor points may be bothering you: "What will my co-workers think?" and "What about putting on makeup?"

People will think whatever they want to think, no matter what you do. And who cares? Over the last 20 years of cycling, I have become accustomed to gawking, staring, and rude questions about my rather weird-looking cycling attire, my shaven legs, and what not. If I let the general public shame me into giving up cycling, what would other cyclists think? The fact is that somebody might think something awful about you no matter what you do, so you may as well do what you think is right and let the world gossip.

Suppose one of your fellow workers kids you about riding your bicycle to work. You might just as easily kid him or her about wasting fossil fuels in a most extravagant way. You might point out that you are taking a positive step toward improving your health, fitness, and appearance, and saving money in the bargain. Or you might smile and ask him or her to join you the next day, because you had such a great time getting to work.

If you fear that your boss will think you have lost some marbles or that your secretary will shriek when you arrive with your legs exposed, you can just tell them ahead of time what you are planning to do. You can forewarn your co-workers as well, perhaps sending around a notice that you are looking for commuting companions. Then if there is to be a truly embarrassing or awkward situation just because you plan to do one of the most sensible things on earth, you will get an inkling of the problem before you ever wheel your trusty machine up to the door. Maybe there will be some talk behind your back, but what of it? The worst outcome is that some people will eventually decide that you are "a character," that you are "a bike nut," that you have personal idiosyncrasies. Oh, my. For what it's worth, some career counselors claim that having a harmless quirk is better than being a bland conformist, in terms of career advancement. What quirk could be more harmless than cycling?

Many women will insist that they cannot ride a bike to work because they must put on their makeup at home and the ride would ruin their face. I have to say that of the women I have seen finish a foot race, bike race, or triathlon, most are wearing no powder, lipstick, rouge, or false eyelashes and they are just as beautiful as they can be.

If you are a woman and you think you need a lot of cosmetic help to look naturally beautiful, I have a little challenge for you. Ride your bike to work—at least part of the way—every day for a month. Let the sun shine on your face without any makeup to block it, and let the wind blow your hair and cheeks every morning and evening. I bet you will look and feel better next month than you do right now, and you even may put your makeup kit away for good.

Carrying the Briefcase or Purse

Whether you use your briefcase to carry your lunch, the sports section, or your briefs, you will probably want to continue transporting those items as a bicycle commuter. One solution is to leave the briefcase in the office and just carry your essentials in panniers or in a knapsack. But many people will still want to take their briefcases or purses with them. Your question then is, "How do I do that?"

Many briefcases and purses are too large to fit in panniers, but you may find a back pack big enough to accommodate your briefcase or purse and it will work well enough, although I personally prefer not to carry anything on my back when I ride. It can cause lower back pain, problems with stability due to a higher center of gravity, and greater chance of catching the wind.

If you are exceptionally creative or blessed with excess leisure time, you might try crafting your own briefcase sling to serve the same purpose as a back pack. You also can try tying your briefcase or purse down on the top of your bike rack—either front or back rack—with straps or bungie cords. This can be risky, though. I've seen more than one parcel fall off a bike. If it survives the spill, it may not survive being run over by a motor vehicle.

Another idea is to fit your briefcase with small, permanent attachments that couple with attachments on your rack. I know one college professor named Jack who rides to school and back daily with his briefcase apparently resting on top of his inexpensive rear rack. His briefcase has a reflector on the end and three small belt buckles riveted to the underside that attach to three small belts on his rack. Jack doesn't care if you use his idea for your own briefcase. In fact, here's a great money-making idea for you, free from me: start your own company manufacturing and selling briefcases that attach to bike racks, or conversion kits for briefcases, or just plans. You can call your company BikeCase Corporation or CaseRack—something catchy like that—and after you start making more money per month than you can possibly spend, quit your present job. Everybody there gossips about you behind your back anyway.

Transporting Clothes

Unless you have only a very short, flat stretch to cover to get to work, you will not want to wear your work clothes on your bicycle. Short trips in street clothes are easily accomplished with a pants clip on the right leg, but generally your comfort, safety, and efficiency will require that you wear cycling clothes for the trip and change at work.

The easiest way is to carry them in a back pack or in panniers. For many people this is quite satisfactory, especially if the clothes are not particularly bulky. I know a bus driver in Southern California who leaves his shoes, belt, and ticket puncher with the dispatcher each day and carries his shirt and slacks on his bike. He gets a short workout both before and after a long day behind the wheel, and the few items he carries are easy to handle.

For others, an automobile trip to the office to drop off several changes of clothes allows up to a full week of cycling without having to carry any baggage. You also could send them with a co-worker, or leave your car parked at work with clothes in the

It looks like someone has already come up with one solution to the attache problem.
(Courtesy Kirtland Tour Pak)

trunk. Sally is a graduate student with an office on campus. Her hours are long and varied and this prevents her from riding her bike to school every day. But she keeps a change of clothes in a file cabinet drawer, bikes as often as she can, and never has to take clothes with her on her bicycle. If you do take your clothing with you on your bike, whether in panniers or in a pack, I have a tip about packing. Most items will travel better if they are rolled rather than folded. They pack easily that way and they are less likely to wrinkle.

Routes

As a bicycle commuter you may have to take a different route to work, since your bike will not be allowed on freeways, railway tracks, and some bridges. No doubt your new route will be more scenic and pleasant than the old one—not to mention safer and less polluted. But it also could be longer. Plan carefully for your first commute to avoid getting lost, riding on roads under construction, arriving late, hitting nothing but stop lights and signs, or traveling through the ugliest parts of town. If you have a problem, call the local bicycle club or the city road or recreation department for help in planning your route.

Some things to consider when thinking about which streets to take are traffic density, width of the streets, number of controlled intersections, aesthetic appeal of the area, and variations in the terrain. For starters, you will probably want to take the flattest and shortest course possible with the least amount of traffic. If you live very near work, consider a longer route. And as your skill and fitness level increase, you may wish to take longer and more varied routes just for the fun of it.

You should drive possible routes beforehand, taking note of distances to various landmarks and noticing what features the routes present for you as a cyclist. Is there a big hill that you would rather not have to face each day? Are there just too many stop signs on Elm Street? Is the surface smoother on Third Avenue than on Fourth? Is it prettier to go a little closer to the lake? Is there any way to avoid all those railroad tracks? Is there another street parallel to this one that has a bike lane painted on it? As you drive remember that the minor ups and downs you hardly notice in a car translate into more challenging climbs and more exhilarating descents when cycling.

Once you have decided on a good route to take to work, ride it. Take one of your days off and set out with your bike set up and loaded just as it will be for the real thing. It's a good idea to take it easy without dawdling, and time your commute. Get a conservative estimate, one that will serve you on days when you want to loaf. If your days off are Saturday and Sunday, then you will have to allow a little time for increased weekday traffic. The test ride(s) will indicate not only how long your commute will take, but also how much energy it will require. You may be surprised at how many miles you can cover at a leisurely pace without tiring, unless you force the pace or are out of shape.

COMMUTING PLANS: VARIATIONS ON A THEME

The Full-On Bikie Plan

The rarest and purest breed of bicycle commuter is the full-on bikie, the person who does all his or her commuting by bicycle. No matter what the weather, working hours, or job requirements, this type of commuter gets there and back by bike. Usually the full-on bikie cycles everywhere else too, and may not even own a car.

The motto of the biking commuter who relies solely on the bicycle is, "Be Prepared." If you're not ready for that sudden shower or heat spell, you'd better be willing to grit your teeth and bear it. Biking means moving through the elements, and this can be fun in any circumstances. But if you prefer to stay dry, warm, and safe as a daily bicycle commuter, you have to keep an eye on the weather forecasts and the ever-changing sunrise and sunset times.

If you become a full-on bikie, you will get the maximum benefit from cycling to and from work, and every day you will have the pleasure of knowing that your health, mental well-being, and bank balance are better off for it.

The Alternate-Days Plan

Let's suppose you have to take your daughter to her piano lesson on Tuesday afternoon, and you coach a Little League team on Thursdays. Or maybe you teach at a school where there is a late faculty meeting every Wednesday and a game to attend every Friday. Or perhaps you don't feel you can spare all the time it takes to commute by bike every day, due to time constraints, fitness level, or other physical activities. You can still ride your bike every other day.

Most months have 21 working days to them, so the alternate-days commuter will get back and forth by bicycle 10 or 11 days per month. It's a good idea to keep track of which days you actually ride to work and back as a way to document your mileage, and to serve as a reminder to take your bike whenever possible. You might find it helpful to set a goal of the number of days you will commute by bike each week or month, then check your weekly and monthly totals on your calendar.

For two years running I commuted this way while working in Texas. I couldn't ride my bicycle to work every day, but I managed to go that way about half the time, using the weather and time constraints to guide my day-to-day commuting plans. Note that the alternate-days plan makes transportation of clothing and other goods quite simple. You can take two days' worth of apparel every time you drive to work and never have to carry anything with you when you cycle.

The Alternate-Trips Plan

If you live a relatively long way from work, an alternate-trips commute might work out best for you: on any given day, you either will drive to work with your bike on your car and then ride your bike home; or, you will cycle to work, where your car is parked, and drive home that evening. All you need is a bike rack on your car (unless your bike will fit inside your car) and a good memory.

Suppose you start alternate-tripping next Monday. You drive your car to work on Monday morning, but you have your bike on a rack, and after work you ride your bike home. The next morning, Tuesday, you have to ride your bike to work because your car is not at home, but Tuesday evening you return home by car. Wednesday is a repeat of Monday, and Thursday is just like Tuesday.

One thing to consider is what to do with your bicycle on days that you cycle to work but drive home. Since you will be driving to work in your car the next morning, it would be preferable to leave your bicycle at work so that you don't have to fool with carrying it home and back to work again the next day. On the other hand, if you think you will want your bicycle in the meantime, you don't want it to be sitting in your office.

Another thing to consider is how to work it on Friday. If you follow the above routine, you will ride your bike to work on Thursday and drive home Thursday night. Friday morning you have both your bicycle and your car at home, so you have four choices: Just drive both ways; ride your bicycle both to work and home; cycle to work and take public transportation home; or drive to work and ride your bicycle home. If you don't cycle home, then you can always retrieve your bicycle over the weekend or the following Monday. Or if you decide not to ride your bicycle on Friday, you can promise yourself a long ride over the weekend.

This style of commuting is ideal for the person who drives a long distance to work every day—too long to make it practical to cycle both ways. It works best with the support of a car pool. Ideally, if you can get four cyclists to collaborate on this, you can work out a rotating driving-cycling plan that will take only one car per day rather than four. Consider, however, Lon Haldeman, the winner of the first coast-to-coast Great American Bike Race. He rides his bike over 40 miles to work each morning and back home each night. Then he may take an evening ride to stay in shape!

The Bike-and-Train Plan

This might also be called the bike-and-bus or bike-and-subway plan. Many people drive to the station each morning and take the train, bus, or subway to work. As often as not, the spouse drives him or her to and from the station. This makes four unnecessary automobile trips every day. If you normally travel to work this way, and if you live fairly close to the depot,

Public bike lockers enable cycling commuters to leave their bikes protected from the weather and from thieves. (Courtesy Christian Paul)

consider cycling to the station in your normal working attire, with your briefcase or lunch pail on a rack and appropriate protection such as trouser clips for your garb.

Bicycle security may be somewhat of a problem for the bike-and-train commuter, more so than for other cyclists, since the bike will be left unattended all day. Some depots are better than others, of course, and you'll have to decide for yourself whether you want to leave your best bicycle locked up at the station, at the mercy of the weather and a temptation to the bike snatcher. A clunker bike secured with a stout cable and lock is one solution; meanwhile, you can lobby the depot management for better security, bike lockers, or some sort of check-in room for bicycles. Some places have excellent facilities, such as the San Francisco-area BART stations, while others are still in the Dark Ages with regard to cyclists.

The better the accommodations for commuting cyclists, the more people will be encouraged to ride their bikes to the depot, thereby cutting down on traffic jams and parking problems at the station.

The Drive-and-Bike Plan

This is a flexible way to commute when the trip is too long to cycle every day. Drive part of the way to work with your bike on a rack, park in a safe spot, and cycle the rest of the way to work. At the end of the day, you'll have another chance to ride your bike, taking as direct or as meandering a route as you wish.

The beauty of this plan is that you can adjust your bike commute every day depending upon time pressures, your energy level, the changing daylight hours, the weather, etc. If you like to train on a hard-easy schedule, you can easily work that into this plan. Or if you are just trying to get into better shape before going the whole distance to work, you can gradually increase your cycling distance as your fitness level improves. One good training method is to park farther and farther away from your place of employment while trying to keep the amount of time it takes to ride the distance constant.

Combining Commuting Plans

Your plan should be your own creation. Given the above possibilities, there's no excuse for not working your bicycle into your commute in some way. For example, the person who rides to work and back nearly every day may have to use the drive-and-bike method some days when time is short. The bike-and-train commuter occasionally may wake up early enough to bicycle the whole way to work, perhaps getting picked up at the station at the end of the day. The possibilities are endless, but the main idea is to use your bicycle as a practical form of transportation for the daily commute.

THE PROS AND CONS

I am convinced that the biking commuter has much to gain, but there are some very real costs as well, and you should be aware of them. By costs I don't mean money; the bicycle is the cheapest form of transportation next to walking. But you will have to invest some time and physical energy into commuting by bicycle. The benefits, however, are great enough to make up for these costs many times over. I'll give you the bad news first.

Time Investment

Without question, the bicycle is slower than the train, the auto, or the bus, when they are all going at top speed. Although some commuters actually get to work faster by bike than by bus or even by car, most people will have to allow more time for their commute when they switch to the bicycle depending upon speed and distance.

Your daily commute already takes you some time. Any extra time that cycling takes is time spent exercising, which you (hopefully) would spend that way anyhow. The time you normally waste just getting back and forth to work now can be spent fruitfully, strengthening your heart and legs.

Let's suppose you normally drive to work, spending 15 minutes to travel 8 miles. (This may sound slow, but in fact even if most of the trip is on the freeway at 55 miles per hour, that's about how long it will take you door to door.) Now imagine yourself cycling to work, taking a different route of course, and spending 35 minutes to get there. That works out to under 14 miles per hour, a leisurely pace. The extra 20 minutes you have spent getting to work certainly is a cost in time, but the 15 minutes you might have sat behind the wheel would have been totally wasted. Instead, your commute is a combination of exercise and transportation, in which a little time is saved and a little time is spent.

There are ways to shave time off your bike commute. Try to shorten the route, decrease the obstacles in your route, flatten out the trip, or speed up.

Finding a shorter route to save time can be a pleasant exploration. But with bicycling, the shortest distance is not always the fastest course because there are stop signs, traffic signals, other vehicles, and road conditions that can slow you down considerably. A 30-second wait at a traffic light may not sound like much, but slowing to a stop and then re-accelerating take up still more time; five or six stop lights can add up to a significantly longer ride. Rougher roads also will slow you down, perhaps more than it seems at first and, of course, a smoother surface makes for a more comfortable and enjoyable ride. Another factor that can slow you down is traffic. Not only is a heavily traveled route more dangerous, but waiting for cross traffic at intersections greatly increases time on the road.

Sometimes just a slight variation in routes will make a big difference in terms of elevation changes, so it is worth scouting around for a flat, or flatter, route. Which brings up the last way to speed up your commute: going faster. As you stick to the same route, your skills, strength, and stamina will increase as you commute. What starts out as a 40-minute trip can soon become a 25-minute jaunt without appreciably altering the effort you put into the journey. You can work toward increasing your commuting speed, but even if you don't you will get faster over time.

Maintenance

The more use a machine gets, the more maintenance it requires. This is true for all machines, and so it is with your bicycle. Once you use it regularly you will have to devote some quality time to it or pay someone else to do it.

As a regular bicycle commuter, you should inspect your machine daily, if only to be sure all the parts are still there. It doesn't take a lot of time to be sure that the brakes are not malfunctioning, and that the tires are properly inflated and not too worn. The one sure thing about riding your bike daily is that you will be aware of most problems before they become overwhelming. You will notice if a brake shoe starts rubbing, indicating that a wheel is out of true or that the brake itself is out of alignment. You will hear when your crank begins to squeak or your front derailleur begins to rub the chain. And it usually doesn't take long before a punctured tire makes itself known. Get into the habit of taking care of these little problems right away, before they get out of hand. I recommend that you follow the guidelines in the maintenance chapter religiously. Every day, you want to be able to put your bike away knowing it is set to go for the next time.

Money

The more commuting you do by bicycle, the more money you will save. Even if you buy the most expensive tires and inflate them with helium, you will get more miles per dollar out of any bicycle than out of any car, train, bus, or jet plane. The savings you realize will be not only in gasoline, but also in repair bills, parking, and speeding tickets (unless you get *really* fast on your bike). These add up. The current estimated cost of operating an automobile, according to some car rental agencies, is fifty cents per mile. Let's use that as a benchmark. Now let's suppose you get a two-week vacation each year and work five days per week. If you live 7 miles from work, you have a 14-mile round trip to make 250 times a year, for a total of 3,500 miles, costing $1,750. How much do you pay for parking? How much do you spend on

parking tickets and moving violations on your commute? Add
those costs. For that kind of money, you can treat yourself to a
new bicycle every year, pay for *all* its maintenance, and still
have enough left over to buy any required accessories.

Every mile you ride is money in your pocket. Let's say you use
the drive-and-bike method to get to work tomorrow, and you ride
only the last two miles to work, parking your car somewhere
that saves you $.50 over where you usually park. Those two
miles both ways make four, equaling a $2.00 savings. That little
bit of exercise will save you $2.50—enough to pay for lunch.
Just think what kind of a lunch you could afford if you rode
farther!

Additional savings add up with reduced insurance rates. If
you can truthfully claim that your car is used only for pleasure
and recreation, and not for commuting, you can find much
cheaper insurance rates for your automobile. And your car will
still have all those miles "left in it" and so will last you longer.
That new bike you *could* buy every year (but probably won't)
could be sold for some fraction of its original value as well.

Pollution

The bicycle is a non-polluting vehicle, while the auto, the
train, the bus, the subway are all highly polluting machines.
They consume limited energy resources and they befoul the air.
The average automobile drips more oil in a week than a bicycle
uses in a year. And nobody ever choked on fumes while following a bicycle.

It has been estimated that a million bicycle commuters would
save 3.2 million barrels of oil per year—oil that would otherwise
go up in smoke, carbon monoxide, and sulphur dioxide. How
many gallons of gasoline will go unburned this year because of
your efforts?

I would like to see more places like the Lawrence Livermore
Laboratory, in Livermore, California. Once I happened to have a
long plane layover in San Francisco, so I uncrated my bicycle
and went for a ride. As I proceeded eastward, I kept passing
cyclists—commuters—some in cycling clothes and others in

business suits. I was intrigued and asked why there were so many commuters on the road. It turned out they were all going to the Livermore Lab, an energy research facility that employs 6,500 people. With the encouragement of the Lab about ten percent of them—650 people!—commute by bike daily.

The Livermore facility maintains bicycle racks and showers for the commuters as well as many company-owned bikes for transportation within the sprawling complex of buildings. This is the direction that large corporations *should* be going, encouraging a sensible, healthy alternative to the automobile for the employees. How many gallons of gasoline do those 650 Livermore Lab workers save every year? How much clearer and cleaner could the skies be in your community?

Physical and Mental Well-Being

I have already written about the fitness benefits of cycling. Here I just want to repeat the basics: that cycling will help you lose weight effortlessly and will improve your physical appearance; that your heart rate and blood pressure are almost certain to decrease when you ride your bike a little bit every day; and that the tensions and problems of everyday living and working are much less likely to bother you when you cycle. These alone make it worth considering riding to and from work, using one or more of the plans mentioned in this chapter.

Above all, you will find that you are more aware of your surroundings when you cycle to work. You will notice the seasons more, be in touch with the sunrise and sunset patterns, and watch the weather working even as you ride through it. The earth is a beautiful place, and if you ride your bicycle enough, you gain a deeper appreciation for that beauty than you ever could sitting in a train or steering an auto between the stripes. You will learn to relish your commute rather than dread it, because every trip is an adventure and an experience worth having. And you may find, as others have, that the best part of your working day is that time spent getting to work and returning home.

I like what Neil Goldschmidt, President Carter's Secretary of

Transportation, had to say about commuting by bicycle: "Most adults still associate bicycling with something they did as kids, and gave up when they were old enough to drive. And even though some have taken it up again, it has been primarily for recreation—for fun. For some reason, people are uneasy with the idea of having fun getting to work!" I say, ride your bike to work, and have that fun.

8

Touring

Perhaps you have seen them pedaling through your town or city. Maybe you sometimes join their ranks. I see a steady procession of them when I train on California's scenic Pacific Coast Highway. They are the tourists. No, I don't mean overweight motorists with cameras dangling from their necks. I mean a special breed of bicyclist.

They can travel long distances across Europe or America or simply explore their home state. Occasionally they travel light; sometimes they overload their poor bicycles until the tires flatten and the frames groan. Some of them stop only at the fanciest restaurants and most posh hotels. Others practically live off the

Not all tourists travel light. Here Wrong-Way Wooten pedals his 300-pound bicycle (which carries a functioning TV and stereo and a plastic model of a kitchen sink) backward while juggling. Wrong-Way has toured many thousands of miles in this fashion, using the resultant publicity to raise money for charities. (Courtesy Al Gross)

land, either carrying most of their provisions or foraging for them, and camping wherever there is a legal campground—or lenient enforcement of vagrancy laws.

Many people call any long bike ride that isn't a race a *tour*. But for the purposes of this chapter I define a tour as a bike ride that takes longer than one day, requires equipment for comfort and survival, and requires the bicyclist to camp or seek other sleeping accommodations. Other types of long bike rides, such as one-day trips to the mountains or beach, and century (100-mile) rides, sometimes are called tours, too. But this chapter is devoted to touring on overnight or longer bike trips.

What constitutes a tour can vary greatly. On one extreme there are organized group expeditions replete with motorized sag wagons to support the exhausted and carry the equipment between nightly bivouacs. On the other, there are tours for self-sufficient cyclists who carry tents and sleeping bags, cooking equipment, bike tools—in short, everything needed to survive and travel.

Thousands of cyclists participate together in such highly organized rides as the Tour of the Scioto River Valley in Ohio. But tourists can also travel alone or with only a few close companions. No matter what the physical arrangements, the cycling tourists of today may be the last of the free spirits. Be they rich or poor, fleet or ponderously slow, wide-ranging or weekend voyagers, bicycle tourists follow in the tradition of Huck Finn. On your bicycle, you can meet people, see things, and soak in the local atmosphere. If you have never toured I recommend you give it a try.

Those who have gone touring by bicycle will often say that their bicycle trips were among their most memorable vacations. Whether or not the tours also were among their most enjoyable depends on how much the tourist knew about why, how, when, and where to tour.

WHEN AND WHERE TO TOUR

The human spirit is indomitable. You might be able to tour across Death Valley at high noon during the summer, north to Alaska on the AlCan Highway during a blizzard, up a 20,000-

Think what it would be like to leisurely pedal your bicycle through this lush mountain scenery. (Courtesy Rich Landers, Bikecentennial)

Get a horse. (Courtesy TOSRVPHOTO)

foot pass in the Andes into the teeth of a windstorm, or across Afghanistan during a civil war. You could tour virtually anywhere there is a road or, with the right mountain bike, even some places where there are no roads. You could tour any time of year. But would you want to tour under extremely adverse conditions, and if you did, would you survive?

Don't rule out touring during any season of the year or in interesting, even hazardous, places. Just plan your trip with foreknowledge of the obstacles you will encounter. The majority of tourists will want to plan their trips in peaceful, scenic locales with manageable terrain (few hills steeper than a 6 percent grade), at times of the year when the temperature will be somewhere in the range of 55–80°F. It's also good sense to avoid touring in any locale during its rainiest season.

There are several sources of information that you will want to tap when you are planning a tour. The U.S. Weather Bureau can give you reliable, long-range forecasts for anywhere in the United States and for many other countries as well. Gasoline companies and automobile clubs supply general road maps of most areas which include secondary roads where bicycle travel is legal. In some cases, where there is no other route available, it is legal—if not encouraged—to ride a bicycle on the shoulder of interstate highways. (Check in advance by calling the local road department or state police.)

Bikecentennial is a nonprofit, member-supported organization that furnishes valuable information to bicycle tourists. That association publishes 35 detailed, waterproof tour maps that form a nationwide network of good routes. Bikecentennial actively promotes use of the Trans-America Bike Trail, established in 1976 to commemorate America's 200th birthday. Appendix A includes their address and a list of official and volunteer contacts in 48 states and the District of Columbia from which you can obtain a wealth of touring and commuting information.

Some transportation departments also are listed in Appendix A. In many states they maintain bicycle support offices, which often publish special maps and information bulletins for cyclists. The California Department of Transportation (Caltrans), for in-

Cycle-tourists really can ride wherever there is a road. Here June Siple rides through a village in Colombia, South America. (Hemistour Photo courtesy Greg Siple)

stance, publishes wide-area bicycle route maps for each of that state's transportation districts. Additionally, for about $2.00 you can obtain a highly detailed, illustrated map book of the Pacific Coast Bicentennial route, which describes an ocean-view tour the length of California. The book fits in the map window of a handlebar pack and is keyed to distinctive signs en route and a network of State, Forest Service, and National Park Service campgrounds, where a bicycle tourist can stay for fifty cents per night without advance reservations.

The most inexpensive accommodations are American Youth Hostels (AYH). A nonprofit corporation, AYH is affiliated with youth hostels throughout the world. You can join AYH for a $20.00 membership fee ($10.00 if you are under 18 or over 60 years old). You can get information by visiting a local hostel which may be listed in your local phone book, or by writing: American Youth Hostels, National Administrative Offices, 1332 I Street, N.W., Suite 800, Washington, D.C. 20005.

Membership entitles you to stay for as little as $5.00 per night at any of a network of hostels, whose nationwide locations are listed in the annual *AYH Handbook*. One word of caution: if you join by mail, allow plenty of time before you leave on your tour. The membership card will come right away, but the *Handbook* travels by 4th-class book rate and could take weeks to arrive.

I have found that many people are willing to extend hospitality to bicycle tourists. The hosts vicariously enjoy the tourists' adventures by talking to them about their travels. A friend of mine, who lives near the Pacific Coast Bicentennial route, is an avid tourist. He's working too hard starting a business to go touring now, but occasionally he invites homeless bicycle tourists to stay at his house. He has not done so nearly as frequently, however, as the renowned "Cookie Lady" of Afton, Virginia. Charles Kuralt, who does news features for CBS-TV, has spread the legend of the Cookie Lady, June Curry. She attracts bicyclists to her Blue Ridge Mountain home alongside the Trans-America Bike Trail with a sign that says "Water For Bikers." Her hospitality has become legendary among those who pedal

Tourists riding down a steep grade on a desolate gravel road in the Yukon Territory, Canada. (Photo by Dan Burden, courtesy Hemistour)

across this wide country. She has given cookies, food, and a place to stay the night to the more than 3,000 cyclists who have called on her since the Trans-America Trail was inaugurated in 1976.

There are a number of books written just for the bicycle tourist that describe particularly enjoyable tours. The two-volume set, *Best Bicycle Tours,* by the editors of *Bicycling* magazine, describes approximately 40 specific tours, mostly in the United States and Canada. Karen and Gary Hawkins provide the international tourist similar information in their book, *Bicycle Touring in Europe,* and you can find other tour information in sources listed in the Recommended Reading section. Additionally, organized group bicycle tours often are advertised on flyers at bike shops, in travel magazines, and in bicycle publications.

A bicycle tour that starts and finishes at your own doorstep is great. It is exhilarating to turn your bicycle onto the street where you live at the conclusion of hundreds or even thousands of miles. Keep in mind, however, that it is possible to combine forms of transportation and enhance your enjoyment of the sport of cycling and of sightseeing in unfamiliar environs.

During my career as an Olympic cyclist (1968, 1972, and 1976) I did my share of sightseeing in Mexico, Europe, and Canada, but I've often thought how much fun I could have touring those lands by combining bicycling with other modes of travel. For instance, I would like to fly to Europe and do some traveling via EurRail and thereby increase the number of places I would be able to see by bike. I also hope to take a bicycle tour of the People's Republic of China, organized by Robert Carpenter, a United States Cycling Federation board member.

If you are concerned about how to transport your bicycle, one option is to buy a bike at your destination. If you happen to be in the market for a new bicycle and are traveling overseas, you may be able to pick up a bargain in the country where it was manufactured. I'm not aware of any companies that arrange for bicycle pick-ups at a foreign port the way some companies do for cars. You could do a little shopping when you arrive, or maybe you are lucky enough to have a friend at the destination who can shop for you in advance.

It's not all that difficult to ship a bicycle. The people at bike shops often can save you a box from which they have unpacked a new bicycle. It is a simple matter to take off your handlebars, pedals, and saddle, and pack your bicycle in that free box. You can then take the bike with you on airplanes, buses, ships, and trains. Most airlines charge anywhere from a $10.00 to $25.00 baggage fee to transport a bicycle, but you should always check in advance to verify that any given common carrier will accept a bike box as accompanied baggage.

Be sure to use sufficient padding when you pack your precious bicycle for the gorillas in baggage handling. Besides protecting your bike with padding, you may also want to reinforce the box by nailing a frame of inexpensive 1-inch by 2-inch wood furring strips to its inside edges. If you are particularly well-heeled, you can put the bike in one of the expensive new airbags now available for shipping fragile merchandise. When you arrive at your destination you can reassemble your bicycle right at the depot, and be off on your tour without the expense and inconvenience of finding taxis or other transportation.

Taking a ferry can give you an entertaining respite from the constant work of pedaling, and such boat trips can easily be planned into your itinerary. Rarely will a ferry company require you to pack or disassemble your bike to bring it on board. Most likely you'll only be charged the pedestrian rate—no fee for the bicycle—and usually you can board without waiting in the interminable lines that drive the motorists crazy. (Even if you are compulsive about exercising during your entire tour, a ferry ride is justifiable. Of course, the triathletes will consider swimming across while pulling a raft that holds the bicycle.)

In planning your tour you needn't rule out visits to cities. More than anywhere else on earth, Los Angeles is reputed to be a city where the automobile is king, a well-earned reputation. It is less widely known that greater Los Angeles is criss-crossed by numerous bicycle lanes and some bike paths totally separated from auto traffic. Thus, without worrying about auto traffic you can cross the Los Angeles area on the north-south axis by the beach bike trail, and on the east-west axis by several different, separated bike paths that follow flood control channels.

Not all U.S. cities are as well-suited for safe bicycle travel as

Los Angeles. Again, do a little research prior to your trip by calling or writing letters to state transportation departments and city road departments. There is always a way to bicycle into, through, or around major urban areas. Rather than being an impediment, traveling through a city may be an asset to your tour. Some of the most interesting sights and much of the best entertainment and accommodations are found in urban areas.

THE SECRET OF SUCCESSFUL TOURING

There is one essential key to enjoying a tour: deciding on your objectives. Why are you taking this tour? Do you want a long, strenuous workout or are you just traveling from Point A to Point B by a somewhat unconventional mode of transportation? Do you want to see some sights you have never seen before? Are you using the tour to cement a relationship with one or more of your traveling companions? Do you want to enjoy comfortable resort facilities between daily bike rides, or is camping and roughing it more your style? If you initially decide on some specific objectives for your trip you're more likely to have a good time. Knowing your priorities will help you make choices during the tour. If weather or injury or some other unplanned contingency makes your original plan too difficult or costly, you would benefit by adopting enjoyable alternatives.

Make sure that all participants in your tour group are aware of each other's goals. Things are a lot simpler when touring partners have the same aims. Decisions about routes, pace, equipment, accommodations, expenses, and schedule are greatly facilitated by common goals and prior discussion.

However, don't rule out the possibility of enjoying a tour in the company of others who have compatible but different goals. For instance, a friend of mine named Jack wished to use a tour from San Diego to San Francisco as an opportunity to train for participation in the Ironman Triathlon. His secondary objective was to enjoy the sights in the company of his girlfriend, Elena. Elena wanted to vacation along the California coast, travel up to

This well-equipped cycle-tourist can travel long distances in comfort and safety. Yet he is clearly not overloaded. Three water bottles and a plastic bottle of juice crammed under the sleeping bag make dehydration unlikely. Extra clothing strapped conveniently outside the rear pack permits adding and subtracting layers as the temperature changes. He can easily check his map in its clear plastic envelope atop the handlebar pack. He even carries a foam rubber sleeping pad. (Courtesy Bikecentennial)

Berkeley to visit her sister, and get some challenging exercise, in that order. My friends were able to enjoy their tour together even though their objectives were so different. On the way up they went slowly, which gave Jack time to go for training runs after the day's riding was complete and to take swim workouts when they stayed at motels with pools. Thus, Jack was able to use the tour for athletic training, while Elena, who wasn't similarly obsessed with getting a workout, was able to enjoy a relatively leisurely pace. The two of them took over ten days to reach San Francisco—about 50 miles per day. Elena stayed in San Francisco to visit her sister and later returned to San Diego by bus. Meanwhile, Jack turned around and pedaled back down to San Diego alone, this time getting a more difficult workout by completing the return trip in only 4½ days. The secret to their successful tour was that they made their own goals known to

Of course there are alternatives to panniers and packs. This tourist is able to carry more than he probably should by using a kiddie trailer. (Courtesy Bikecentennial)

each other and struck a workable compromise before they ever packed their bags.

You would be amazed how many bicyclists have sabotaged their tour by failing to plan adequately. Maybe you can take other trips without much preparation, but a bicycle tour is somewhat like a safari: if you are not prepared, the lions may eat you. If you have decided on your objectives, and if you have decided when and where to tour, you need to get information about road conditions, decide what equipment to take, prepare your bicycle for the trip, and even obtain appropriate shots, passports, and visas for visiting foreign countries.

EQUIPMENT

One of the most important aspects of your tour preparation is the choice and acquisition of your equipment. Ultralight bicycle frames and components that are ideal for racing and some recreational uses usually are unsuitable for touring. Touring with a support vehicle to carry your clothes and equipment is about the only way you can tour on a racing bike, which won't even have eyelets for attaching racks anyway. A good, lightweight racing machine would be strong enough to take the punishment meted out by the road and as much as fifty pounds of touring luggage, but its rigid frame would give the tourist a very stiff ride. A good touring frame generally will be somewhat heavier than a racing frame and more flexible because it will have a longer wheel base and more comfortable angles. It also generally will be less expensive than a racing frame, and therefore won't break your heart as much when it gets the scratches and dings inevitable on tour.

You almost certainly will want to put wider gauge (1⅛" or 1¼") clincher tires on a touring bike rather than the narrower sew-ups customary for racing bikes. Touring-tread tires, such as those made by Specialized, and thorn-resistant tubes will help combat the bicyclist's bugbear, flat tires. If you know that you are flat-prone you might even consider a puncture-resistant strip (such as Mr. Tuffy) around the inside of your tires. If you can stand the constant rubbing sound, think about using Tire Savers, light wire devices that brush tacks, broken glass, and thorns off your tires before your weight can push them in on the next rotation. Lately, some heavy, puncture-resistant, steel-belted bicycle tires have come on the market that may help.

These precautions will all make your tires heavier and thereby increase your bicycle's rolling resistance. I am reminded, however, of one friend who practically wore the skin off his hands changing five flats in one day on the seventeenth day of a 2,000-mile bike tour. He almost gave up in despair only a half-day's ride from his destination. You decide whether flats are a bad enough problem for you to justify heavier wheels.

Keep touring tires inflated to a high pressure. Heavyweight bicycles traveling at 8 mph use more energy overcoming rolling resistance than they do overcoming air resistance or any other retarding force. Fully inflated tires waste less energy on rolling friction.

Racing bikes usually use 3-cross light-gauge spokes. On a touring bike you would be well-advised to use heavier, less responsive, 4-cross 14-gauge stainless-steel spokes. Popping spokes in the middle of nowhere can ruin a bicycle tourist's whole day.

My bicycle career has been focused on competition, so I am very aware of the different needs of the tourist. For me, top-of-the-line derailleurs, gears, and brakes are worth the slightly higher cost. However, the best, most expensive derailleurs usually don't accommodate the wide gear ranges found on touring bikes. On a racing bike every bit of mechanical efficiency counts, but when you are carrying a heavy load on less-than-ideal roads you want equipment that is less likely to break your budget.

Tourists carry a much heavier payload than do racers. Consequently, to accommodate hauling the load up steep hills, a touring bicycle should be set up with a wider range of gears than you would want for a racing bike. At the front end you'll want maybe a 52-tooth chain ring for extra speed on level ground and down hills, and as low as a 36-tooth or smaller ring for grinding up steep hills. Similarly, the gears on the cluster might have as few as 13 teeth for speed to as many as 28 or 32 teeth for climbing.

Thus, your lowest gear would be truly an Alpine granny gear (36 × 32 ratio) that could get you up most steep hills, and your highest gear (52 × 13) one that could push you along at a smart speed.

Choosing a saddle for touring or any other purpose is highly individual. Because it's harder to climb hills out of the saddle with a lot of baggage, look critically at your current seat and choose one that you can sit in without rising for longer periods. For the past 13 years I have used the same two Brooks racing saddles, and I wouldn't trade them for anything.

EQUIPMENT CHECKLIST

If you are touring with a group and most or all of your equipment is being carried for you, it's not too difficult to decide what to take. If you think you need the kitchen sink, just throw it on the tour wagon. However, few experiences give you a greater feeling of self-reliance than touring independently, carrying all your own equipment. When you're traveling alone or in a small group, then you need to evaluate carefully what you or your group will carry, because it's always better to travel light on a bicycle. I offer here an annotated equipment checklist that you can use as you prepare for a tour. Climate, itinerary, cost, availability, needs, and personal preference will influence your choices, but I have put a star next to those items considered to be essential touring equipment:

WHAT TO BRING ON TOUR

★ ☐ **SPARE TUBE(S)**

☐ **Spare Tire**

Specialized and some other manufacturers make foldable touring tires, which can be stowed in a pack or beneath the seat. Almost any other bicycle tire can be lashed to your bike once you have folded it into three circles held together by string.

★ ☐ **PUMP**

Zefal and Silca make excellent pumps with quick-release connectors to the valve stem. You lose air with a threaded hose connector. Be sure you have the attachment that matches your tire valve: Presta or Schrader. There is a product called Quikfil, which is a tiny CO_2 cartridge for inflating bicycle tires. Quikfil could make a pump unnecessary, provided you carry a few extra cartridges and replace them as soon as possible after using them.

☐ **PATCH KIT**

The Rema Tip Top patch kit is compact and includes glue and abrasive for roughing the puncture area. Other kits are usually satisfactory, too.

★ ☐ **BIKE TOOLS**

—A pair of open-end wrenches (8-mm/10-mm combinations are available at most bike shops and fit most bicycle nuts and bolts, but check).
—Allen keys. (Optional: If your bicycle has Allen bolts, you probably at least need a 5-mm and a 6-mm key.)
—Flat-blade screwdriver.
—Phillips-head screwdriver.
—6″ adjustable wrench.
—Needle-nose pliers (preferably with a cutting capability for cables).
—Spoke wrench.
—Freewheel remover.
—Tire irons.
—Small tube or aerosol can of a high-quality chain lubricant (e.g., Triflon).

☐ **SPARE BRAKE AND DERAILLEUR CABLES**

★ ☐ **EXTRA SPOKES**

Some friends of mine really wished they had these when they rode across the Arizona desert. Spokes can be taped to the upright support of your bike rack.

☐ **Maps**

Not essential if you know exactly where you're going.

☐ **Paper and Pen**

☐ **Warm Clothes**

Determined by season and climate. Leggings for bike shorts are great and a warm sweater or jacket is nice even for summer. Wear layers of clothes and anticipate your body-temperature changes. Add clothes before you chill and take off clothes before you overheat.

☐ **Rain Gear**

Breathable fabrics such as Gore-Tex will keep rain out without allowing perspiration to soak you.

☐ **Tent**

☐ **Ground Cloth**

☐ **Air Mattress or Pad**

☐ **Sleeping Bag**

I recommend a lightweight, down-filled bag, necessary only for emergency use if you'll be staying in motels.

☐ **Toilet Paper**

Only the last few hundred sheets of a roll, so you can flatten it for easy packing.

★ ☐ **SOAP AND TOWEL**

Cleanliness is next to Godliness.

☐ **Toothbrush and Toothpaste**

☐ **Other Toilet Articles**

☐ **Tube of Waterless Hand Cleaner**

You'll enjoy your tour more if you can clean up after you've worked on your chain.

★ ☐ **BIKE LOCK AND CABLE**

You'll have to leave your bike unattended sometimes.

☐ **First Aid Kit**

☐ **Bicycling Shoes**

☐ **Lights**

Necessary if you travel after dark.

★ ☐ **HELMET**

A well-ventilated one should be on your head to prevent scrambled brains.

★ ☐ **WATER BOTTLES AND CAGES**

☐ **Food**

(You can eat at restaurants instead.)

☐ **Eating Utensils**

☐ **Cooking Utensils**

☐ **Sunscreen**

Sunburn can be unbearably painful.

☐ **Knife**

Useful when camping.

☐ **Camera and Film**

☐ **Cycling Gloves and/or Padded Handlebars**

★ ☐ **MONEY**

Travelers checks and credit cards are fine if you prefer, but remember some merchants only accept cash.

Note: If you bring everything on this list, don't try to lift your bike!

TOURING LUGGAGE

How do you carry all that stuff on a bicycle? A friend of mine once saw a tourist battling a very stiff head wind while wearing a top-heavy, wide back pack and frame. While this tourist's pack was ideal for hiking in the woods, nothing could have been worse for bicycle touring. In effect he was wearing a large sail that was pushing him backward. Not that you can't travel that way. When my friend saw him, the back-packing tourist was already north of San Francisco on a tour from San Diego to Seattle.

Racks and panniers are better for touring. A cheap Schwinn rack is adequate for the rear, but Blackburn makes a lighter,

These large, lightweight panniers can be mounted on either a front or rear rack. A sleeping bag can then be strapped on the top of the rack. Notice the reflectors. (Courtesy Cannondale Corporation)

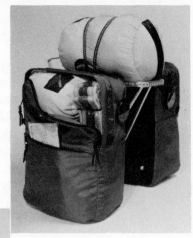

This knobby-tire mountain bike has been equipped with both front and rear panniers. It's ready to tour on any type of road. (Courtesy Madden Touring Equipment)

more elegant, more expensive rack for the rear and other racks for over the front wheel. The current recommendation for touring is to put some luggage over the front wheel to avoid disproportionate weight in the rear. Also, for stability it is advisable to carry your luggage as low to the ground as possible.

Panniers usually are made of lightweight but sturdy nylon dyed with reflective colors. A first-class bicycle shop should display a good inventory of panniers with various compartments, pockets, fastening arrangements, and other features. Most commercially available panniers will attach to standard bicycle racks.

Munchies, tools, first-aid kits, and other paraphernalia can be carried conveniently in the handlebar and seat packs. Some handlebar packs have a plastic window behind which you can place a folded map to be read while riding. You can find handlebar and seat packs constructed of the same lightweight, reflective materials as panniers, and they, too, are readily available at quality bike stores.

HOW TO RIDE

After I set the world record for distance covered in 24 hours at the 1983 Pepsi Marathon Bike Race, a journalist asked me to explain the psychological tricks I had used to pedal 514 miles. I was tired and soaked by 19 hours of rain, so all I could manage to say to the reporter was, "You do it with your goddamn legs." The way you cover long distances during a bicycle tour is by staying in the saddle and keeping the cranks turning until you get where you are going each day. No tricks.

That doesn't mean you have to try and cross the United States in under 11 days, as I once did in the Great American Bike Race. That tour was a little bit manic and wouldn't even have been possible without an elaborate support team, including a motorhome, motorcycles, a nurse, a masseur, a bicycle mechanic, other assistants, and several bicycles. What I am saying is that if you have set realistic objectives for your tour, you will achieve them only if you stay focused on the cycling required.

Notice how these two tourists are riding single file, while carrying reflector triangles, for safety. (Bikecentennial Photo)

On tour I like to break camp early in the morning, get where I'm going, and then relax. However, your circadian rhythms might make you more effective later in the day. Whatever you do, remember you're not a machine. You need to warm up during the beginning of each day's ride, at least for the first 20 minutes. If you make a prolonged stop, particularly if you stop for a heavy meal, the lactic acid from your earlier riding will build up in your muscles. Your circulatory system also will divert some blood from your muscles and brain to help digest anything you ate. You won't be able to just turn on the ignition and get back on the road; you'll have to warm up again.

Pedaling a bicycle with a heavy set of packs is different from competitive cycling. You will be less aerodynamic and your weight will increase the effects of tire friction. Because of these factors, I recommend pedaling in easier gears than you otherwise would, so you don't strain your knees and leg muscles. The effect of the extra weight is particularly stressful going up steep hills. On the down side of a hill, extra weight may make you go a bit faster and will almost certainly make it harder to steer your bicycle. I once met an unhappy tourist in Colorado whose bandaged and stitched body was tangible evidence that 50 pounds of touring equipment made it extremely difficult to negotiate a hairpin turn while speeding downhill at 45 mph.

DO'S AND DON'TS

Finally, some gratuitous advice:

- **DO RIDE SAFELY.** The general safety rules in Chapter 4 are even more important when you're riding in unfamiliar territory on a bike made less maneuverable by touring equipment. You could easily hit an open car door with your extra-wide load, or worse yet get hit by a passing motorist who isn't used to wide bicycles. Your panniers cause other safety problems that aren't necessarily apparent. For instance, panniers would hide a leglamp that might otherwise make you highly visible at night to motorists behind you.

- **DO WEAR A HELMET.** This not only will help to protect your head if you have an accident, but it also will shield your head from sunlight.

- **DO PICK YOUR COMPANIONS CAREFULLY.** They should be socially compatible, and capable of meeting the physical challenges of the tour.

- **DO BE IN ADEQUATE PHYSICAL CONDITION.**

- **DO LEARN HOW TO FIX YOUR BIKE.** At a minimum you should know how to change flats, adjust brakes and derailleurs, and replace a spoke. It's too late to learn these things when you're stranded in the desert, so practice.

- **DO TAKE CARE OF YOUR BIKE.** During your tour, continue the preventive maintenance, cleaning after use, and lubricating.

- **DO PACE YOURSELF.**

- **TAKE KNEE-STRAIN PRECAUTIONS.** During cold weather keep your knees warm by wearing leggings, knee warmers, or long pants. (Remember a speeding cyclist is vulnerable to wind-chill effects.) Avoid stressing your knees by pushing big gears. Use a lower gear and pedal a bit more rapidly instead. Some doctors recommend aspirin as an anti-inflammatory for bicyclist's knee.

- **DO STAY DRY AND WARM.** On a winter tour, ride during the warmest parts of the day and stop occasionally for a warm drink or hot soup.

- **DO DRINK WATER BEFORE YOU ARE THIRSTY.** By the time you are thirsty, you are already on your way to dehydration.

- **DO HAVE FUN.** Touring is a hobby, not a chore.

- **DON'T GO ROAD CRAZY.** Each day of your tour, stop before it is dark and before you are exhausted. The road can exert a seductive, hypnotic force on tourists, which keeps them riding to "just one more" campground or one more town, long after they are tired.

- **DON'T OVERLOAD.** Anything you lack and really need can usually be acquired along your route, and it's a pity to burden yourself with useless ballast.

- **DON'T RIDE ON AN EMPTY STOMACH OR EMPTY WATER BOTTLE.** Plan ahead. Dehydration or low blood sugar can make you a hazard to yourself in traffic.

- **DON'T BREAK THE TRAFFIC LAWS.** In particular obey signs that limit bicycle access to most (not all) interstate highways. If the highway patrol officers or state troopers don't put you in jail, they will probably drive you many miles back to where you first got on the forbidden road. You could waste hours of pedaling.

- **DON'T ANTAGONIZE THE MOTORISTS.** Most of them are only out for short trips, so you almost always will be affronting someone on his or her own turf.

A friend of mine, Steve, toured Washington State by himself. He gave an obscene hand salute to the driver of a huge logging-truck, who had just run him off the road. The logger stopped the truck, apparently to take revenge for my friend's truculent gesture. Steve hightailed up a nearby narrow side road where he knew the logger would be unable to bring his unmaneuverable rig. After he thought it was safe, my somewhat foolhardy friend got back on the road. Within minutes a large sawdust truck tried to run him down. No doubt the two drivers had communicated via CB radio. My friend is now far less aggressive toward the drivers of much larger vehicles, for he learned the lesson that discretion is the better part of valor.

9

Competitive Cycling

We now come to my favorite part, cycling as a sport. In two decades as a bike racer, I am happy to say that I have had a fair degree of success—winning a few, losing a few, loving them all. Competitive cycling is the most specialized type of bicycling, and in this chapter I want to talk a little bit about it, not only to help aspiring and practicing racers but to inspire other types of cyclists. I believe information about the esoteric world of the competitive cyclist can facilitate the use and enjoyment of the bicycle by cyclists of every stripe.

Those of you who aren't already hooked on bicycle racing may be somewhat skeptical about what I've just said, and may be ready to skip this chapter. I would ask you first to consider two things: (1) the sport of bicycle racing is fun to the participant and spectator alike, and (2) competition greatly increases the fitness benefits to be derived from bicycling. Commuting, errands, cruising along scenic streets, and touring are all legitimate, wonderful uses for a bicycle. However, the bicycle is such an efficient machine, it doesn't provide you the aerobic workout that Kenneth Cooper and the American Heart Association recommend, unless you ride fast enough to raise your heart rate.

That's where competitive cycling comes in. Training to *compete* necessitates really getting fit. To make your bicycling *less* energy efficient, training and competing on the bicycle at high speeds will do the trick. Competition gives you the incentive to bicycle fast, and to kick the habit of leisurely cycling. It's fun *and* good for your heart when you get an aerobic workout on your bike.

One word of caution: bicycle racing is a dangerous, demanding sport. First, see how much fun it is by watching a bike race. Perhaps you will be inspired to test yourself in a local club time trial, which is far less dangerous than a mass-start race. Whether you are a time trialist or full-on road racer, competitive cycling is a sport that can be pursued by male and female, young and old alike.

BICYCLE RACING FOR FUN AND PROFIT

Many are called, but few are chosen. In ghetto neighborhoods in the United States many poor youngsters dream of following the footsteps of Khareem Abdul Jabbar into a six-figure contract in big-league basketball. In poor neighborhoods and rural villages of Europe, kids who don't dream of a soccer career fantasize about making their fortune as a winner on the professional bike racing circuit.

During the early years of this century, bicycle racing was a major spectator sport in the United States. Attendance often exceeded that of baseball, the national pastime. A legendary love affair with automobiles—and I love them too—is probably responsible for contemporary America's relative disinterest with the sport of bicycle racing. Whereas the spectator appeal of bicycle racing is now increasing in America, bicycling has been among the top *participation* sports for the past 15 years. The renaissance of American competitive cycling is attributable in part to the fervor over the Los Angeles Olympics, and in part to a generally heightened awareness of fitness.

In Europe the enduring public enthusiasm for bicycle racing has made Eddy Merckx and a handful of other professional cyclists wealthy athletes. But it may be a while before American professional and amateur cyclists can make a living on the meager prize money offered in this country. One of the few Americans who has made it work did so by showing well in European races. Greg LeMond, who at 22 won the 1983 World Professional

Here I am (#7) in the thick of things, out of the saddle to climb a hill. That's Phil Anderson just to my right, who has done well as a pro. (Courtesy Kim Howard)

Road Championship, could not hope to equal his overseas earnings by racing in the United States.

I have been able to make my living in this country as an athlete largely because I have worked in the bicycle industry and, more recently, because the burgeoning sport of triathlons has attracted some financial support. Unless I had conceded to competing in Europe, I could not have dreamed of earning a living purely as a competitive cyclist. Most bicycle races in America offer some prize money, but not even enough to make the U.S. Olympic Committee very fussy about the line between cycling amateurs and professionals. Until recently it was not at all uncommon to win such items as electric toasters and $10 gift certificates for office supplies—nothing compared to European purses and prizes.

A handful of Americans have become bicycle bums, forsaking other meaningful careers in order to support their bicycle racing with short-term menial work. However, the majority of American racers are amateurs who have full-time occupations from which they draw their personal income and much of their self-esteem. Cycling is secondary to family and profession; the competition is largely for the fun of it.

And it is fun. Few things are more exhilarating than zooming down steep hills or taking a fast corner. Breaking away from a pack or reeling in the leaders can be tremendously exciting. For sheer thrills, a raucous mass start of an Olympic road race, with 250 rock-hard tubulars singing at 40 mph, is hard to top. Even long hours of training alone are fun for me; I'm out in the open and moving through interesting country. Conquering new terrain, I am content in the knowledge that I have done it on my own, whether it's 10 miles or 200. I can think about my life, plan, and generally sort things out on a long solo training ride.

About half of my training I do with other cyclists, so my sport also provides social opportunities. You can't be a total recluse as a bicycle racer. There is no such thing as the loneliness of the long-distance bike racer. If nothing else, you'll have to connect with other cyclists in order to compete against them. Training alone exclusively makes you wheel-shy and non-aggressive— the kiss of death for a racer.

I find the camaraderie of long workouts with cycling buddies to be both fun and beneficial to my training. You work harder when you ride with equally skilled companions. Sometimes they will keep up an interesting conversation, or engage in a little friendly competition. Your cycling buddies may also push the pace at times you otherwise would be lazy. What is more, training companions can swap taking the lead in a pace line.

There is a lifestyle and mystique that goes along with my demanding sport. The mystique is deeply rooted in its history, as the final chapter describes. I am a member of the bike-racing subculture, and I love it. Yes, I even shave my legs. Some people believe that cyclists shave to cut wind resistance, but I decided to start shaving my legs after the bandages were removed from abrasions suffered in my first crash.

Bike racing is a sport for thinking men and women. Because the sport involves a machine, technology as well as physiology plays a role. As you read on, you will learn some of the intricate strategy and tactics of bike racing. Being clever helps; occasionally, the tactics of racers are downright funny. Sometimes bike racers play malicious tricks too, which aren't so funny.

There is even a special jargon to bike racing. Terms such as "attack," "breakaway," "drop," "paceline," "bonking," and "wheelsucker" have special meaning to competitive cyclists.

HOW TO BECOME A BICYCLE RACER

Competitive cycling is a social sport. To become a bike racer, your first step is to join a bicycle club. If you're good at striking up a conversation, you might learn about bike clubs from cyclists you meet on training rides. The folks at almost any pro bike shop will be able to give you information about bicycle clubs in your area. If you are a beginner, you probably will want to find a club that encourages neophytes. Some clubs are really designed to support elite athletes, and if you're an experienced, talented racer, new to a particular community, you'll *probably* want to seek out that kind of club. An active club most likely will sponsor a busy schedule of time trials, races, training meetings, informational meetings, and other events. Additionally, the club may publish a calendar of major races, or a newsletter, and certainly members of the club will know about nearby competitions.

Once you have learned about competition and training by cycling with a club, your second step should be to obtain a United States Cycling Federation (USCF) license. The USCF is the primary governing and sanctioning body for traditional competitive cycling in the United States. It is a federation of local bicycle clubs. If you want to compete in a USCF-sanctioned event, you will need to hold a valid racing license from that organization.

You can obtain a USCF license by requesting an application from: United States Cycling Federation, 1750 East Boulder, Colorado Springs, CO 80909. At this writing the fee for a new membership ranges from $10 to $25, depending on the category. Your annual USCF dues include a copy of the rules and a monthly subscription to *Cycling USA,* a bicycle-racing publication that includes up-to-date racing calendars and results. Male and female USCF-licensed racers can compete against members of their own sex in five age categories: midget (8–11 years old), intermediate (12–14), junior (15–17), and senior (18 and older). Additionally, there is a veteran class for men (age 35 and over). Within most of the age and gender classes the USCF has established four ability categories.

New licensees race as Category IV and advance to categories III, II, and I by participating in or winning a specified number of events at their present ability level. The USCF sanctions and supplies licensed officials for many races and race series, including district and national championships. And it is the USCF coaching staff that selects the U.S. Olympic cycling teams.

The Professional Racing Organization of America (PRO) supervises and promotes professional competition. Two separate divisions of the Union Cycliste Internationale (UCI) manage amateur and professional international competition, including the Pan Am Games and the Olympic Games.

The sort of traditional bicycle competition that the USCF governs includes track races, time trials, road races, and criteriums. Track races and some time trials are staged in velodromes (banked, oval tracks for bicycles), while road races, criteriums, and most time trials are held on the roads.

BIKE-RACING EVENTS

Velodrome events at the Olympic Games include a 1000-meter time trial (individual cyclists against the clock), the 4000-meter pursuit (pairs of riders starting on opposite sides of a velodrome trying to catch up with each other), the 1000-meter matched sprint (pairs of riders matched against each other). Olympic competition also includes a 4000-meter team pursuit, in which 2 four-person squads (working as teams in pace lines) pursue each other around a velodrome. Additionally, there is a mass-start points race in the Olympic velodrome. I have competed in a few pursuits, but in the Olympics I never did any track racing. I chose to specialize in road races, because I am better suited to long-distance events.

Road races usually vary from 25 to 150 miles. Nonetheless, I have competed in such gargantuan road races as the Quebec-Montreal Race (170 miles) and the Great American Bike Race (2975 miles from the Santa Monica Pier in Los Angeles to the Empire State Building in New York). However, don't be intimidated; most road races are 50 miles or less.

Criteriums and stage races are two other race varieties. A criterium is a multiple-lap road competition around a closed circuit of at most a few miles in length. Most of the scars on my knees came from criteriums, such as the Summerville Criterium

National track team members Young and Barczewski take a spin around the velodrome. These track bikes have no brakes and no derailleur, and the single fixed gear forbids coasting. (Courtesy Omni Sports)

The pace line strings out around a turn at the Red Zinger Classic, 1979. (Courtesy Kim Howard)

How innocent we looked as we lined up for a group photo in Santa Monica, California, before the Great American Bike Race. (Left to right: the author, John Marino, Michael Shermer, and Lon Haldeman.) All four of us crossed the United States in under 13 days, and three of us (Marathon Lon, Sherm, and I) made it under the previous record. Lon won in 9 days 20 hours and 2 minutes. We were all much wiser when we got to New York. (Courtesy Robert Hustwit)

National Champion Joe Ryan's legs show the mud spatters that prove he's in a cyclo-cross race, as he takes an obstacle of the course on foot. (Courtesy Kim Howard)

and the Tour of Nutley. I recall riding right into a competitor who fell in front of me at the University Park Dallas Criterium; by the time I crossed the finish in that race—which I won—I had lost much blood and skin. I like the criterium, but I won't pretend it isn't a dangerous race.

Stage races, such as the Coors Classic and the famed Tour de France, are really a series of road races, criteriums, and time trials that stretch over several days or weeks. (I won the Coors twice; to date, Dale Stetina and I are the only people ever to win that race more than once.) In stage races, the riders get a rest period overnight or at least a few hours between each segment of the race. The Tour de France, the best known, most prestigious stage race, covers approximately 2300 miles (the course is changed from year to year) in 22 days. The Giro d'Italia, the ultimate test in Italian bicycle racing, includes 24 stages and covers about the same distance as the French Tour.

Non-traditional bicycle racing has blossomed in the past few years. A cyclocross race is something like a criterium over unpaved, rugged ground. Cyclocross racers are forced by the terrain to get off their bicycles and run while carrying their bikes over parts of the difficult courses they traverse. I have had some

199

experience with cyclocross, having won the 1969 National Cyclocross Championship, held that year in Chicago.

Mountain bikes, those recent entries into the bicycle marketplace, also are being raced. In 1983 I competed in my first mountain-bike race, the notorious Whiskeytown Downhill. I won in my class (35–40 age group) and I still have the scars to prove it.

In biathlons, triathlons, and other multi-sport events, bicycle road racing is combined with one or more sports, such as swimming, running, rowing, cross-country skiing, or even racquetball. I've already mentioned that I won the 1981 Ironman Triathlon, and I'm proud of that particular achievement. Interestingly, that hybrid event brought me more publicity and notice than any bicycle race has in a 20-year athletic career that has included participation on three Olympic teams and a gold medal in the 1971 Pan Am Games. Many athletes have been introduced to bicycle racing through the sport of triathlon. I think this new sport has done nothing but good for cycling as a sport and athletics in general.

RACING EQUIPMENT

In general, I would say that what you do to your body during training is far more important than what you do to your bank balance at the bike shop. In the beginning, concentrate on your training efforts and gradually accumulate better equipment. If you train hard on a garage-sale special for a long time, just think how well you're going to do if you finally acquire a custom-built racing frame outfitted with your favorite top-of-the-line components.

My first "racing" bicycle was a 3-speed Schwinn, and my first 10-speed was a Schwinn Continental. I now ride on a bike frame made by Dave Moulton, the builder of the John Howard line of bicycles. At the risk of discouraging someone from buying one of my company's frames, I have to say that my competitive performance is much more dependent on my health and training than the equipment I'm using: "you do it with your legs." The finest equipment in the world might make a small difference at the finish line of a national or world championship, but even there the extravagant claims made by manufacturers say more about how badly they want to sell their merchandise than anything else.

There are, however, some relatively small equipment investments that the beginning competitor should make long before considering a super-lightweight, thousand-dollar-plus racing bike. Of course you should have toe clips, straps, and cleated shoes, else your stroke will be too inefficient to race. And a good set of racing wheels is imperative. Even if you train on 1½" steel rims with heavy clinchers and save your good wheels only for races, you should have a set of strong, light alloy wheels with sew-ups, otherwise you can never hope to excel in competition. You also should have a good alloy crank set and pedals. Only if the wheels and cranks are light and strong can you really get maximum speed out of your machine.

After making certain that your spinning parts are high in quality and low in weight, you might improve your bike by replacing any other parts that are heavy, unresponsive, or worn. Get rid of those heavy steel handlebars and stem, and put on some alloy bars. Put on a set of top-quality brakes; your stopping power is more critical in a race than anywhere else. Buy derailleurs that are light, responsive, and durable, so that you won't lose time getting hung up between gears or stuck in the wrong gear because of an inexact shifter. If you have a heavy bike— say, more than 25 pounds—think about getting a lighter one, perhaps one with tighter angles than your present bike. Remember that if you can't afford new parts you might be able to get them used from other cyclists who themselves are upgrading. A well-made, used frame may look shabbier than a new one, but if it's been treated right it should serve you well for many years.

Whether you have new or old equipment, don't go into a race with anything extra on your bike. Racks, kick stands, handlebar bags, reflectors, and so on should be removed. Carry a pump and bottle and, if you are riding in a road race with little or no support, have your spare tire under your saddle. Get rid of everything else before the start of the race. Your bike should be in good condition, meaning clean and in good repair. The USCF

Bradley on a Raleigh (left) and Phinney on a Murray (right) led an American team to a 1983 Pan Am Games gold medal for the team time trial on these "funny bikes" with the 24" front wheels. The small front wheels lower the bicyclist's profile, making him go faster because of reduced air resistance. (Courtesy Robert F. George/*Velo-News*)

specifies that race promoters should disqualify any competitor whose bicycle is not in good order. You should make sure that your machine is going to last you at least until you cross the finish!

TRAINING FOR RACES

The right way to train is a highly individual matter, determined by such factors as your goals, athletic background, age, sex, time commitments, and genetic endowment. The training program that is right for me may be all wrong for you, but I can

suggest five universal, cardinal rules, which can be boiled down
to the acronym: TRAIN.

T means *take it easy sometimes*. In fact, train "hard/easy." If
you work out *hard* today, then tomorrow take it *easy*.
Allow your muscles to recover from today's stress and
they will adapt by becoming stronger. Continually stress
your muscles, joints, and tendons, and you will eventually
be injured. Challenge your body, but don't fatigue it by
avoiding rest.

R stands for *ride regularly*. "Weekend warriors" eventually
become *weakened* warriors. They are begging for trouble,
injuries and maybe heart attacks. In any case, you'll
never make any progress in competitive cycling by training for 10 hours on Saturday and 12 on Sunday while you
let your bicycle rust from Monday to Friday. If all you can
manage is half an hour's daily bicycle workout and one 5-
hour ride on Saturday (8½ hours per week total), you'll
benefit and improve more than you would by riding a total
of 22 hours on Saturday and Sunday. If you can fit as
much as a daily hour or two of quality training into your
lifestyle, perhaps by using the bicycle for commuting or
errands, then you'll make even better progress.

A stands for *aerobic*. On level terrain it's easy to bicycle too
slowly to get an aerobic workout. If you are not getting an
aerobic workout you won't build your strength and endurance for racing. Exercise physiologists sometimes call
aerobic workouts in running and bicycling *l*ong, *s*low *dis*-
tance (LSD). On the bicycle make sure it isn't *too* slow; but
maintain the aerobic effort as long as your schedule and
physical condition will permit.

I stands for *intervals*. Your body will stop you from sprinting before too long, but sustained bursts of speed are just
what you need to break away from a pack or win a race.
Along with the LSD training, which predominates on the
easy days, you need to throw in some high-speed,
anaerobic intervals on the hard days. Interval training
requires that you go slowly until a designated moment
and then sprint a predetermined distance. Slow and fast
intervals are alternated repeatedly. Phone poles or signs

along the road make good landmarks to govern the spacing of your speed intervals. If a sufficient number of races and time trials are scheduled near your home to permit weekly competition during the race season, you can get some of your interval training by entering races. You can use the less important races as preparation for the more important events.

Long-distance runners use the Swedish word *fartlek* (literally speed play) to describe one form of interval training. In running, fartlek workouts are done over varied terrain with other runners. The object is to jog along, challenge each other to short sprint races from time to time, tumble around, and generally act like a child during the workout. On the bicycle, little impromptu races or games of tag with your training buddies can serve as enjoyable, effective fartleks.

The first goal of interval training is to raise the threshold of your anaerobic level so that you can ride faster without losing your breath and being forced to slow down. The second goal of interval training is to increase the length of time you can tolerate anaerobic exertion.

N is for *no burnout*. Even God rested on the seventh day. A day or two off from training each week won't turn you into a lump of lard. No matter how dedicated you are about your training, you can afford a day off every couple of weeks. The best day to rest is the day you are tired from a particularly difficult workout or competition. If you are constantly fatigued and get bored with your training, your performance in cycling (and probably in other areas of your life as well) will suffer. Before you burn out and drop an enjoyable, healthful activity altogether, take a break from cycling. The best athletes I have met lead full lives, which include time for personal relationships, professions, and other avocations as well as training.

If you are worried about losing endurance and muscle tone when you are not cycling, then take up some other athletic activities to maintain your fitness. Eric Heiden, the American Olympic gold medalist in speed skating, and basketball star Bill Walton have used cycling as an alternative athletic activity to avoid burnout in their sports. Why not do the reverse and use activities such as skating, basketball, cross-country skiing, or racquetball to maintain your edge while you take a holiday from cycling? Since I revived my childhood interest in swimming and running to become a successful triathlete, I have become increasingly convinced of the merits of cross-training. My running and swimming not only help me avoid bicycle burnout, but they help me train for cycling competition. In fact, I am so convinced of the merits of cross-training that I am working with two other writers on a book devoted exclusively to that topic.

That sums up my advice on training for bicycle competition. When you train for a race, remember to TRAIN!

RIDE SMARTER, NOT HARDER

Bicycle races are not always won by the strongest or most fit athlete. Technique, strategy, and tactics all play a role in determining the outcome of a bike race. It takes more than brute force. It takes a fair amount of skill and savvy to win on the bicycle.

Let me first speak of pedaling technique. What I said earlier about pedaling is valid for competitors as well as tourists and recreational cyclists. In their training, however, competitors additionally should pay attention to building leg strength and maintaining an efficient cadence. Racers need to pedal a bit differently from other cyclists.

You can build leg strength for competitive cycling by pedaling occasionally in the "wrong" gear. When pedaling against the wind or up an incline, stress your muscles by riding in a higher gear than the situation would usually warrant. When riding with the wind or down the hill, learn to spin pedals at a high cadence by riding in a low gear, which normally would be more appropriate for uphills and headwinds. This technique, which I call high-gear/low-gear training, will build strength, endurance, and pedal speed. Be careful, though: you can injure your knees by pushing too hard against the wind and up the hills.

In general, you should strive to maintain a fast, fluid pedal cadence of 85–95 revolutions per minute. Learn the feel of different cadences and do some high-cadence intervals in a variety of gears. Vary the routine. As always, use moderation in your training.

Early in the season I do workouts on a track bike to rebuild both my strength and suppleness, thus increasing my effective rpm range. If you stop pedaling a track bike, you don't coast: the fixed cog forces the chain to keep turning, which in turn forces the pedals to push the rider's legs around. I take a track bike out on the road and get an intense workout going up and down hills without the help of a variable-gear cluster and derailleur. Up hills I'm building strength by working the single gear. Down hills I'm building pedal cadence as the fixed gear pushes my feet. Note: Track-bike workouts on the open road are difficult and can be dangerous, so I recommend those workouts only for advanced cyclists. Be sure to put a brake on the bike before taking it on the street. A track bike is *not* street legal.

Many competitive cyclists occasionally train by motorpacing behind a mo-ped or motorscooter. I do that myself, when I feel that I have gotten slow and lazy by training alone. Motorpacing shields me from the wind and makes it possible to cycle faster, restoring my flexibility, snap, and ability to turn a fast cadence. But even more so than track-bike workouts, motorpacing is *dangerous*. Only the most experienced cyclists should train by motorpacing.

What about adjustments of the bicycle? How does the bicycle's set-up affect competitive performance? You should review the earlier comments about riding position. Find the best set-up for you on your bicycle and stick with that. Some top-level racers tinker with their bikes a little for races, but most people don't need or want to make drastic adjustments. It's better, in general, to set up your bike right in the first place, and race on it that way. Find the best spot for the saddle and stem and leave them there.

A different type of adjustment sometimes is made in the cranks. In criteriums and in road races that have many sharp turns, some racers ride on shorter cranks and on criterium bikes that have higher bottom brackets. The more time you spend coasting around sharp bends while the competition is pedaling,

Tight quarters at a tight corner. Notice how these two take the turn in perfect synchrony, inside pedal up and ready to crank as soon as there's clearance. (Courtesy Mike Hodges)

the harder you'll have to work on the straights just to keep up. The top-level riders whose sponsors will give them the most exotic equipment can afford different bikes for different races. Most cyclists, though, ride their one bike in criteriums, road races, and time trials alike.

Training yourself to pedal correctly in an efficient racing position will improve your performance and get you ready for your first competition. After you have tried some local club time trials, you might want to try a road race. That's when it's important to know something about pace and riding in a pack.

How well I remember my first race, the 50-mile Tour of Florissant, in 1966. I had no experience riding in a pack and felt totally intimidated at the (seemingly) blinding speed we were

207

going. When another rider crowded me I was completely unprepared and rode straight off course and into a ditch. I wrecked my front wheel and my chances to even finish my first race, but fortunately that was only at the beginning of my career. I learned to ride in a group for my next race.

The best advice for a novice riding in the pack (or peloton as the French call it) is to avoid the death grip on the handlebars. Stay relaxed; keep your arms and shoulders loose. Club riding or riding with several buddies will get you used to maneuvering at close quarters. You might even try a few workouts in which you and your friends purposely bump each other to get the feel of pack riding. When riding in the pack, be sure not to panic; learn to trust your fellow riders. Don't overlap your front wheel with the back wheel of another rider.

In order to perform well in a road race, try to stay in the first third of the pack and conserve your energy by staying close to other riders who will block the wind for you. In criteriums and road races, you always should ride aggressively, but never heedlessly. Choose carefully the riders you follow; if the person ahead of you continually brakes or swerves, escape and let that menace take someone else down.

Avoid getting boxed in by other riders at crucial points. As a novice you probably won't want to initiate attacks, but if you are alert to what the top riders are doing, you will be able to go with them when they try to break away from the field (when one or more riders pull ahead of the main pack).

The success of a breakaway is usually determined by four things: (1) the strength of those in the break; (2) the number of bicycles in the break—three or four is perfect, but more is trouble—(3) the ability of those in the break to work together, alternating through a pace line to counter the aerodynamic advantage of the numerically superior pack; and (4) the ability of teammates left behind to block other strong riders from counterattacking to bridge the gap to the first break.

The success of the individual rider in the lead break is determined by knowing when and how to sprint away from the break. Those who don't pull their share in a break are derisively known as "wheelsuckers." However, all's fair in love and bike racing, and unless the rest of the riders manage to shake a wheelsucker that low person may have just enough oomf left at the end to sprint to victory. Knowing the right time to sprint and conserving enough energy to do it are abilities that separate the winners from the losers.

For the most part, the experienced bike racer accepts the group's pace for the majority of a race. Unless you are exceptionally strong and have great endurance, you won't benefit by setting the pace or breaking away early. If you are out there in front all by yourself nobody will decrease air resistance for you. You will be doing 30 to 50 percent more work than the pack, and they'll just reel you in and drop you once you have exhausted yourself. Bicycle racers sometimes call that state of exhaustion "the bonk" or "bonking out." Conserve energy during a race as much as possible by riding in the lowest gear practicable. Spin fast to stay up in the pack and don't try to muscle your way to the lead unless you know you are clearly superior to all the competition.

Just staying with the pack is a challenge for which you will have to train. As I've said before, don't slack off every time you train. You need some LSD training to build your base, but some of your training also should simulate racing. There is no let-up in a race. The key is your heart rate. Monitor your heart beat, and increase your ability to cycle at an elevated heart rate. Decide on your goals before each training session. If you really wish to be scientific about heart rate, cadence, etc., I recommend one of the many computer devices on the market such as the Velo Coach. The Coach is a digital speedometer for cyclists and runners that also can give you a continuous readout on your heart rate. What feedback could be better for assessing aerobic achievement and charting progress?

POINTING TO A RACE

I follow a definite procedure for specific races, which includes long-term preparations, preparations the day before the race, and day-of-race preparation.

Long before the race I set my goals and institute a training program to meet them. I try to simulate the event in my training. If I'm training for a short event I concentrate on speed work, even throwing in some motorpacing. If I'm training for a long event, I pile on the miles. For team events I train with my teammates, and decide with them on strategy and tactics. Along the way in the long-term preparation, I set and meet realistic short-term performance goals to build my confidence. I draw up charts and calendars to record and monitor my progress on such performance tests as time trials and less important races. I find and maintain my optimum body weight.

While I'm readying myself for a race, I keep my bicycle in tip-top condition, cleaned and lubed and ready to go, to avoid the need for stress-producing last-minute overhauls. If I live close enough, I check out the course to determine the difficult points and to avoid being surprised by any dangerous areas. For races far from home, I try to arrive a day or two early to inspect the course. As the race day approaches I "image" the actual race,

Dale and Wayne Stetina relax and chat about team strategy before a race. (Courtesy Kim Howard)

riding it in my mind several times and working out several alternative plans for the race.

The day before the race, I eat good food that won't upset my digestion, continuing a high-carbohydrate diet if it is going to be a long race. For several days before the event I get plenty of sleep, and stay relaxed by avoiding conflict and other stressful situations. Sleep and relaxation are doubly important on the last day before the race. I convince myself to be confident about the race because I have prepared correctly. It is important not to procrastinate about final preparations. I pack all my race equipment well in advance, making a checklist to avoid omissions. I always bring along some extra equipment and clothing in case I need it.

On the day of the race I warm up and stretch before the event. I make sure not to go into the competition upset or on edge. I stay close to the other cyclists in order to get to know the competition.

THE DIRTY TRICKS DIVISION

One last issue: bicycle racing has an image as a somewhat cutthroat sport. In part that image is well-earned, although I like to differentiate carefully among legitimate strategy, cute tricks, and foul play.

In a road race, when a breakaway cyclist's teammates get in front of the pack to block the road and widen the lead, that's legitimate strategy. That's part of the game; it's up to the other cyclists to get around and catch the break if they can.

In the Tour of Coconut Grove a few years back, a well-known sprinter caught up with us in the lead pack and told us he had just been lapped—fallen a whole lap behind the leaders. The course had many turns, and it was raining, and we had lapped numerous riders, so it was easy to lose track. We believed him. Sometimes the rules call for an overtaken rider to drop out; but in any case, a lapped rider is forbidden to take pace from the lead pack. So it seemed a little fishy when he said he was just going to "sit in" with the leaders, but no one said anything. Remember, we were in a race and had our minds on other things. By drafting, this "lapped rider" was able to keep up with us right to the end when he surprised us by suddenly sprinting out in front to win the race. That wheelsucker had made suckers of us. All along, he was fibbing about being lapped. To me his tactic seems like a dirty trick, but it's in the cute category, not the vicious category.

At crucial moments during a race, I have been known to imitate the sound of a tire blowing out. If my competitor is somewhat of a novice, my amateur ventriloquism may distract him just enough to allow me to successfully attack. To my devious mind that dirty trick seems more cute than vicious.

When cyclists intentionally force a competitor to crash or purposely knock over another cyclist, those are vicious—not to mention artless—dirty tricks. In the 1983 Giro, commercial sponsors of one competitor allegedly tried to prevent world champion Giuseppe Saronni from winning by putting strong laxatives in his food. Poisoning someone with laxatives is a vicious, dangerous, dirty trick. It's a deed that justly attracted the interest of the Italian police, whose undercover agent foiled the plot.

Unfortunately, the American press has a tendency to report only the tricky side of competitive cycling. Bicycling is not a first-rank spectator sport in this country so American sport commentators don't report on it much. When they do report on cycling it's because something exceptional or outrageous has happened. Thus, the only bicycle race that the American press covered in the 1968 Mexico City Olympics was the team time trial. They covered that race because a Mexican radical, standing a scant 20 feet from me, blew his own brains out with a revolver. American news organizations reported on the gory, dramatic, sad incident and scarcely gave the results of that or any other bicycle race.

Another, less morbid example comes from the 1983 national championships. Rebecca Twigg won the 57.6-mile senior women's road race by pulling away from Connie Carpenter on a steep hill in the next-to-last lap. According to the local San Diego paper the next day, Twigg's teammate, Cindy Olivarri, had blocked Carpenter on that hill while Twigg made her break. The account made it look like Olivarri had nearly ridden Carpenter off the road, and it went on to report an alleged punching match between the two during the last lap of the race. Both Carpenter and Twigg deny there is any animosity between them other than the natural rivalry of competitors. Carpenter later told reporters that she had just begun to fade at that point in the race and had not been blocked by anyone. In my opinion, the alleged fight and supposed rivalry gave the ill-informed reporter something juicy to write about.

Cycling is neither dirtier nor more corrupt than any other sport. American coverage is merely distorted. It seems basketball and football stars regularly get involved in drug scandals; yet, people know that it is just one aspect of these highly publicized sports. At present, bicycle racing usually is written up by American journalists when something suggests scandal. I hope the increased popularity of American bicycle racing soon will change all that.

10

A Brief Maintenance Manual for the Bicycle Engine

The bicycle is a curious vehicle whose passenger is also its engine. In over 30 years of cycling, I've been inundated by information about the nutritional and physiological factors that determine whether and how comfortably that engine will keep going. I hope I have successfully sifted through that bicycle lore to separate the facts from the myths because in this chapter I present what I know about the engine itself, the fuel that you put into it, and the accidents and mechanical breakdowns it can experience. I also discuss some physiological factors that are specific to women cyclists.

ENGINE SPECIFICATIONS

I'm not a physiologist, and I don't pretend to know everything there is to know about the human body and sports. However, there are some facts about physiology that the cyclist should know and that the average medical doctor may not be able to talk about.

First of all, if you are thinking about competition you have to accept that your potential ability is *largely* determined by heredity. Don't get me wrong; success in competition requires hard training, but genetic endowment sets the limits. Enthusiasm and effort can stretch you to meet your limits, but your max-

214

imum lung and heart capacity, body contour, and muscle characteristics all are inherited determinants of your potential. Regardless of your gene package, though, you still can use training science to make yourself a better cyclist for recreation, exercise, touring, commuting, or club racing. Realistic appraisal of physiological limits and personal preferences should tell you what type of cycling to pursue; you merely need to find the cycling niche where you are most comfortable, and then you will be able to enjoy the sport without frustration.

Ed Burke is a pioneer in cycling physiology. As the assistant to the cycling staff at the U.S. Olympic Training Center at Colorado Springs, he has tested and observed some of America's best bicycle racers to determine the physical characteristics that predict success in competition. He also has systematically studied the training and coaching methods used to develop those characteristics. Burke and Eddie Borysewicz, the national coaching director and former Polish team coach, have used this knowledge to choose the national teams that represent America at the World Championships and the Olympics. Their philosophy is to use the limited resources and training facilities to develop the skills of only those cyclists who show the most promise of becoming world-class bicycle racers. Cyclists who lack those characteristics are encouraged to continue racing, but they are counseled to be realistic about their aspirations. Of course, motivation, competitiveness, raw drive, and other emotional factors determine how well cyclists capitalize on their potential, so not all of Burke's candidates become top cyclists. But Ed's track record is good; he has discovered some outstanding athletes.

What are some specific characteristics that determine success? Among several other things, Burke looks for cyclists with the correct proportions of slow- and fast-twitch muscle fibers for their events; he searches for candidates who have a high maximum VO_2 uptake; and, since the cardiovascular systems of the most successful sprinters differ from those of the most successful endurance riders, Burke also seeks cyclists with the right kind of heart for their particular events.

I will explain the above terms, such as fast-twitch and slow-twitch muscle fiber, but it's not my purpose to help you decide if you should go out for the Olympic cycling squad. This book is for all kinds of cyclists, and everyone should better understand what makes the engine perform the way it does.

The Basics

Our legs push the pedals, but the musculature of the rest of the body holds the torso in place so that leg power is translated primarily into useful movement. The heart, lungs, liver, digestive system, nervous system, and every other major organ and system play a role in making the legs turn the cranks. Failure of any organ or system can disable a bicyclist.

The Neuromuscular System

This system ultimately controls everything that happens on a bicycle. In order to cycle at peak form the nervous and muscular systems must interact with flawless coordination. The nerves release a fuel called adenosine triphosphate (ATP) that stimulates muscle fibers to contract. (Neither muscles nor individual muscle fibers are capable of pushing; they only contract.) Since each fiber relaxes soon after it contracts, it is the sequential firing of individual fibers in a bundle of fibers (the muscle) that produces the sustained effort necessary for a pedal stroke.

Muscles are composed of two types of fibers: fast-twitch and slow-twitch. Fast-twitch fibers, which resemble a turkey's white meat, also are known as white fibers. The fast-twitch fibers obtain their ATP from the phosphoryl creatine and glycogen already in the fiber. Since the fast-twitch fibers can burn their fuel without taking any oxygen from the blood, they are responsible for anaerobic effort. Because an athlete has only a limited number of such fibers, and each fiber has only a limited capacity for fuel storage, anaerobic effort can last only for about five minutes. The body uses fast-twitch fibers for sudden bursts of activity, and sprinters need a high proportion of these fibers to perform well.

The slow-twitch fibers are brown in color; they resemble the turkey's dark meat. These are the fibers that the endurance rider needs in abundance to be successful. The slow-twitch fibers can work for long periods of time because they obtain all their fuel from glucose and fatty acids carried by the blood. Those fibers oxidize (or burn) their fuel, so they also need to obtain oxygen from the blood. The body's aerobic activity is the result of slow-twitch fiber contractions.

All fibers are not strictly divided into the two categories; they often fall in between the two extremes in their aerobic capacity and rate of contraction. Any individual will have some of both types. Supposedly the proportion of fast- and slow-twitch fibers is an inherited trait, with most people having about an equal number of each.

It is believed that long-distance riders may be able to develop some of the aerobic capacity of fast-twitch fibers, and that sprinters can develop fast contractions by slow-twitch fibers. Physiologists believe that a fiber's *type* can never be changed, but that training can alter the aerobic capacity of either type. So the proportion of slow- and fast-twitch fibers will determine your potential for either endurance cycling or sprinting, but training can influence the outcome somewhat.

The human body has energy-storage capacity for about 2,000 calories of glycogen and about 50,000 to 70,000 calories of fat.* Glycogen is a fuel stored in the muscle fibers, ready for immediate use. We obtain our glycogen by eating starchy food (bread, rice, pasta, etc.) and sugars (fruit sugar, refined sugar, etc.). Such foods collectively are known as carbohydrates. Humans vary considerably in their ability to store glycogen, with the male's greater muscle mass being an advantage. Previous activity, training, and conscious storage ploys, such as "carbohydrate loading" (to be discussed later), can influence the amount of glycogen in the muscles at any given time. Remember, the

---

*You may remember from some physics or nutrition class that a calorie is a measure of the amount of heat a fuel can produce. In physics we usually talk about small calories, while in nutrition we talk about large calories or kilocalories. A nutritional Calorie is 1,000 small calories. It is the amount of heat necessary to raise 1,000 grams of water 1° Celsius, measured at sea level. A morsel of food (whose fuel value needs to be determined) or an animal's glycogen or fat deposit is burned in a device called a calorimeter to determine how many calories of heat it can produce.

fast-twitch fibers burn glycogen anaerobically, that is, without oxygen from the blood, to produce fast bursts of activity. Thus, the sprinter rides primarily on glycogen (the body's high-octane fuel) that is obtained from carbohydrates. Since there is usually only about 2,000 calories of glycogen stored in the body, and because oxygen debt and lactic acid build-up occur rapidly, most humans can't keep up anaerobic activity more than five minutes or so.

Aerobic activity is a different story: it is the work of the slow-twitch muscles, which oxidize glucose and fatty acids. The fatty acids, glucose, and oxygen all are taken from the blood by the slow-twitch fibers. The blood first gets the fatty acids and glucose from sugars, fat, and protein that have recently been eaten. When that's mostly gone, the blood also can get fuel by breaking down some of the body's stored fuel—the kind that many of us are embarrassed to have in abundance. The fuel was stored previously as fat deposits in the muscles themselves (intramuscular fat—similar to the marbling in a high-quality beefsteak) and in the more unsightly, lumpy variety as fat deposits between the muscles and skin (subdermal fat—lardlike in appearance). The body is very frugal with the bon-bons and fatty steak dinners we give it; much of what we don't burn today it "banks" for tomorrow as fat deposits. Then, when we want to bicycle longer than the glucose and fatty acids already in the blood will permit, the slow-twitch muscle fibers make withdrawals from our fat deposits. Given enough time, endurance riding can set the skinny person inside of you free from his or her fatty prison.

Humans vary in their ability to store and use the glucose and fatty acids. With a higher percentage of body fat and an ability to endure longer before running out of fuel, women seem to have an advantage over men.

VO₂ Max

The quantity of oxygen that a bicyclist can use in a given period, the oxygen uptake, is called maximum volume of oxygen (or VO_2 max). The VO_2 max determines the athlete's ability to use fat. For the same workload, a cyclist with a higher VO_2 max will produce less lactic acid than a cyclist with a lower VO_2 max. This is because lactic acid is one of the end-products of anaerobic muscle contraction. The muscle ache and fatigue you may have felt during or after exercise are the result of lactic acid building up, when the muscles produce more than can be removed by the lymphatic system. Occurrence of those painful episodes usually sets the limit on how long you can continue to cycle. Obviously then, the cyclist with a high VO_2 max will be able to perform better on an endurance ride or race than the one with a low VO_2 max.

Riding aerobically, or by "fat metabolism," gives you vast reserves of calories and prevents the build-up of lactic acid. Cyclists riding anaerobically depend upon carbohydrate metabolism; they'll soon run out of fuel and simultaneously fatigue their muscles. When I ride a road race, I pace myself so I will use fat reserves most of the race and conserve the carbohydrate/anaerobic metabolism for an all-out sprint during the last miles. One key to successful racing is to raise your anaerobic threshold so you can pedal faster using aerobic metabolism. To do so, you have to follow a balanced training regimen that includes both LSD (long, slow distance) and intervals (alternate sprinting and slow cruising). Now you know the theory behind my recommendation.

The Cardiovascular System

Training probably makes the heart adapt to the kind of riding you do. It also may be that particular bicyclists excel at either endurance or sprinting because of the inherited characteristics of their hearts. In either case, we know that endurance athletes have hearts whose left ventricles have larger-than-average volume, while sprinters have left ventricles that are more muscular than average. Endurance requires that a large amount of blood be available to deliver the necessary oxygen and metabolites to the muscle tissue, but the delivery does not have to occur at a particularly high pressure. On the other hand, sprinters need to get the blood pumped more forcefully because contraction of skeletal muscles constricts blood vessels.

Cyclists and other endurance athletes commonly have a lower resting heart rate than other people. (My own resting pulse is 38 beats per minute, practically not alive!) A conditioned aerobic athlete develops a more efficient pump that works slower than a non-athlete's heart. Aerobic cyclists also have greater-than-average total blood volume and a higher percentage of hemoglobin in the blood. Both those adaptations make sense to me because the hemoglobin carries the oxygen you need for aerobic muscle contractions, and it stands to reason that sustained strenuous activity requires more blood to deliver the fuel and oxygen. Interestingly, research shows that the trained cyclist's blood pressure is lower than the untrained cyclist's during a ride, but there is no difference while they are at rest. However, a program of training on the bicycle can somewhat lower the overall blood pressure of a person who has a pre-existing problem with high blood pressure. If you are such a person, be sure to see your physician before embarking on any exercise program.

The Respiratory System

Trained cyclists have bigger lungs than untrained athletes. Yet it appears that lung volume by itself is a poor predictor of athletic performance. The key variable seems to be how well the network of alveoli in the lungs do their job of taking the oxygen out of the lung cavity and putting it into the blood where it joins with hemoglobin to form oxyhemoglobin.

The VO_2 max uptake I spoke of earlier can be improved 15 to 20 percent not only by LSD training but also by over-distance training. Sprinters do over-distance training to prepare for their relatively short races. In over-distance training you practice at distances longer than your event—say 5000-m wind sprints interspersed with 5- to 10-minute rest periods to prepare for a 4000-m pursuit—but you don't take the ponderous 25- to 125-mile rides you would on an LSD program. Both methods increase lung capacity and uptake, but the over-distance training (like other forms of interval training) also conditions the rest of the body. A rider who trains exclusively by LSD won't be prepared for the rigors of the faster race pace.

ABOUT THE FUEL: NUTRITION

At a Los Angeles panel discussion that Julie Leach, Dave Scott, and I gave shortly after the 1982 Ironman Triathlon, a member of the audience asked us what triathletes eat. It was just before lunch, and I was hungry, so I answered that I eat a wide variety of foods, and lots of it. I added that I take vitamin supplements, shy away from red meat, and eat a lot of carbohydrates. Dave Scott, who had repeated an earlier Ironman Triathlon victory a week before the panel discussion, answered that he adheres to a strict vegetarian diet. Julie Leach, who had won the women's division of the 1982 Ironman, answered, "I eat a *see*-food diet: everything I *see*, I eat." Other endurance athletes, like marathon great Bill Rodgers and endurance cyclist Lon Haldeman, are sometimes chided in magazine articles for eating lots of junk food or sticking to a single item, like cheeseburgers. So it seems a wide variety of diets are followed by successful endurance athletes. The common denominator among athletes who engage in aerobic sports is that they burn many calories and they need to replenish them.

How Much Fuel Do You Need?

Using the graph on page 223, you can determine approximately how many calories you burn on a ride. You need to know three things: how much you weigh, how much your bicycle weighs, and how fast you are riding. Note: this graph is only valid for rides on level terrain with no head wind. Throw in hills and winds and the calorie consumption goes up. It's simple to use the graph. Just follow the six steps that accompany it.

How To Use This Graph

1. Add your weight to your bicycle's weight (or just step on a scale while holding your bicycle completely off the ground) to get total "vehicle weight." If you carry anything heavy on the ride be sure to add its weight too. For instance, Erica weighs 120 pounds and her bike weighs 25 pounds, so that brings her vehicle weight up to 145 pounds. On her daily commute to work the other morning Erica carried panniers weighing 15 pounds, which contained her briefcase and a change of clothes, so that makes her *total* vehicle weight 160 pounds.

2. Next compute your average speed for the trip in miles per hour by the most convenient method available. If you own a digital bicycle speedometer, such as the Coach, it should have a function for average speed. If not, merely determine your distance and elapsed travel time as best you can, and divide the distance in miles by the time in hours. For example, Erica knows that she lives almost exactly 5.1 miles from her office. The other morning she made her commute to work in 17 minutes. Seventeen divided by 60 equals 0.283 hours. Then she divided 5.1 miles by 0.283 hours and got 18 mph. Not bad speed!

3. Next sight along the horizontal axis of the graph until you find your average speed.

4. From that point sight a line vertically up the graph until it crosses the curve that corresponds to your total vehicle weight.

5. Then sight across horizontally and read the number of calories you burn per hour on the scale of the vertical axis.

For example, Erica did steps 3, 4, and 5; so, with her speed of 18 mph and her total vehicle weight of 160 pounds, Erica burned 500 calories per hour on her trip to work.

To find out how many calories of fuel you burn on a given bike ride, multiply the number of calories per hour obtained from this table by the number of hours you cycled. Erica multiplied 500 calories per hour by 0.283 hours and found that she burned 142 calories.

One more thing about using this graph: you may have noticed that your total vehicle weight is not the same as any of the weight curves drawn on the figure. Look again at the graph: If Erica's total vehicle weight had been as much as 60 pounds greater her calories per hour would have gone up by only 50. Likewise a crash diet and loss of 60 pounds would decrease her fuel consumption by only 50 calories per hour. So, if your total vehicle weight is between the curves available on the graph, you still can estimate the difference between the numbers for the curves above and below where your weight falls.

From the graph you can also see that increases in speed affect your calorie consumption much more than increasing the weight of the vehicle. That's why streamlining is so much more important than buying a super-light bicycle if you want to work less while riding.

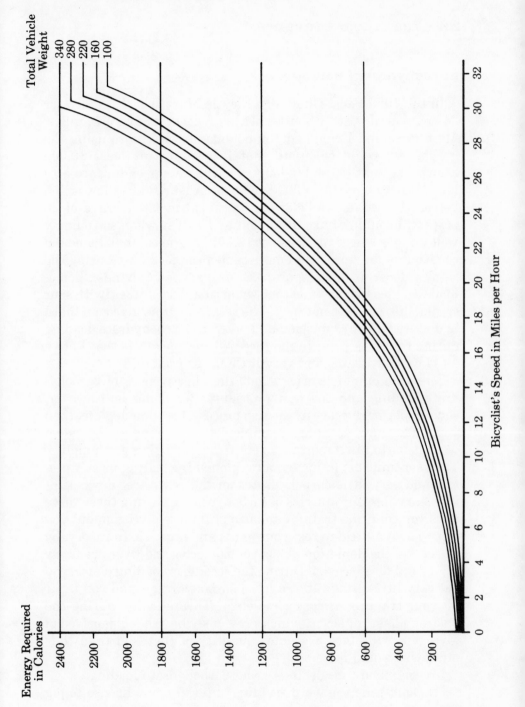

Total Vehicle
Weight

340
280
220
160
100

Energy Required
in Calories

Bicyclist's Speed in Miles per Hour

223

Carbohydrate Loading

In the 1983 Pepsi Challenge Bicycle Marathon, I pedaled for 24 hours at almost 21.5 miles per hour, covering over 514 miles. My bicycle and I weighed 180 pounds altogether, so using the graph, you could calculate that I consumed at least 19,000 calories on that little day-long ride. Like other endurance athletes, I carry very little fat. I've been measured at as low as 3.5 percent body fat, far below the national men's average of 20 percent. I couldn't burn all my fat and still survive, so you may well wonder where my legs got 19,000 calories of fuel. Some did come out of fat stores, and more came from food I ate during the rainy ride: fruit (apples, oranges, grapes, and bananas), homemade cookies (whole wheat, no sugar), baked potatoes (with sour cream), hot tea, and hot soup. The rest came from glycogen that I had stored in my muscles and liver by carbohydrate loading during the week prior to the race. All that means is that I ate a lot of carbohydrates and very little fat or protein.

Scientific opinion varies about the effectiveness of carbohydrate loading and the best procedures for doing it. However, some experts advocate a two-step process: first you deplete, then you load. They recommend you deplete by taking a long ride a week prior to the important event to burn off glycogen supplies. Then continue depletion by not replenishing, eating mostly protein and very little carbohydrates for the next three days, actually starving your muscles of carbohydrates. During those three days you continue training to burn still more glycogen, but you taper down a little to rest your joints and muscles. In theory, by the end of the depletion phase your muscles and liver are fairly crying out for glycogen. During the second, or loading phase, you eat very little protein but a lot of carbohydrates, and you taper off your training almost completely. Theoretically, during the loading phase, muscles, which previously have been deprived of glycogen, will store a greater quantity of that fuel than they otherwise would have.

I recommend three things about carbohydrate loading:

(1) Don't take the word "loading" literally as a license to pig

out. Carbohydrate-loaded muscles are measurably larger than non-loaded muscles, and you don't want to carry too much extra weight on your long ride.

(2) Don't carbohydrate load for any exertion that will burn fewer than 2000 calories. From my graph that would mean a 190-pound bicyclist on a 30-pound bicycle would have to ride for three hours at 20 mph before carbohydrate loading is worthwhile. That's 60 miles at race pace.

(3) Alter the proportions of carbohydrates and protein during the two phases, but don't totally abstain from either. It's damaging and fatiguing to your body to forego *all* carbohydrates during the depletion phase. Doing so can cause a nutritional ailment known as ketosis, which will be evident from flatulence, body odor, and the presence of ketones in your urine. (Most pharmacists can sell you test strips for detecting these ketones.) Likewise, your body needs protein for tissue repair during the loading phase. I do take depletion rides and continue my training during the depletion phase, but I don't usually lower my carbohydrate intake at all during that phase. I continue a balanced diet that includes both carbohydrates and protein. I figure that at my level of training my body is constantly deprived of carbohydrates anyway. Why add insult to injury? During the last three days I just raise the proportion of carbohydrates and rest up for the event by decreasing my training. No matter what advice I give, you'll probably have to do what I did long ago: experiment and see what works best for you regarding carbohydrate loading.

Weight Reduction

Overweight bicyclists are seen more often than overweight runners. The calories-burned graph partially explains this. If you look at the speeds below 10 mph, you'll notice that no matter how much weight you are carrying, you burn relatively few calories, fewer than 250 per hour. That's less than you'd get by eating a few donuts to reward yourself for your bike ride. If you get going fast enough, air resistance comes into play, so the number of calories burned rises rapidly.

According to Jim Fixx, running burns up 800–1000 calories per hour, the equivalent of going over 20 mph for a 190-pound rider. That's pretty fast going for most people! What's more, slow runners use up almost as much energy as fast runners, but the disparity between slow and fast cyclists is huge. The reason is rather complicated, but it boils down to the fact that high-speed bicyclists are proportionately more hampered by air resistance than are fast runners.

In spite of all this I still advocate cycling as a fitness activity, even in preference to running, since runners greatly stress their joints, muscles, and tendons. Besides, you can always learn to bicycle faster. I should also point out that the bicycle calorie-consumption estimates on my chart are conservative, because the assumed riding conditions (still air and no hills) rarely exist.

Most important, cycling, like running, elevates your heart rate to give you aerobic exercise. It is now widely believed that training generally elevates the metabolism of aerobic athletes so they burn more calories per hour even when not exercising—even when they sleep—than do non-athletes. Therefore, the number of calories you burn directly by exercising is less important than achieving an athlete's metabolic rate. Imagine that; you will be able to trim down while sitting and reading this book! Just be sure to exercise aerobically at *least* four days per week.

I want to recommend two books: Covert Bailey's *Fit or Fat* and Peter Wood's *California Diet and Exercise Program.* Both of those books assert that dieting won't help you decrease your body's fat deposits. Wood makes the startling claim that you should eat *more* to lose fat. Notice I have written, "lose *fat,*" not "lose weight." The objective is to maintain or increase muscle mass while using up fat deposits. Both of these books advocate a fitness lifestyle that includes aerobic exercise and a balanced, nutritious diet. I wish to add my voice to theirs.

What Kind of Fuel

The men and women I know who practice endurance sports provide evidence that the most sound nutritional principle is to eat a varied, balanced diet that always includes a lot of carbohydrates (other than refined sugar), protein (mostly from sources other than red meat), raw fruit and vegetables, and fluids to replenish those lost in exercise. Less than two decades ago nutritionists recommended high-protein diets for athletes, but now research suggests that athletes stay healthier and perform better if they eat more carbohydrates than protein and very little fat. I know I am peppier on a carbohydrate diet than a protein diet. Your body first has to break down fats and protein in order for the muscle fibers to get the glycogen they need. To the consternation of many, the body very efficiently turns excess fuel into fat stores, so you don't need to help this along by eating a lot of animal fat. You do need protein for general body maintenance, muscle building, and repair of tissues strained by exercise. However, I feel lethargic the day after the rare occasions when I eat a lot of red meat. Cereal grains, beans, and soybeans are probably better protein sources than meat because they don't have the saturated fat and cholesterol, two substances suspected of causing heart disease and cancer.

Plain old beans and rice, which together have lots of carbohydrates and safe protein, may provide a better basis for nutrition than any other diet. This is especially true if you add tomatoes or citrus fruit for vitamin C, leafy vegetables for roughage, and other fresh fruit and vegetables. Such a diet is even high in fiber content and therefore may help prevent diverticulitis and cancer of the colon.

Fuel Additives: The Racer's Edge?

Like many other people, I take vitamin supplements to make sure I get enough vitamin B_{12}. This is one of the few essential nutrients supplied almost solely by meat. I can't hope to treat the topic adequately here. I only can recommend you learn what you are doing from reputable sources before you radically alter your vitamin intake. Be especially careful about taking massive doses of vitamins. While taking too many of some vitamins merely will cause you to excrete your investment, other vitamins, such as A and D, are fat-soluble and may become toxic as they build up in body tissues over the years. It just may be that cravings for particular foods are requests from your body to obtain naturally the vitamins it lacks. The large quantities of varied food I eat to fuel my training efforts make it highly probable that I will get most of the vitamins and minerals my body requires, even without supplements.

What about the legal and illegal "secret" fuel additives advocated by some? Invariably, the topic of drugs comes up in discussions of athletic nutrition. Other than an occasional beer when I'm relaxing or socializing late in the day, I abstain from most drugs except aspirin to reduce swelling in my poor battered knees. I do use a little caffeine as a mild stimulant to get the adrenaline going before a race or training session. (With cream and no sugar, please.) The long-range effects of most drugs, such as steroids for muscle building and stimulants for immediate performance, are much too devastating to justify their use by athletes or anyone else. For the most part, I feel drugs are for sick people; they certainly won't help athletic performance. Tobacco use, which reduces oxygen capacity by as much as 33 percent and causes cancer, is so far out of the question for athletes (or anybody else, for that matter) as to be unworthy of any further comment.

To summarize, bicycle more and faster, eat more, eat better, take vitamins cautiously, avoid almost all drugs, and you will lose fat and live a healthier life.

ENGINE REPAIR: ACCIDENTS AND OTHER BREAKDOWNS

Stalin is reputed to have said, "You can't make an omelette without breaking some eggs." Uncle Joe's aphorism may or may not be sufficient justification for violent revolution and upheaval, but it is apropos of bicycling. I know some things about bicycling injuries because I have experienced many of them. If you ride as much as I do, you can't avoid them entirely; injuries are just part of the game. Although cycling is a gentle form of exercise, you need to know how to avoid injuries as much as possible, and how to care for them when they are unavoidable.

Broken This and Broken That

The most serious ailment suffered by bicyclists is an occasional bad case of *autosquashedunder*. This condition is to be avoided at all costs. Among others, telltale symptoms are: broken collarbones, arms, legs, ribs, and skulls; perforated organs; abrasions; cosmetic trauma; and (with distressing regularity) death. Other non-automobile-caused encounters with the pavement result in similar symptoms, with injuries to the collarbone, skull, wrist, and hamate (the bone under the fleshy part of the palm) being particularly frequent consequences. Wearing a helmet can save the rider's life, and wearing padded cycling gloves can mitigate hand injuries. Also, practicing how to fall, as do parachutists, high-jumpers, and acrobats, might be a good injury-prevention measure for cyclists. (When falling, tuck your head, protecting it with your arms as you roll away from the bicycle.)

As far as treatment is concerned, immediate, life-saving first aid is essential at the scene of the accident, and the rest needs to be left to competent medical personnel.

Contact the American Red Cross to enroll in a first aid course so you will know what to do to help yourself or a fellow bicyclist after an accident. Basic first-aid measures are as follows. First make sure the victim is breathing. If not, perform cardiopulmonary resuscitation and mouth-to-mouth artificial respiration. Then stop any bleeding, using pressure and a clean cloth to stanch the flow. Step three is to treat for shock by reassuring the victim and keeping him or her warm and comfortable, with feet elevated if possible. Never move victims with neck or back injuries unless they are in imminent danger where they are. Inspect for further injuries and keep victims who can't move to shelter as warm, dry, and comfortable as possible until the doctor arrives. It's also a good idea for bicyclists to have up-to-date (within the past 5 years) tetanus immunization.

Rubbing

Skin irritations caused by friction with the bicycle seat can be avoided almost entirely. Wear clean, properly fitting cycling shorts and you probably will not be bothered by any irritation in the seat or legs. If you are a triathlete and have just swum in salt water, be sure to rinse off before hopping on the bicycle.

Cyclists sometimes confuse a case of "jock itch" (tinea cruris) with chafing. The rubbing may be a complicating factor. If you simultaneously are suffering from "athlete's foot" (tinea pedis), that is a good sign that you have been attacked by a bona fide fungus rather than just experiencing some irritation due to rubbing. The fungi that cause jock itch, athlete's foot, and so-called "ring worm" are, contrary to popular belief, not "caught" by walking barefoot in the locker room, but almost always are present on our skin. During hot, humid weather the little devils get active in dark sweaty areas on the skin of susceptible people. I'm lucky—my skin doesn't seem to be a good home for fungus. However, I know one bicyclist who predictably in June gets jock itch, athlete's foot, and an embarrassing line of ringworm on his face that perfectly traces the edge of his helmet. Fortunately, there are over-the-counter fungicides that hold the fungus in check when applied at least daily after washing and drying the affected area. (Tinactin is one brand that comes as both ointment and drops.) Of course, if the itching persists or worsens, you should see a physician.

Pressure

Pressure due to the force of gravity causes two other major types of physical ailment for bicyclists: butt aches and nerve problems in the hands.

In one sense the aching backside problem gets worse as you get more fit; you have simply lost a lot of your padding. In another sense, the problem is alleviated as you build muscles in your thighs, back, arms, and shoulders to take the weight off your rear end. Getting out of the saddle occasionally to climb hills, riding on varied terrain, and putting some of the weight on your arms and legs all help protect your derriere.

You can also help reduce this kind of problem by riding on the saddle proper for your anatomy. Another part of the cure is tolerating the pain until both you and your saddle are broken in. I would be devastated if I lost the two Brooks saddles I've used for the past 13 years. If it's any comfort, most good cyclists experience saddle soreness early in their riding careers, but rarely after they have become proficient.

Circulatory and nerve problems in the hand result from riding long hours with your weight shifted forward to give your behind a break. During the 1982 Great American Bike Race I rode 22 hours a day for 10½ days, and I became a victim of what doctors call carpal tunnel syndrome: the radial and ulnar nerves are damaged by putting prolonged pressure on your hands' blood vessels. For at least six months after the GABR I had numbness and tingling sensations in my fingers, and dexterity problems so severe that I had difficulty working keys in a lock with one hand. The problem largely disappeared as nerves regenerated, and I regained most of the sensation in my hands. As is common with this ailment, some of my damage is permanent, but most function has returned. The majority of cyclists won't experience this problem; unless you go on very long bicycle tours, or regularly ride for more than 10 or 12 hours at a stretch, you don't have to worry about damaging the nerves in your hands.

Muscle Soreness

Training pains or muscle soreness are to be expected if your muscles are unaccustomed to exercise. In particular, cycling works your quadriceps (thigh muscles) more than almost any other activity, with the possible exceptions of mountain climbing, cross-country skiing, and uphill running. Bicycling can also make the muscles in your back, neck, shoulders, arms, and calves sore.

The best way to treat this malady is by breaking your body in gradually. Don't make your first ride a trek the length of your state. You'll just injure your muscles before you can strengthen them for the challenge. You'll be laid up for weeks and feel so punished by the pain that you probably will abandon cycling altogether. Progressively increase the stress on your muscles over many rides and they will respond by becoming stronger. Learn to recognize benign, mild training pain and let it be a guide for deciding when you're ready to try something more. Allow yourself an occasional day off or a day of leisurely riding to permit your muscles to recover and rebuild.

Tears and Pulls

Bicyclists' legs take quite a beating, although not as much as a distance runner's. They suffer a variety of pulls and tears, aches, and pains. Three injuries to look for are Achilles tendinitis, pulled hamstring, and sciatica. If you are suffering from either of the first two, you can usually take care of yourself. But if you are the victim of sciatica you'll need the help of a physician to get better. Thus, it's useful to know how to diagnose these ailments so you can decide whether to go to the doctor.

Sciatica is an inflammation of one of the two sciatic nerves, the longest nerves in the body. These nerves run from your lower back to your toes, and they can be irritated by rubbing against a vertebral disk or a joint. In an excellent book called *The Runner's Repair Manual,* Dr. Murray Weisenfeld recommends a simple test that runners can use to detect whether their leg pain is sciatica. Your body doesn't know whether it was hurt by running or cycling, so I can heartily recommend both Weisenfeld's book and his two-part diagnostic procedure: (1) If your pain is on the exterior side of your thigh and is accompanied by hip or lower back pain, then according to Weisenfeld there's a good chance you have sciatica rather than a pull. (2) Lie on your back, raise one leg with knee unbent, and have someone push your toes toward your shin while supporting the leg. Repeat this test with the other leg. If, during the test, you feel strong pain or a burning sensation down the back of either leg, in the buttocks or in the lower back, proceed directly to your doctor without passing GO and without collecting $200—you probably have sciatica. Don't go there by bike, either. In fact, stop cycling until your doctor tells you that you can resume that activity.

Achilles tendinitis is an inflammation of the tendon that attaches the heel to the calf muscle. If you experience pain anywhere between the calf and the foot, the tendon may be rubbing against the sheath within which it moves. A hamstring pull makes your thigh hurt and is often the result of not warming up sufficiently before riding in cold weather.

If your problem is Achilles tendinitis, you'll need to lay off cycling for a few days. Relieve the swelling by icing the injury and taking aspirin or acetaminophen. To ice an injury, use a plastic bag filled with ice cubes, or some moist towels that you put in the freezer. Both the icing and the aspirin will relieve the pain, but don't resume riding before you heal. In particular, don't risk masking the pain warnings by taking aspirin during a ride.

Once you have recovered from your tendinitis, get in the habit of stretching before and after riding. Probably the problem was caused by exercise shortening the calf muscle. To stretch this muscle, push against a wall with one leg thrust back straight and the other leg bent at the knee. Gradually and smoothly push down on your rear heel as you continue to press against the wall. Repeat by switching legs, bending the one knee and straightening the opposite leg. Stretch a lot and often. It's hard to overdo it when it comes to stretching.

I've been told it's all right to continue riding with the pulled hamstring (strengthening that muscle will help), but only in the easier gears. Again, icing and aspirin help, but don't take the aspirin before a ride. Exercises to strengthen your leg muscles, including moderate use of either a Nautilus machine or a Universal gym, are good preventive measures. Stretching before and after cycling is not only helpful to prevent the injury, but, in this case, sometimes is prescribed by doctors as part of the treatment. Of course, see a doctor if your problems persist.

Bicyclist's Knee

Some orthopedists consider the knee to be the worst designed joint in the human body. Cyclists, among other athletes (most notably football players, basketball players, and runners), are plagued by bad service from this joint, and it comes with no warranty. Chondromalacia of the patella, literally the softening of the cartilage of the kneecap, is the medical name for bicyclist's knee. It can hurt like the dickens. I know because I suffer from this one myself.

Basically, the cause of chondromalacia is failure of the four muscles that comprise the quadriceps to hold the kneecap straight. The rubbing that results from twisting irritates the kneecap. Therefore, strengthening your quadriceps will help prevent this ailment. Cycling itself should strengthen the quads, and off the bike you can exercise your quadriceps by doing leg lifts, with your knees unbent, while standing with your back against the wall—sort of a stationary goose-step. Cycling up hills in too high a gear contributes to chondromalacia, because as you strain your quadriceps they can't hold the kneecap in the correct position. Cold-weather cycling also poses a special hazard to the cyclist's knees, because cold synovial fluid does not properly do its job of lubricating the joint surfaces. Thus, you can protect your kneecaps from damage by doing four things: (1) ride in gears that don't strain your quadriceps; (2) strengthen your quadriceps; (3) ride with toe clips and cleats to keep your legs planted squarely on the pedals; and (4) keep your knees warm by wearing leggings or leg warmers when the air is cold.

If your knees already hurt, lay off cycling for a few days, icing them at least daily and taking aspirin to reduce the swelling. When you resume cycling, follow my preventive advice, in particular changing your gearing habits to avoid future strain, and exercising the quadriceps to make them more effective at guiding the kneecap. If the pain persists see a doctor, but be sure to get a second opinion if the doctor suggests surgical removal of cartilage. You need that cartilage for cushioning, and today most doctors prefer that you keep it.

Sick in the Saddle

Many noncycling-related ailments are aggravated by riding. For instance, few experiences could be more unpleasant than trying to ride while you have some sort of intestinal or digestive illness. More than discomfort is involved here; first-rate athletes have killed themselves (mostly due to heart attacks) by doing even a lighter-than-normal workout with a fever. Add to that risk the fact that illness and fever adversely affect your reactions, judgment, and dexterity. Bicycling in traffic under those circumstances is virtual suicide. When I'm ill I take a rest from the bicycle, treating what ails me and seeing a doctor if my illness merits professional attention. I recuperate and live to ride another day.

Exposure to the Environment

Bicyclists are vulnerable to the atmospheric conditions that prevail where they are riding. Hot weather threatens the rider with sunburn, heat exhaustion, dehydration, and eye damage from glare. Cold weather brings with it the risk of frostbite, chapped lips, knee damage, hypothermia (excessive loss of body heat), and even a chronic runny nose. In all kinds of weather rapidly moving cyclists can get insects or other airborne debris in their eyes, ears, noses, or mouths. In traffic the cyclist is always getting a snoot full of such auto exhausts as poisonous carbon monoxide gas. At very high altitudes, bike riders have to watch out for the headaches and light-headed discomforts of hypoxia (oxygen deprivation). And when smog is bad, cyclists are particularly affected because they are using more air than the sedentary victim.

This almost sounds like a litany of "ain't life awful." Well, before you permanently hang up your bicycle, don a gas mask, and crawl into your hermetically sealed fallout shelter, keep in mind that you can do many things to protect yourself from these environmental hazards. Admittedly there are some things, like smog and blizzards, that you can't avoid or escape. But you can take sensible precautions and simultaneously decrease your level of exertion as a way to handle many atmospheric conditions.

In the winter you can dress warmly, adding or subtracting layers of clothing to maintain correct body temperature. Awareness of your body and a healthy respect for prevailing conditions will tell you when to seek shelter before you experience teeth-chattering, bone-chilling hypothermia. Chapped lips can be prevented by wearing a lip wax, and runny noses are avoided by covering exposed areas of your face with scarves and ski masks. Warm gloves and ski masks are essential, in fact, for fighting the wind-chill factor and avoiding frostbite.

In warmer seasons, carry extra bottles of water, wear protective, light-colored clothing, apply sunscreen ointments, wear a hat with a visor underneath a ventilated helmet, and wear dark sunglasses to fight the ravages of the sun. It is particularly important to combat dehydration by drinking water and other fluids *before* you get thirsty. If you wear goggles or sunglasses, you will probably be able to avoid catching insects and debris with your eyes. If you do get something in your eye, the natural tendency to tear in those circumstances should help, but a good squirt from your water bottle will wash out most objects. Whatever you do, don't rub it. If your efforts to clean your eyes fail, you may need help from either your cycling partners or a physician if there is a risk of scratching the eye.

Beast Bites Cyclist

If you follow the earlier advice about coping with dogs, you probably won't ever be bitten. But if any animal bites you, you must give the matter prompt attention. Rabies is always a risk. In order to avoid a painful series of shots in the stomach, try to have the animal examined, preferably alive and with as little damage to its head as possible. Healthy wild animals usually flee unless they are cornered, so you'll especially want the rabies issue investigated if ever you are bitten by a wild critter. Poisonous snake bites also require prompt medical attention.

Some people have a known allergic sensitivity to bee stings, and occasionally such allergic shocks are fatal. If you are allergic to bee stings you should consider carrying prescribed antivenom with you when you cycle farther than a leisurely 20 minutes ride from medical assistance. In cases of bee-sting allergy or poisonous snake bites, you shouldn't try sprinting for help; the elevated heart rate will only accelerate the reaction.

Looniness of the Long-Distance Cyclist

Crossing the United States in the 1982 Great American Bike Race damaged my hearing somewhat. Hours and days of having enormous 18-wheelers and other loud vehicles pass a few feet from my ears had to take its toll. In my opinion the GABR should be turned into a stage race, because it's too dangerous the way it is now. For instance, Michael Shermer, one of the GABR competitors, dozed momentarily on his bicycle and fell on a guard rail, trashing his bike and slightly injuring himself. He could just as easily have fallen into traffic.

Along with such physical effects, I believe that ultra-distance riding subjects cyclists to psychological stress. I have experienced those effects myself. But, I hasten to add that after my long rides I make a rapid and complete recovery. Nothing's wrong with me! . . . with me! . . . with me! . . . with me! . . . with me! #$&*#%&!!

All fooling aside, during the GABR I experienced powerful hallucinations that doubtless were caused by lack of sleep and by physical exhaustion. In my mind, the cracks in the pavement turned into Egyptian hieroglyphics. In the desert, I repeatedly saw an imaginary man on a horse at the side of the road. Some of the hallucinations were frightening: at one point, the road and sky ahead of me seemed to be pressing together to squeeze the life out of me. Some were merely frustrating: when I was hungry and exhausted, my girlfriend Sandy appeared in a flowing white gown at the side of the road holding out food; but, when I reached out for it, it vanished, and she along with it. I repeatedly saw visions of a black dog, a retriever I know, age and then turn into a pile of dusty bones. I rode on the ragged edge between sanity and the frighteningly irrational void, though eventually I was able to come back to the "real world." But I would caution anybody who wants to try ultra-distance cycling to be prepared for some psychological toil.

There is one more psychological trap to endurance riding: I call it "road craziness." Delusions that you can ride forever, or that you are invincible to traffic, or that you are actually part of the highway are symptoms of road craziness. Motorists as well as cyclists can become victims of this malady. Long-distance truck drivers compound the hazards of this ailment when they fry their brains with "speed" to keep going.

I believe that a case of road craziness develops in two stages. The first stage occurs when the victim literally becomes hypnotized by the monotonous and seemingly endless repetition of the same stimuli and scenery on a highway or interstate. Victims who survive the hypnosis without running off the road or having some other accident enter a euphoric stage in which they believe they can go forever. Ultra-distance cyclists, who are exerting themselves considerably, can drive themselves past exhaustion when they are in this second stage. For instance, instead of stopping at dusk at a perfectly good campground, a bicycle tourist suffering stage-two road craziness might press on 40 miles to the next town or campsite. Road-crazy cyclists make errors in judgment about stopping, about their own physical condition, about food and water supplies, and about the mechanical condition of their bicycles. Cycling over a period of days, with inadequate rest between the days, compounds stage-two road craziness into an advanced case.

Like the hallucinations I mentioned earlier, road craziness is, I believe, the result of irrational mental interpretations of real stimuli. In the case of the hallucinations, cracks in the road became hieroglyphs, hunger became a mirage involving emotional and nutritional support, etc. As for the road craziness experienced by ultra-distance cyclists, the real stimulus is the indisputable fact that they are doing something remarkable. If I really can ride my bike from Phoenix to St. Louis in just a few days, I'm superman, and I may as well just keep on going until I drop.

My theory is that the less experience cyclists have with ultra-distance riding, the more likely they will fall victim to road craziness. It would seem then that a good defense against this road hazard is the knowledge that it exists. Cyclists who are aware of the danger are able to consciously be more conservative about how far they will push themselves. A second defense against this psychological trap is the buddy system. There is a low probability that two cyclists simultaneously will be driven nuts by the road.

FEMALE CYCLISTS

Most of my readers are probably aware that public attitudes and scientific opinion about female athletics have altered radically in the past few decades. Popular opinion and the male-dominated athletic establishment prevented women from competing in endurance events for decades. It was not until the late 1960's that Katharine Switzer first broke the sex barrier in long-distance running by crashing the previously all-male Boston Marathon. The race director tried to prevent her from running by tackling her, and it took almost 15 years before women were "allowed" to run that distance in the Olympics. In bicycle competition, the USCF's Women's Road Championships are still much shorter than the men's. The rationale for excluding women from endurance events was an erroneous belief that female bodies could not withstand the stress. Ironically, recent evidence suggests females endure better than males.

In recent years Title IX of the U.S. Civil Rights Act has been interpreted by Federal courts to mean that schools receiving Federal aid must spend the same amount of money on female as on male athletic programs. While some big-time academic football and basketball coaches bitterly oppose the equitable distribution of funds, most Americans have realized that previous discrimination against women was based on prevalent misconceptions about women, rather than on any real need to protect an inherently less durable form of human. Still, men and women are physiologically different from each other; hence, a female bicycle engine has different characteristics and needs slightly different care and maintenance than a male.

Female Advantages for Cycling

Mother Nature seems to have given her daughters a few advantages over her sons for bicycle performance. I already have explained that differences in the ability to store and use fat probably favor women for long-distance riding, although it may handicap them for sprints.

Female cyclists are blessed with a higher concentration of muscle mass in the lower extremities than their male counterparts. The strong muscles in the arms and upper body of a male cyclist are mostly ballast that contributes little to propelling the bicycle. What is more, the distribution of muscle mass gives the female cyclist a lower center of gravity than the male, and that makes her more stable on the machine.

Female cyclists have at least two other advantages over males. Women are smaller overall than men and thus are hampered less by air resistance. Since they may age slower and lose their aerobic capacity more slowly than males, some women may only have to wait a sufficient number of years in order to be able to leave their male cycling companions in the dust.

Benefits to Women

Laboratory research and coronary statistics both suggest that women generally have lower cholesterol levels and less risk of developing heart disease than men. After menopause, however, this advantage diminishes. Over the age of 50, the incidence of heart problems in women is greater, and the benefits of aerobic exercise become even more desirable. Also, after menopause women's bones tend to become brittle; again, frequent exercise is thought to be beneficial because it retards that degeneration.

Menstruation and Pregnancy

Most of the difficulties mentioned earlier in this chapter apply equally to bikies of either sex. In addition to the problems common to all cyclists there are a few unique difficulties which are suffered only by the women.

Specifically, performance of women on the bicycle can be adversely affected by menstruation and pregnancy. Medical authorities generally believe that the athletic efforts of women are hampered by menstruation. Some physicians (primarily male doctors) have gone so far as to suggest that women avoid exercise entirely during their period. My own informal discussions find female bicyclists divided on this issue. A few women say that exercising during menstruation is very uncomfortable. On the other hand, others say that not only is bicycling comfortable during that time, but exercise seems to diminish cramps and other pains associated with menstruating. Being neither a woman nor a physiologist, I'm hardly an expert on this topic, so I would suggest that women do what their own comfort and available medical advice seem to dictate.

Much the same can be said about cycling during pregnancy. Again medical opinions seem to vary. If examples make any difference in your choices, I can report that in 1973 Jeanne Omelenchuk finished among the top 10 in the Women's National Road Race while five months pregnant. Likewise, Audrey McElmury, who won the 1969 Women's World Championships, continued her training until the day before she gave birth, and then she resumed bicycling within a few days of delivery. Of course, you should listen to advice from your own doctor and heed your own feelings rather than follow anybody else's example.

For any number of reasons a doctor may prescribe that you not bicycle during pregnancy; although, in recent years, it seems that doctors often tell their pregnant patients that it is not only safe but probably beneficial during gestation to continue exercise programs begun earlier. Conversely, doctors discourage beginning any new physical activity during pregnancy. If you are unaccustomed to exercise, that new stress could be harmful while carrying a child.

Attacks Against Women

While cyclists of either gender can fall victim to foul play, women are far more vulnerable to attack than men. The high incidence of rape and other violent crimes against women is a scandalous blemish on our culture. What can a cyclist do to defend herself?

The first line of defense is to avoid attack. While a woman's rights and freedom are violated by the fact that she can't safely go everywhere men can, in this instance discretion seems to be the best idea. Women should avoid routinely riding alone through dangerous locales, such as deserted neighborhoods in urban areas. Women can avoid attacks while bicycling by using the buddy system. Cycle with friends, male or female.

The second line of defense is to keep moving. Limit your stops to well-lit and safe areas. Traffic permitting, move to the inner lane if anybody on the sidewalk looks threatening. On your bicycle you can outdistance most pedestrians and outmaneuver most motorists. If the threat comes from an automobile you may do better by dismounting, since you are more stable off the bicycle. If you can do so without being hit, stay in the road to avoid being cornered and jump back on the bicycle and take off when a potential assailant leaves an auto.

Your third line of defense is to be as self-sufficient as possible. Carry critical tools, a pump and a spare tube or patch kit, and learn how to quickly and efficiently make roadside repairs so you are not a sitting duck. Make sure your bike is mechanically sound so that breakdowns are unlikely. Tape some money under your saddle so that you can take a cab in an emergency, and carry a few coins to phone a friend or family member for assistance. Don't be bashful about asking your cycling companions to stay with you if you have a mechanical breakdown. Hitchhiking is illegal in many states; it is dangerous for men and even more so for women. If your cycling companion is male, borrow a spare tire or wheel from him and let him do the hitchhiking if necessary. If it comes down to it, ride home on a flat tire and risk ruining a rim. That's preferable to risking injury to your person by hitchhiking.

Experts on rape defense advise against carrying firearms, knives, and other weapons. Like as not your weapon would be used by the attacker against you. Also, fumbling for a weapon on a moving bicycle would destabilize you sufficiently to cause a fall, which would increase your vulnerability. Irritant aerosols such as mace may well end up in your own face in a struggle, and they are impossible to aim in the artificial wind experienced by a rapidly moving bicyclist. However, experts generally recommend that victims of an attack try to escape, to resist, and to obtain help by shouting out.

In summary, women cyclists should avoid attacks by not cycling alone in dangerous areas, should keep moving when attack seems possible, should be self-sufficient, should try to escape or resist attack, and should cry out for help.

SO WHO CARES?

After reading all the information in this chapter you may now be asking, "What difference does it make?" Does it matter what makes the muscles work, or what diet is best? Is it important to know how to deal with injuries? Are the special concerns of female cyclists worthy of discussion? I emphatically say "Yes!" to all those questions. Unlike any other propulsion system, the bicycle engine can be self-regulating, it can give itself a tune-up, and it can learn to operate better. It is hoped this chapter provides enough information so any rider can make the bicycle engine work correctly.

11

A Thumbnail History of the Bicycle: From the Boneshaker to the Gossamer Albatross

The bicycle has played an important role in shaping our civilization, our technology, and our lives. I have difficulty imagining a world without bicycles, yet the modern bike was invented only about a century ago when in 1885 John Kemp Starley built the Rover Safety Cycle. But I'm getting way ahead of myself. First there were hobby horses, then the high-wheel ordinary (also known as the penny farthing), and eventually the safety bicycle. The key ingredient of this development was the discovery of increasingly more efficient ways to harness human power for locomotion.

THE HUMBLE HOBBY HORSE

The earliest form of bicycle was invented between 1816 and 1818 by a German, the Baron von Drais de Sauerbrun of Baden-Wurtemberg, the keeper of the forests of the Grand Duke of Baden. In France, where his invention was soon adopted, the machine was known as a draisienne, in honor of its inventor. The English, never satisfied with the French way, adopted the draisienne but renamed it the hobby horse or dandy horse. In the 1800's use of the hobby horse was quite the rage among

244

The hobby horse or dandy horse. Also known in France as the draisienne for its German inventor, the Baron von Drais de Sauerbrun. This machine, which dates between 1816 and 1818, is generally regarded as the earliest form of the bicycle. (Illustration from Sharp, Archibald, *Bicycles And Tricycles* [Longmans, Green. London: 1896/ MIT Press. Cambridge, Massachusetts: 1982.])

English gentlemen. Prince Albert, the consort to Queen Victoria, was known to use one. The hobby horse was really little more than a prop for its rider to sit upon while walking or running—sort of a two-wheeled walking stick. The rider sat on a beam mounted between two equal-sized wheels and pushed along the ground with his (or very rarely her) legs.

Such contrivances were primarily for the gents and not too often used by ladies, but a London coachmaker, Denis Johnson, built a ladies' model with a drop frame to accommodate skirts as early as 1820. Thus, very early on the bicycle earned its reputation as a machine that facilitated the struggle for women's equality.

Crude as it was, the hobby horse was a giant breakthrough because it was the first machine to attempt to efficiently use leg power for transportation. The earliest human-powered machines, such as hand tools and most agricultural implements, made poor use of the strongest source of human power, the leg muscles. Later, the invention of the wheel permitted more efficient use of leg power on treadmills and capstans (giant rope-winding wheels turned by people or animals).

Even though our legs are used for walking and running, the most primitive forms of human transportation, the design of machines that use leg power for self-propulsion is a relatively recent development. Much earlier the force of the upper body had been harnessed for rowboats, canoes, and other oared vessels. And human leg power had also been harnessed for transportation in the rickshaw and sedan chair, but these are not examples of "self-propulsion"; one or more servants were required to perform the function of beasts of burden. David Gordon

An English inventor, Louis Gompertz, introduced this hand-operated velocipede in 1821. (Illustration from J. T. Goddard, in *Wheels and Wheeling,* S. H. Oliver and D. H. Berkebile, eds., Washington, D.C.: Smithsonian Institution Press, 1974.)

Wilson, an MIT professor who has specialized in bicycle engineering, speculates in *Bicycling Science,* a book he co-authored with Frank Rowland Whitt, that von Drais or one of his assistants probably discovered that their steerable hobby horse could be balanced to coast down hills. Wilson says the chance discovery of coasting was a momentous development that could give von Drais priority for the title "inventor of the bicycle."

Louis Gompertz improved on von Drais's invention by attaching a sector gear and pinion to the front wheel. The sector gear was attached to a pull handle, which also served as the steering lever, and the gear was fixed with a one-way ratchet. The rider was able to lean forward on a padded chest support and assist the leg efforts by arm power. My legs are much stronger than my upper body, but I'd like to try riding the Gompertz hobby horse anyway because it is reported that early bike could cruise at a respectable 10 to 14 mph. Not bad.

Gompertz's machine probably looks comical to you. However, it was a major step toward getting the bicyclist's feet off the ground and making human-powered locomotion more efficient. Essentially, Gompertz added more muscle groups to the effort, permitting the rider to become a little less like a supported walker and a little more like a bicyclist. More recently, some designers of human-powered vehicles have tried adding arm and leg power to multi-person machines, going on the theory that every little bit helps.

It remained for Kirkpatrick MacMillan, a Scottish blacksmith, to make the breakthrough that turned the hobby horse into a bicycle. In about 1839, MacMillan took the rider's foot off the ground by adding cranks to the rear wheel. The cyclist turned the cranks by walking or running on swinging pedals, which were attached to the cranks by long connecting rods. At last the rider's legs were supplying power directly to the wheels.

The MacMillan machine finally looked like a bicycle, and it is surprising that it didn't catch on more than it did. MacMillan did obtain some notoriety for a widely publicized 140-mile ride from Dumfries to Glasgow, during which he bumped into a child in a crowd of onlookers and consequently became the first in a

A Scottish blacksmith built the first true bicycle. MacMillan's velocipede, invented about 1839, used a swinging pedal arrangement that allowed the rider to propel the machine without touching the ground. (Illustration from Sharp, Archibald, *Bicycles And Tricycles.* [Longmans, Green. London: 1896/MIT Press. Cambridge, Massachusetts: 1982.])

long line of bicyclists to receive a traffic fine. Whitt and Wilson advance the theory that the "railroad mania" that gripped England and Europe in the 1830's and 1840's is probably the reason MacMillan's major contribution was not followed immediately by further bicycle development. And apparently MacMillan never attempted to sell or manufacture any of his machines. The same basic scenario was to be repeated later when the automobile was introduced. The popularity of a much heavier vehicle, which burns a fossil fuel, retarded the acceptance of human-powered transportation.

THE MICHAUX BROTHERS BUILD A BONESHAKER

In the 1860's Pierre and Ernest Michaux of Paris contributed the next machine in the evolution of the bicycle. The Michaux bicycle had two equal-sized wheels and was powered by two cranks directly attached to the front hub. They got the idea for their propulsion system from cranked grindstones used to mill grain at the time, and it turned out to be a profitable fusion of ideas for the Michaux brothers. It is unclear whether the Michaux or their assistant, Pierre Lallement, actually built the first "velocipede," as such machines were originally called in the 19th century, but the idea was evidently that of the brothers. Lallement later had a falling out with the Michaux family and emigrated to the United States, where he introduced a veloci- pede to the Americans. The Lallement machine quickly gained the uncomplimentary nickname "boneshaker," and it enjoyed a brief, fad-like, American popularity in the late 1860's.

The Michaux family was talented at both industrial organiza- tion and marketing. Their shop produced two velocipedes in 1861, 142 in 1862, and 400 in 1865. The family also promoted

This Michaux velocipede circa 1861 had a steel frame with saddle sus- pended on a spring strip, and rear brakes controlled by a cable at- tached to turning handlebar grips. Doubtless the almost-round wooden wheels are responsible for this velocipede's American nickname: the boneshaker. The front wheel is 35½" in diameter and the rear wheel is 32". The boneshaker weighed in at a hefty 110 pounds, five times the weight of a modern racing bicycle. (Courtesy Cycles Peugeot)

their product by sponsoring races and demonstrations. Thus, they established a procedure in bicycle and later automobile marketing that persists to this day, and to which I indirectly owe my current livelihood and career as a bike racer. Thank God for the Michaux brothers—they founded both bicycle manufacturing and the sport of bicycling.

The first bicycle trade show was held in Paris in 1869; and the same year, *Le Vélocipède Illustré*, an early French cycling journal, sponsored the first formal, long-distance bicycle road race. The race covered approximately 130 km from Paris to Rouen, and was staged specifically to demonstrate to the public that cycling is superior to running, from the points of view of speed, efficiency, and endurance. The race attracted 203 contestants, an international field that included six women racers. Englishman James Moore was the victor in that first race.

JAMES STARLEY AND THE PENNY FARTHING

War often interferes with commercial development, and the Franco-Prussian War (1870–1871) shifted the base of the infant bicycle industry from France to England in a curious way. At that time in England a remarkable inventor named James Starley took over the world's fledgling bicycle industry and sent it in many directions. Here is how it happened.

Starley was born in Albourne, Sussex, in 1831, and began work on his father's farm at the age of nine. By the time he was 15, Starley was bored with farm life, and he decided to join the legions of young English farmers who forsook rural life to find their role in the industrial revolution. He walked to London, where his first job was as a gardener for a wealthy man named John Penn. Before he left Penn's employ, the young Starley already had invented a mechanized bassinette, an adjustable candlestick, and a single-stringed window blind. In 1855, at 24 years of age, Starley found his next position in London, this time as a mechanic. In that job he distinguished himself by improving the design of sewing machines. Later, Starley invented a new sewing machine, for whose production a new company was formed in Coventry.

As managing foreman of the Coventry Machinist's Company, Starley also produced some velocipedes of the Michaux "boneshaker" design. That's where the Franco-Prussian War comes in. Starley had intended to send his bikes to France, but since France was at war he decided to market them right in England. They sold, and he continued to produce boneshakers for the English. Not surprisingly, the inventive Starley subsequently improved on the Michaux designs. Beginning with the introduction of his Ariel model, Starley and his family produced a succession of bicycles that ultimately evolved into the high-wheeled "ordinary" or "penny farthing." The ordinary was called a penny farthing because the front wheel was large like a British penny, while the rear wheel was small like a farthing.

The ordinary or penny farthing introduced by James Starley in the 1870's. (Courtesy Cycles Peugeot)

The ordinary had a direct front-wheel drive, like its predecessor, the Michaux velocipede. But unlike the velocipede, the ordinary's front wheel was huge to overcome the problem of low gearing and consequent slow riding. Usually a cyclist would have an ordinary built with as large a front wheel as his (and again rarely her) legs would permit. Thus, riders of ordinaries could travel a good deal farther for one turn of the cranks than they could on the Michaux machines. Ordinaries with 60-inch front wheels were quite a common sight at one time.

Starley also adopted the lever-tension radial-spoke wheel from France, where it had been used experimentally. He then improved upon it, inventing the tangent-spoked wheel, which resists the radial-spoked wheel's tendency to twist apart as torque is applied to the hub. With very minor mechanical improvements, Starley's wheel design is still in use.

James Starley was one of those prolific 19th-century inventors

These drawings by Brian Walker commemorated the hundredth anniversary of Stevens' historic ride across America in 1884. (Courtesy Bikecentennial)

of the Edison genre, who made many technological contributions and obtained numerous patents. From the point of view of bicycling, his major contribution was to allow cyclists to use their legs for locomotion nearly as efficiently as they could. The ordinary was in many respects a practical, effective machine. Some early ordinaries weighed in at well under 25 pounds, despite their strength and usefulness.

I feel a special kinship with Thomas Stevens, who rode an ordinary across the United States in 1884. When I crossed the United States in the Great American Bike Race in 1982, I didn't have to carry my bike across railroad trestles and I never passed a covered wagon, so I stand in awe of what Stevens did. On my difficult trek across America, I often thought about those early years before the widespread use of macadam road surfacing. I wondered what it must have been like for Stevens to negotiate his huge ordinary along the dirt paths and log roads on solid rubber tires. The ruts and potholes in the road surely sent him sprawling more than once. This pioneer bicyclist (or was he a bicycling pioneer?), camping alone at a stream, must have wondered how safe the Santa Fe Trail was from wolves and hostile Indians.

I know how good a machine the ordinary must have been. A year before Stevens's ride, in 1883, an English cyclist by the name of J. H. Adams was able to cover 242½ miles in 24 hours on an ordinary. In this instance I feel a special kinship, too, because exactly 100 years later I set a 24-hour record of 514 miles on a modern bicycle in the Pepsi Bicycle Marathon held in New York. To my way of thinking, Adams's performance compares quite favorably with my 1983 record. I'm very impressed by Stevens's tour and by Adams's record, because I've ridden ordinaries, and they must have been a handful to balance on narrow cobblestone roads. With nervous horses pulling wagons, and pedestrians darting heedless of bicycles, the ordinary rider did not have an easy time. As good as the machine was, though, it wasn't perfect: it had no gear transmission. I have to struggle to negotiate even a slight grade on an ordinary, so my helmet is off to those strong, talented riders.

The principal problem with this efficient, elegant, sophisticated machine is that it's dangerous. If you fall, it's from a great height, and the instability inherent in an ordinary makes that event highly probable. On the ordinary, the rider's center of gravity was high and very far over the front wheel, and it was not uncommon to pitch forward and land on one's head or shoulders. Add to that the problems imposed by turning one's legs as they straddle the front wheel, and you can see the potential for disaster in the ordinary. Something better—and safer—just had to come along.

THE ROVER SAFETY CYCLE: THE MODERN BICYCLE

The safety problems of the ordinary led H. J. Lawson to invent a rear-driven "safety" bicycle in 1879. Unfortunately there wasn't a market for Lawson's machine when he first invented it, so it remained for another Starley, James's nephew John Kemp Starley, to introduce the Rover Safety Cycle in 1884. This was a machine with two equal-sized wheels and a chain to the rear hub—in short, the modern bicycle. The frame of the Rover

The Rover Safety Bicycle, first marketed by John Kemp Starley in 1884, was the prototype of the modern conventional bike. All this machine lacks is a seat tube to form the present-day diamond frame. (Illustration from Sharp, Archibald, *Bicycles And Tricycles*. [Longmans, Green. London: 1896./MIT Press. Cambridge, Massachusetts: 1982.])

By 1896, this diamond-frame bike by Humber had set the form of the modern bicycle. (Illustration from Sharp, Archibald, *Bicycles And Tricycles*. [Longmans, Green. London: 1896/MIT Press. Cambridge, Massachusetts: 1982.])

lacked only the seat stays to form the "diamond" frame so popular today. By 1890 Humber and Company had manufactured a bicycle with a nearly diamond-shaped frame, and by 1896 a Humber diamond-frame safety bicycle became the model for most subsequent bicycles.

Archibald Sharp published his *Bicycles and Tricycles: An Elementary Treatise on Bicycle Design and Construction* in 1896. That book, which MIT Press reissued in 1982, is still the definitive work on the physics and engineering of bicycles. Sharp says:

> till a few years ago, a great variety of bicycles were on the market, many of them utterly wanting in scientific design. Out of these, the present day rear-driven bicycle, with diamond frame, extended wheel base, and long socket steering head—the fittest has survived.

Sharp's words in 1896 were prophetic. Although advocates of the ordinary linger even to this day, within a few years of the publication of Sharp's book the safety cycle had largely replaced the ordinary. Some alternative frames such as the mixte also have been successful in the marketplace, but the present-day bicycle can be traced directly to the machines produced by Lawson, Starley, and Humber.

Brakes of various design were invented along with the early forms of the bicycle, and a primitive, derailleur-system transmission was shown at the Paris velocipede show in 1869. During the years 1901 to 1906, J. J. H. Sturmey and J. Archer obtained several patents for epicyclic gears, and they began manufacturing what we now know as the Sturmey-Archer 3-speed hub. At the moment, Sturmey-Archer gears are less popular than derailleur transmissions, but they are still widely in use.

After the introduction of the Rover Safety Cycle and its modifications, only two major developments remained before modern bicycling had arrived: the flat tire and the pneumatic tire to go flat. An English patent for an inflatable tire was granted to R. W. Thompson in 1845, but there weren't any modern bicycles or other appropriate vehicles around to use them.

The low top tube and skirt protector on this 1913 bike were designed to protect priests' robes. Notice the nice Peugeot logo on the chain stay. (Courtesy Cycles Peugeot)

If this sleek 1899 bike looks a little too bare, that's because it's missing the chain. It used gears instead. Weighing about 31 pounds, this bike was available in three sizes—52, 62, and 67 cm—and came with either steel or wood wheels. (Courtesy Cycles Peugeot)

This tricycle, built about 1890, features spring front suspension and a double-sprung saddle. The rear wheels are 90 cm in diameter. It weighs about 63 pounds. (Courtesy Cycles Peugeot)

This 1889 "popular" bike, with a cross-shaped steel frame and bronze hubs, was built after the diamond frame had been invented. It weighs about 45 pounds. (Courtesy Cycles Peugeot)

Toe clips, wooden rims and fenders, and a safety bell were standard on this 1910 diamond-frame road bike. Frame sizes available: 52, 57, and 62 cm. (Courtesy Cycles Peugeot)

Railroad cars did not need tires and horse drawn carriages were already protected by heavy-weight suspension systems. As long as the horse was doing the work, who cared how heavy the carriage was?

When John Boyd Dunlop, a veterinary surgeon in Belfast, reinvented the pneumatic tire, there *were* bicycles around to use them, and Dunlop became fabulously wealthy from his invention. Here we have a classic case of profiting from reinventing the wheel. As early as the boneshaker days, bicycle manufacturers had nailed solid rubber strips around their wheels in order to somewhat soften the jarring ride, but the inflatable tire worked so much better that Dunlop's fortune was assured. Some say he invented the pneumatic tire for his son's tricycle, so I have to assume that the young Dunlop was the first person in history to have a flat. In any case, once the tire was invented, the bicycle was complete.

THE BICYCLE COMES OF AGE

As soon as the bicycle had evolved to its present form it was put to numerous uses besides transportation. Most of these applications still persist. Commercially, bikes fitted with large baskets were used for package and message deliveries. I'm just old enough to remember bicycling with George, a Western Union telegraph messenger, who was practically the only other teenager who rode a bike in my hometown of Springfield, Missouri, in the early 1960's.

In the early days of the bicycle, enterprising promoters quickly realized that a bicycle could move more rapidly and thus be seen by more people than could a man carrying signs. To this day in the Orient, and as a novelty in some American cities, wiry pedicab drivers use their leg muscles to transport their fares around town.

U.S. soldiers mounted on bicycles comprised a self-propelled unit that saw action in World War I, a sort of wheeled cavalry. Even now heavy-frame bicycles are widely used for transportation between far-flung hangars at military bases and between shops at huge civilian industrial plants, such as the Livermore Labs.

Early on the bicycle acquired a reputation as a fun way to travel, and its use for recreation and exercise has endured to this day. The romantic connotations of travel on a tandem were recognized by songwriter Harry Dacre, who penned "Daisy" way back in 1892.

Although the bike was first built for use by adults, the American bicycle industry has survived only because scaled-down bikes were produced for children. Just as railroad mania probably retarded progress with MacMillan's early bicycle, so did auto mania slow later bike development. When the automobile literally pushed the bicycle off the road, and minimum ages were established for driving licenses, the bike became the Kiddie Cadillac. A shiny new bicycle was the archetypal Christmas gift among the well-off, and poor youngsters often earned money to buy a bicycle by doing odd jobs. Well into the 1950's, many newspapers were delivered by adolescents on balloon-tire Columbias, machines built by America's first bicycle company, founded by Albert A. Pope in 1878. Newspapers are still delivered that way in some places, but the bikes are different.

THE ROLE OF BICYCLE RACING

The sport of bicycle racing developed early; it had its first major acceptance in the Paris-Rouen race of 1869. At first, bicycle races all were held on the road. But in order to capitalize on the spectator appeal of the sport, some promoters arranged races on dirt horse tracks. Paved tracks were soon to follow, then banked tracks to allow the riders to speed around the bends. In the heyday of American bicycle racing more than 100 velodromes were located in cities all over the United States. Compare that to the dozen or so American velodromes in use now.

At the turn of the century, bicycle racing served the important function of demonstrating that the self-propelled vehicle could outdistance and outrace the horse. Records were set and bettered regularly. In 1898 one brave soul named Charles N. Murphy rode a bicycle on a specially built board path in the slipstream of a Long Island railroad train. He covered one mile at 63.24 mph and earned immortality by picking up the nickname Mile-a-Minute Murphy.

Along with conventional bicycle racing, a sport called "motorpacing" became a crowd pleaser during the first two decades of this century. Mile-a-Minute Murphy was able to set his record because the train blocked the air resistance to his motion. At first, crack teams of as many as six riders on multi-person bicycles were used to block the wind for single riders competing against each other. Later the pace vehicles were partly human-powered and partly powered by gasoline or electric motors. Currently motorcycles are used as pace vehicles, for these races are still an active, competitive sport in Europe.

In the United States the sport of motorpacing is practiced only rarely, usually in pursuit of individual records set behind race cars. In the years since Murphy set his record, others have motorpaced to remarkable speeds. On August 25, 1973, Doctor Allan V. Abbott, a Los Angeles physician and motorcycle racer, attained 138.674 mph behind a car on the Bonneville Salt Flats in Utah. I'm trying to raise Dr. Abbott's record even higher. On January 10, 1983, I achieved 124.2 mph on a bicycle designed for me by aeronautical engineer Douglas Malewicki. That was on a closed-off 5-mile stretch of road in Mexico, riding behind the Pepsi Challenger, a low-slung race car driven by champion driver Rick Vesco.

Mile-a-Minute Murphy was very nearly killed by his record ride, when the locomotive engineer slowed down too soon and caused Murphy to collide with the rear of the train. Only the alertness of his handlers, who pulled Murphy and his bike aboard the train, saved his life. I, too, can attest that such motorpacing speed-record attempts are dangerous, and I intend to quit once I have set a record of around 150 mph. I believe that the expense, danger, and logistical difficulties of the sport will prevent it from ever entering the mainstream of competitive cycling. But motorpacing is an important and colorful part of the history of bicycling.

The author chasing Rick Vesco's race car at 124 mph. The rather stark, flat background is Laguna Salada, Baja California. (Courtesy Campagnolo USA)

Former Olympian Chuck Pranke checking my radio set-up as I spin the wheels on my specially designed motor-pacing bike. The bike weighs about 45 lb. and uses motorcycle wheels and tires for strength and safety. Note the double-reduction gearing, which gives me super-high gears without having to use overly gigantic chain rings. (Courtesy Campagnolo USA)

SUPER-FAST STREAMLINED BIKES

Besides proving the utility of the bicycle and providing public entertainment, bicycle racing and performance tests have served one other valuable function. The sport of cycling, at least initially, spurred engineers to make technological improvements in the machine. Lightweight alloy frames, efficient derailleurs, and the presently popular low-slung handlebars all were developed specifically for racing.

Unlike automobile racing, however, bicycle competition has sometimes served as an impediment to development. Each technological advancement in bicycle design conferred an advantage upon its possessor. Officials of the sport occasionally have resisted the adoption of some advances because they would have changed the sport and invalidated previous records. Thus, race officials at first tried to prevent safety cycles from racing, deferring to the riders of high wheelers by claiming that the chains were dangerous. Later, race officials unsuccessfully tried to ban use of pneumatic tires.

Reason usually has prevailed over conservatism, and competition ultimately has provided an incentive to improve the bicycle. This was not always so, however. In 1896, Sharp noted in his classic bicycle engineering manual that decreased air resistance confers a substantial advantage on a bicyclist. At that early date, Sharp already knew that the advantage was much more than proportionately greater at higher speeds. (Earlier I explained that at 18 mph air can account for 80 percent of the resistance to a bicycle's motion, while at 10 mph air only accounts for 50 percent of the resistance.) In the 1930's Francois Faure, a second-rank competitive cyclist, annihilated several records while riding the Velocar, a streamlined recumbent bicycle designed by Charles Mochet. By using aerodynamics, bicycle technology was making important advances; but then in 1938 the Union Cycliste Internationale (UCI) decided to ban streamlined bikes from competition, simultaneously disallowing Faure's records.

Etienne Bunau-Varilla patented this streamlined human-powered ve-hicle in 1913. (From "The Aerodynamics of Human-powered Land Ve-hicles," Gross, A. C.; Kyle, C. R. and Malewicki, D. J. Copyright ©
1983 by *Scientific American,* Incorporated, all rights reserved.)

*VELOCAR. During the 1930's, riding in this fully-faired recumbent
bicycle designed by Charles Mochet, a second-rank competitive cyclist,
François Faure, upset several previous records. In 1938, compe-tition rules were changed to prohibit streamlined bicycles, and that
substantially retarded later technological development of bicycles.*
(From "The Aerodynamics of Human-powered Land Vehicles," Gross,
A. C.; Kyle, C. R. and Malewicki, D. J. Copyright © 1983 by *Scientific
American,* Incorporated, all rights reserved.)

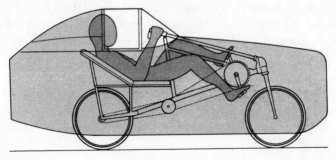

The UCI should have established separate competition for streamlined bikes. Instead, their ban essentially classified the most important contemporary advance in bicycle design as cheating. Only recently has streamlined bicycle development begun to recover from the blow it received in 1938.

In 1976 the International Human Power Vehicle Association (IHPVA) was founded by Chester Kyle, Cal State Long Beach professor of mechanical engineering, and Jack Lambie, an aeronautical engineering consultant. The IHPVA sanctions races by streamlined bicycles and other human-powered vehicles. The only requirement is that the vehicles use no other form of stored energy than muscle power. Kyle and Lambie founded the IHPVA specifically because the UCI's 1938 ban excluded streamlined bicycles from races.

IHPVA competition has demonstrated conclusively that aerodynamic bikes have a substantial advantage over conventional bicycles. They are so fast that three streamlined human-powered vehicles have received honorary speeding tickets from

The VECTOR TANDEM, shown here in top and side view, is the world's fastest human-powered vehicle. The Vector Tandem has sprinted 200 meters at 62.92 mph, and has traveled 40 miles of California freeway at over 50 mph. (From "The Aerodynamics of Human-powered Land Vehicles," Gross, A. C.; Kyle, C. R. and Malewicki, D. J. Copyright © 1983 by *Scientific American*, Incorporated, all rights reserved.)

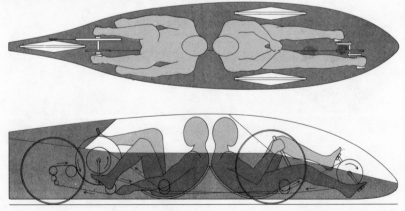

the California Highway Patrol for exceeding the national 55-mph speed limit. (If I ever get a speeding ticket on my bicycle, I'll frame it!) In 1980, the Vector Tandem, a human-powered vehicle designed by Al Voight of Versatron Research Inc., was clocked at 62.92 mph for a 200-meter sprint. By comparison, the record for that distance on a conventional bike is 43.35 mph, held by Russian cycling champion, Sergei Kopylov. Open competition by streamlined human-powered vehicles finally has legitimized exploration in what may be the last frontier of the bicycle's long development: aerodynamics.

It remains to be seen how well the newly awakened technology will be applied to street-worthy machines. Although Voight's streamlined Vector Tandem has covered some 40 miles of freeway from Stockton to Sacramento, California, at over 50 mph, I'm skeptical of riders surviving on the open road. Recum-

The Zzipper. Streamlining for your bike at a budget price. (Courtesy Glenn Brown)

bents are vulnerable to traffic because they are the lowest, least visible machines on the road. Traveling at freeway speeds only increases the danger. Unfortunately, state and federal governments would have to spend billions of dollars building separated bikeways to make HPV's practical transportation, and that's not likely to happen.

Still, bicycle aerodynamics will be useful both for racing and other forms of cycling. The rules of international competition have been relaxed somewhat, and tiny advantages are now available to racers on bicycles with elliptical-frame tubing and aerodynamic components. There are also frames designed to reduce frontal area, some of which utilize small (24″) front wheels, for instance. I've mentioned several times that sometimes a fraction of a second makes the difference between winning and losing a race. If a "flat bike" gives the cyclist a tenth of a second each lap, over a 4-hour race that could be enough.

I occasionally have tried race-legal aerodynamic bikes in competition and, like other bicyclists, I always race in skin-tight aerodynamic racing clothing. In fact, I was one of the first to wear a skin suit in competition back in the 1970's. It's likely there will be even more improvements in the future, although no one should expect the upright bicycle to become much faster than it already is.

Outside the restrictive, esoteric confines of cycling competition, a lightweight, polycarbonate, plastic fairing called the Zzipper recently has entered the bicycle marketplace. While the Zzipper is not "legal" for most races, its inventor Glenn Brown claims that using one can reduce air resistance by as much as 20 percent.

MacCREADY'S MARVELOUS FLYING MACHINE

Human-powered flight is another noteworthy foray into the bicycle's aerodynamic frontier. In 1959, Henry Kremer, a wealthy British industrialist, offered a £5,000 prize (subsequently raised to £50,000) for the first group that could successfully navigate a human-powered airplane around a half-mile-long, figure-8 course, while maintaining an altitude of 10 feet. Numerous contestants were able to produce human-powered airplanes that could fly straight lines fine, but they couldn't make the required turns. Finally in 1977, a team directed by Paul MacCready of AeroVironment, Inc., in Pasadena, California, won the prize with the Gossamer Condor piloted—pedaled—by Bryan Allen; whereupon Kremer put up another prize of £100,000 for the first human-powered airplane to cross the English Channel. MacCready's team rose to the challenge and built the Gossamer Albatross; and in June, 1979, Bryan piloted a fragile, 60-pound airplane across the Channel in about 3 hours.

I'm greatly impressed by MacCready's accomplishment, but don't look for an Albatross Airline soon. Human-powered airplanes are fascinating for scientific and recreational reasons; but I fear such airplanes are too fragile, too expensive, and too difficult to fly ever to have any practical use. What is more, Bryan Allen is a superb athlete whose feats of endurance are well beyond what most humans could ever achieve. Very few people have as high a ratio of strength to weight as Bryan Allen. I believe that MacCready's ingenious machine performs at the very edge of what human-powered vehicles can accomplish on this planet.

INFLUENCE OF THE BICYCLE

To a much greater extent than is generally recognized, we live in a civilization whose shape was influenced by the bicycle. If you live in an automobile-clogged megalopolis such as Los Angeles or Houston, you can blame your misery partly on the bicycle. The automobile could not have been developed without the tangent-spoked wheel, ball bearings, bush-roller bearing chain, and pneumatic tires, all of which were invented for the bicycle. The differential transmission system used by automobiles was invented by (who else?) James Starley to allow the two power wheels of tricycles to work correctly on turns. Even the current concern with the effect of aerodynamic efficiency on automobile fuel economy was foreshadowed by early efforts to design streamlined bicycles.

In many cases automobiles owe the very roads they roll on to the bicycle. In late 19th-century America, bicycling was a craze that caught on rapidly. Annual U.S. bicycle production was 200,000 in 1889, but by 1899 had reached 1 million. A mere handful of automobiles were in use at that time. It was the League of American Wheelmen, a bicycle interest group founded in 1880 in Newport, Rhode Island, by Kirk Monroe and Charles Pratt, whose 150,000 members lobbied most persuasively for road construction. It has been said that the bicycle literally paved the way for the auto.

We tend to forget that Henry Ford's first automobile was a motorized quadricycle, and that Ford was a skilled bicycle mechanic. Among the pioneers in automobile manufacture were such bike designers as Duryea, Pierce, Hillman, Daimler, and Benz, all of whose names have meant quality automobiles. Similarly, the most notable figures in early aviation were two brothers in the bicycle business named Wilbur and Orville Wright. The Wright brothers and later aeronautical engineers borrowed from bicycle technology such ideas as tubular parts, use of lightweight engines (first applied to motorcycles), tangent-spoked landing gear, and lightweight construction.

The bicycle also made an essential psychological contribution to the development of present-day civilization. From the railroad age almost to the present, our civilization's technological development could best be characterized by describing successive transportation systems. For good or ill, the present transportation situation in America is based on the notion that the individual should be able to move about independently. The bicycle psychologically prepared us for the auto by making individual transportation accessible to the average person. Before the bicycle, the great expense of maintaining a horse, or a horse and carriage, confined most people to a lifetime lived within a half day's walk from home. Indeed, as autos and fuel continue to climb in cost, it may be the bicycle, whose use is experiencing a renaissance, that will rescue the freedom of individual transportation. In China, a modern society is being built on bicycle transport.

The bicycle has been a source of social change on other fronts as well. It became a liberating influence because it afforded early 20th-century women the same freedom to move about as men. Such garments as the bloomer, which shocked society when first introduced, were developed as part of a movement to permit rational dress for women so they could bicycle without catching their skirts in the chain. Pioneering sportswomen such as Mrs. Jane Lindsay, who in the 1890's once cycled 800 miles in under 92 hours, set very respectable endurance records. Convenient transportation on the bicycle (and later the automobile) gave women the same freedom as men to leave the farm or home and seek employment in an industrial economy.

The first great American national sports heroes were bicyclists, not baseball players as is generally supposed. Arthur Zimmerman, Major Taylor, and Frank Kramer are not as well remembered, but in their day they were as much idolized by the public as was Ty Cobb in baseball a few years later. What is even less well known is that Major Taylor was the first internationally known black American sports hero. Taylor overcame much racism and discrimination in his day, and he paved the way for numerous other black athletes. Major Taylor's life and cycling career are so interesting to me that I have begun a full-length biography about him. For now, suffice it to say that even in the area of breaking athletic color barriers the bicycle made an important contribution.

THE FUTURE

What will the future of bicycling look like? I predict that in America and other industrialized nations the bicycle will become an increasingly attractive alternative to the automobile. Americans bought 5 million bikes in 1980. The number of bicycles purchased most likely will continue to grow in future years. There already are many more bicycles than cars in this country; what we need now are more *cyclists*.

I predict that in the United States competitive cycling will also become increasingly popular as both a participation and spectator sport. The 1984 Los Angeles Olympics has awakened the United States, a sleeping giant in the world of international bicycle competition. As before in the history of cycling, interest in competition is likely to inspire greater recreational and practical use of the bicycle.

Check back with me in a few years to see if I have correctly used the bicycle's previous history to forecast future trends.

Best wishes in cycling!

Recommended Reading

Books

Touring

American Youth Hostels, Inc. *AYH Handbook*. (Available by request from American Youth Hostels.)

A list of low-cost accommodations across the United States. The locations of youth hostels are given in this handbook.

California Department of Transportation. *Pacific Coast Bicentennial Route*.

This book is indispensable to bicycle tourists traveling the west coast bike route. It is a detailed map of the Pacific Coast Bicentennial Bike Route, including some side elevation charts.

Editors of *Bicycling* Magazine. *Best Bicycle Tours*. Emmaus, PA: Rodale Press, 1981.

Here you'll find the location, recommended season, accommodations information, level of difficulty, references, tour outline, and points of interest for about 40 American bicycle tours.

Hawkins, Karen, and Hawkins, Gary. *Bicycle Touring in Europe*. New York: Pantheon Books, 1980.

Competitive Cycling

McCullagh, James C. (editor). *American Bicycle Racing*. Emmaus, PA: Rodale Press, 1976.

This book is a collection of entertaining chapters by Chuck McCullagh, Dick Swann, Dave Chauner, Alice Kovler, and Owen Mulholland about the contemporary bicycling scene and the history of the sport in America. The book includes an excellent chapter about women cyclists.

Matheny, Fred. *Beginning Bicycle Racing*. Lebanon, NH: Whitman Press, 1980.

A how-to book for the neophyte competitor.

Simes, Jack. *Winning Bicycle Racing*. Chicago: Henry Regnery Company, 1976.

A manual for competitive cyclists written by a champion cyclist and coach.

Bicycle History and Technology

Grosser, Morton. *Gossamer Odyssey*. Boston: Houghton Mifflin, 1981.
  An exhaustive chronicle of human-powered flight, with information about Bryan Allen's flying and Paul MacCready's engineering.
Sharp, Archibald. *Bicycles and Tricycles*. Cambridge, MA: MIT Press, 1982.
  This facsimile of the classic book originally published in 1896 is still a valuable source for both modern engineers and history buffs. Many fine drawings of early bikes are included.
Smith, Oliver, and Berkebile, Donald. *Wheels and Wheeling*. Washington, DC: Smithsonian Institution Press, 1974.
  (US Government Printing Office Stock Number 470-00268.) Photos of the Smithsonian Institution's bicycle and early motorcycle collections are embellished by informative descriptions of the machines and their backgrounds. A thorough history, illustrated by many additional photos and drawings, precedes the catalog of the collections.
Whitt, Frank R., and Wilson, David G. *Bicycling Science*. 2nd edition. Cambridge, MA: MIT Press, 1982.
  This book explains everything you ever wanted to know about the physics of bicycling. Included are chapters on the physiology and history of bicycles, and one on unusual pedaled machines, such as lawn mowers and airplanes.

Bicycle Maintenance

Coles, Clarence W., and Harold T. Glenn. *Glenn's Complete Bicycle Manual*. New York: Crown, 1973.
  A truly complete repair manual for all types of bicycles.
Cuthbertson, Tom. *Anybody's Bike Book*. Revised edition. Berkeley, CA: Ten Speed Press, 1978.
  The perfect book for the cyclist who is all thumbs. There is a thorough yet amusing treatment of just about every aspect of bike maintenance, good for the neophyte and the skilled mechanic alike.

Health, Fitness, and Nutrition

Bailey, Covert. *Fit or Fat*. Boston: Houghton Mifflin, 1972.
  According to Bailey, you don't want to lose weight; you want to lose fat. This book can give you information about the essential role of exercise in losing fat and getting fit.
Weisenfeld, Murray F. *The Runner's Repair Manual*. New York: St. Martin's Press, 1980.
  A good owner's repair manual for the bicycle's engine, though written originally for runners.

Wood, Peter. *California Diet and Exercise Program*. Mountain View, CA: Anderson World Books, 1983.

Believe it or not, you can simultaneously eat more and lose weight. Exercise is the key. This book tells you how that works.

Magazines

During the last few years new periodicals about bicycling have blossomed, while some old ones have continued to flourish. Several magazines appeal to cyclists in *general*, be they tourists, recreational cyclists, commuters, or competitors. Some bicycle publications strictly cover *competitive cycling*. In a third category, *trade* and *technical* journals cater to the needs of dealers, engineers, and others working in the bicycle industry, but those publications also would interest any cyclist curious about the business, the machines, or the technology of the sport. The triathlon has spawned some magazines that cover bicycling as a portion of that new, hybrid sport. The following list of magazines and subscription addresses is broken into those four major bicycle publication categories.

General

Bicycling
33 East Minor Street
Emmaus, Pennsylvania 18049

Bicycle Sport
Box 315
Mount Morris, Illinois 61054

Bicycle USA
(Monthly publication of Bicycle
USA, the League of American
Wheelmen)
Box 988
Baltimore, MD 21203

Cyclist
Cycle Guide Publications
20916 Higgins Court
Torrance, California 90501

Competitive Cycling

Cycling
Specialist and Professional Press,
Ltd.
Dorset House
Stamford Street
London, SE1 9LU, England

Cycling, USA
(Official publication of the United
States Cycling Federation)
USCF
1750 East Boulder
Colorado Springs, Colorado 80909

Velo-News
Box 1257
Brattleboro, Vermont 05301

Winning: Bicycle Racing Illustrated
Velomedia, Inc.
1524 Linden Street
Allentown, Pennsylvania 18102

Trade and Technical

American Bicyclist
80 8th Avenue
Suite 305
New York, NY 10011

Bicycle Business Journal
Box 1570
Fort Worth, Texas 76101

Bicycle Dealers' Showcase
Box 19531
Irvine, California 92713

Bicycle Product News
Box 2338
Van Nuys, California 91405

Bike Tech
Rodale Press
33 East Minor Street
Emmaus, Pennsylvania 18049

Cycle Trader
Wheatland Journal, Ltd.
Penn House, Penn Place
Rickmansworth, Herts WD3 1SN,
England

Human Power
(Official publication of the International Human Powered Vehicle Association, Inc.)
Box 2068
Seal Beach, California 90740

Japan Cycle Press
15-4 Higashi-Veno
3-Chome, Taito-Ku
Tokyo 110 Japan

Triathlon

The Beast
(Bicyclists, Endurance Athletes, Swimmers, and Triathletes)
Box 789
Wainscott, New York 11963

Tri-Athlete
6660 Banning Drive
Oakland, California 94611

Triathlon
Box 5901
Santa Monica, California 90405

Ultrasport
Box 27938
San Diego, California, 92127

Bicycle Contacts

National Organizations

American Youth Hostels, Inc.
National Administrative Offices
1332 I Street, N.W.
Suite 800
Washington, DC 20005
(202) 783-6161

Dr. Robert Jones
Director, L.A. Olympic Velodrome
University Relations
California State University, Domin-
  guez Hills
Carson, CA 90747
(213) 516-3699

United States Cycling Federation
1750 E. Boulder Street
Colorado Springs, CO 80909
(303) 632-5551

Cheri Rae Wolpert
Bicycle Sport Magazine
Wizard Publications Inc.
3162 Kashiwa
Torrance, CA 90505

Chuck McCullagh
Editor and Publisher, *Bicycling*
  Magazine
Rodale Press, Inc.
33 E. Minor Street
Emmaus, PA 18049
(215) 967-5171

Ed Paveilka
Editor, *Velo-News*
Box 1257
Brattleboro, VT 05301
(802) 254-2305

Bicycle Federation
1055 Thomas Jefferson Street, N.W.
Washington, DC 20007
(202) 333-3094

League of American Wheelmen
1701 18th Street, N.W.
Washington, DC 20009
(202) 332-2221

Bikecentennial
Box 8308-K
Missoula, MT 59807
(406) 721-1776

State-by-State Contacts

Alabama

Alabama Highway Department
BUR URB PLAN II South Union
  Street
Montgomery AL 36130
(205) 832-5413

Arizona

Arizona Department of Transportation
Rm 310B
206 S. 17th Avenue
Phoenix, AZ 85007
(602) 261-7562

Arkansas

S. Arkansas Regional Planning
Commission
P.O. Box 8398
Pine Bluff, AR 71611
(501) 534-4247

California

Caltrans
Office of Bicycle Facilities
1120 N Street
Sacramento, CA 95814
(916) 445-7345

Colorado

Planning and Research
Colorado Department of Highways
4201 E. Arkansas Avenue
Denver, CO 80222
(303) 757-9506

Connecticut

Transportation Planner
Connecticut Department of Transportation
24 Wolcott Hill Road
Wethersfield, CT 06109
(203) 566-4270

Delaware

President
Delaware Friends of Bikecology
2 Barley Mill Drive
Wilmington, DE 19807
(302) 658-8186

District of Columbia

Office of the Director
District of Columbia
Department of Transportation
415 12th Street N.W.
Washington, DC 20004
(202) 727-5906

Florida

Bicycle Coordinator
Florida Department of Transportation
605 Suwannee
Tallahassee, FL 32301
(904) 488-7950

Georgia

President
Statesboro Bicycle Club
P.O. Box 2713
Statesboro, GA 30458
(912) 681-4360

Hawaii

President
Hawaiian Bicycle League
2476 Waiomao Road
Honolulu, HI 96816
(808) 737-1345

Idaho

Principal Planner
Ada County Highway District
318 E. 37th
Boise, ID 83704
(208) 344-6111

Illinois

Bikeway Coordinator
Illinois Department of Transportation
2300 S. Dirksen Parkway
Springfield, IL 62764
(217) 785-2937

Indiana

Streams and Trails Coordinator
Department of Natural Resources
612 State Office Building
Indianapolis, IN 46204
(317) 633-4677

Iowa

State Legislative Representative
League of American Wheelmen
208 12th Street
Boone, IA 50036
(515) 432-4757

Kansas

Director—Bikelibrary
P.O. Box 276
Emporia, KS 66801
(316) 343-1961

Louisiana

Associate—Enviroplan
145 Benton Road
Pineville, LA 71360
(318) 487-5465

Maine

State Coordinator
Maine Bicycle Coalition
12 School Street
Portland, ME 04102
(207) 773-4204

Maryland

Bicycle Affairs Coordinator
Maryland State Highway Administration
707 N. Calvert Street
Rm 607
Baltimore, MD 21203
(301) 659-1664

Massachusetts

Bicycle Projects Manager
Central Transportation Planning
27 School Street
Boston, MA 02108
(617) 451-5785

Michigan

Bicycle Coordinator
P.O. Box 8647
Ann Arbor, MI 48107
(313) 994-2814

Minnesota

Chief, Bikeway Program
Minnesota Department of Transpor-
tation
Rm 807—Transportation Building
St. Paul, MN 55155
(612) 296-1650

Mississippi

Research and Data Analyst
Mississippi State Highway Depart-
ment
P.O. Box 1850
Jackson, MS 39205
(601) 354-7172

Missouri

Bicycle Federation
1962 B Western Cape Drive
St. Louis, MO 63141
(314) 567-1691

Montana

Bicycle Forum Magazine
P.O. Box 8311
Missoula, MT 59807
(406) 728-4497

Nebraska

Department of Roads
P.O. Box 94759
Lincoln, NE 68509
(402) 473-4795

Nevada

Transportation Analysis
Nevada Department of Transportation
1263 S. Stewart Street
Carson City, NV 89712
(702) 885-5500

New Hampshire

Granite State Wheelmen Inc.
16 Clinton Street
Salem, NH 03079
(603) 898-9926

New Jersey

New Jersey Department of Transportation
1035 Parkway Avenue CN600
Trenton, NJ 08625
(609) 292-3432

New Mexico

Silver City Hill Chasers
P.O. Box 1293
Silver City, NM 88062
(505) 538-5587

New York

Konski Engineers
727 N. Salina Street
Syracuse, NY 13208
(315) 471-2101

North Carolina

N. Carolina Department of Transportation
P.O. Box 25201
Raleigh, NC 27611
(919) 733-2804

North Dakota

Transportation Planner
ND State Highway Department
Capital Ground
Bismarck, ND 58505
(701) 224-2194

Ohio

Miami Valley Regional Bicycle Committee
1980 Winter Bank Tower
Dayton, OH 45423
(513) 226-1444

Oklahoma

Tulsa Wheelmen Bicycling Society
1719 S. Detroit Avenue
Tulsa, OK 74120
(918) 584-6008

Oregon

Oregon Department of Transportation
Rm 200 Transportation Building
Salem, OR 97310
(503) 378-6883

Pennsylvania

League of American Wheelmen
112 S. 16th Street
Philadelphia, PA 19102
(215) 564-0855

Rhode Island

Rhode Island Department of Transportation
Data Ops—State Office Building
Providence, RI 02903
(401) 277-2558

South Carolina

Spartanburg Freewheelers
P.O. Box 6171
Spartanburg, SC 29304
(803) 585-4481

South Dakota

Transportation Planner
SD Department of Transportation
DOT Building
Rirre, SD 57501
(605) 773-3137

Tennessee

Miller, Watt, Estes, Inc.
113 E. 2nd Street
Chattanooga, TN 37403
(615) 267-3333

Texas

State Department of Highways
11th and Brazos
Austin, TX 78701
(512) 926-8260

Utah

Bonneville Bicycle Touring
2133 Commotion Drive
Sandy, UT 84092
(801) 943-1459

Vermont

Vermont Bicycle Touring
RD 2
Bristol, VT 05443
(802) 453-4811

Virginia

VA Department of Highways
1221 E. Broad Street
Richmond, VA 23219
(804) 786-2964

Washington

Department of Transportation
Transportation Administration
  Building
KF01
Olympia, WA 98504
(206) 753-2150

West Virginia

Jackson County Schools
Box 770
Ripley, WV 25271

Wisconsin

Transportation Planner
Dane County Regional Planning
  Commission
Room 114, City-County Building
Madison, WI 53709
(608) 266-9115

Wyoming

Teton Cycling, Inc.
Box 327
Jackson, WY 83001
(307) 733-4386

Index

Accessories and clothing, 96–119
Aerobic conditioning, 15–18, 203, 216–221, 226
Air resistance, 38, 65–67, 102, 194, 265–269

Beach cruiser, 33–34
Bicycle
  Brakes, 25, 52–53, 64, 128–129
  Derailleurs, 51–52, 76, 126–128
  Drive train, 46–48
  Fitting to own body, 54–64, 206–207
  Frame, 23, 37, 42–46, 60–62
  Handlebars and stems, 53, 63–64, 128–129
  History, 244–273
  Influence of, 270–272
  Parts, 23–26, 40–54, 201–202
  Repairs, 119–139
  Technology, 265
  Saddles, 53–54, 62–63, 70–71
  Types of, 26–40
  Wheels, 25, 48–51, 125–126
Blenders and clashers, 97
BMX bike, 30–32
Boneshaker, 248–250
Bonk, bonking out, 15, 209

Calories, 216, 221–226
Carbohydrates, 217–218, 224–226
Cardiovascular system, 219–220

Commuting, 4, 150–166
Cooper, Kenneth, 2, 15, 21
Cross-training, 204–205
Cycling
  Accessories, 106–119, 179–186
  Children, 6–10, 114–118
  Clothing, 96–106
  Costs, 163–164
  Fitting into your lifestyle, 4–22
  Goals, 17, 176–179, 210–211
  Groups, 86–87, 207–208
  Heredity, 8, 214–216
  Injury, 229, 232–234
  Looniness, 237–239
  Nutrition, 221–228
  Physics, 64–67
  Physiology, 214–221
  Safety, 7, 88–95, 190, 229, 237
  Seniors, 11–14
  Stress, 143–146
  Technique, 67–87, 186–188, 205–206
  Types of, 140
  Women, 20–23, 216–218, 239–243, 271–272
  Work, 150–166

Daisy, 35, 261
Dogs, 87–88

Equipment checklist, 181–184

Fartlek, 204
Fitness, 1–22, 165–166, 191–192
Flat tires, 120–124, 257, 260

Gearing, 75–78
Gear ratios, 77–78
Goals, 17, 176–179

Hills, climbing and descending, 80–85
History of the bicycle, 244–273
Hobby horse, 244–248
Human-powered vehicles, 265–270

IHPVA, 267–268
Injury, 228, 232–234

Leaping, 86

Maintenance, 119–139, 163
Motorpacing, 206, 262
Mountain bike, 29–30

Neuromuscular system, 216–218
Nutrition, 221–228

One-speed, 32–33

Pedaling, 72–75, 205–206
Penny farthing, 250–255
Positioning, 69–72
Purchasing a bicycle, 23, 41, 54–67

Racing, 5–6, 13, 18–20, 30–39, 40, 191–213, 249–250, 261–269
Recreation, 140–149
Recumbent bike, 36–39
Respiratory system, 220–221

Safety, 7, 88–95, 190, 229, 237
Shoes for cycling, 103–105
Sport medicine, 15–16, 228–236
Steering, 78–80
Strategy in competition, 208–213
Stress, 143–146, 165–166

Tandem bikes, 35–36
Ten-speed bike, 26–29, 55–56
Three-speed bike, 34–35
Tires and tubes, 48–49, 120–124, 257, 260
Tool kit, 135–136
Touring, 12–13, 167–190
   Equipment checklist, 181–184
Track bike, 39–40
Training, 149, 202–211
Tricks, dirty, 211–213

United States Cycling Federation, 13, 38, 39, 40, 195–196, 201–202

VO$_2$ Max, 218–219

Weather, 100–102
Wheels, 25, 48–51, 125–126
Women, 20–23, 216–218, 239–243, 271–272